Conservative Reductionism

Routledge Studies in the Philosophy of Science

1. Cognition, Evolution and Rationality
A Cognitive Science for the Twenty-First Century
Edited by António Zilhão

2. Conceptual Systems
Harold I. Brown

3. Nancy Cartwright's Philosophy of Science
Edited by Stephan Hartmann, Carl Hoefer, and Luc Bovens

4. Fictions in Science
Philosophical Essays on Modeling and Idealization
Edited by Mauricio Suárez

5. Karl Popper's Philosophy of Science
Rationality without Foundations
Stefano Gattei

6. Emergence in Science and Philosophy
Edited by Antonella Corradini and Timothy O'Connor

7. Popper's Critical Rationalism
A Philosophical Investigation
Darrell Rowbottom

8. Conservative Reductionism
Michael Esfeld and Christian Sachse

Conservative Reductionism

Michael Esfeld and Christian Sachse

LONDON AND NEW YORK

First published 2011
by Routledge

2 Park Square, Milton Park, Abingdon, Oxfordshire OX14 4RN
711 Third Avenue, New York, NY 10017

Routledge is an imprint of the Taylor & Francis Group, an informa business

First issued in paperback 2017

Copyright © 2011 Taylor & Francis

The right of Michael Esfeld and Christian Sachse to be identified as authors of this work has been asserted by them in accordance with sections 77 and 78 of the Copyright, Designs and Patents Act 1988.

All rights reserved. No part of this book may be reprinted or reproduced or utilised in any form or by any electronic, mechanical, or other means, now known or hereafter invented, including photocopying and recording, or in any information storage or retrieval system, without permission in writing from the publishers.

Notice:
Product or corporate names may be trademarks or registered trademarks, and are used only for identification and explanation without intent to infringe.

Typeset in Sabon by IBT Global.

Library of Congress Cataloging in Publication Data
A catalog record has been requested for this book.

ISBN13: 978-0-415-89186-8 (hbk)
ISBN13: 978-0-8153-7189-2 (pbk)

Contents

List of Figures	vii
Introduction	1
1 The Dilemma of Functionalism	**5**
1.0 Introduction to Chapter 1	5
1.1 The Motivation for Functionalism	7
1.2 Role Functionalism	15
1.3 Realizer Functionalism	22
1.4 The Future of Functionalism	27
2 The Metaphysics of Causal Structures	**30**
2.0 Introduction to Chapter 2	30
2.1 The Philosophical Argument for Causal Properties	31
2.2 Physics and Structural Realism	41
2.3 The Argument for Causal Structures	46
2.4 Causal Structures in Physics and the Transition to the Special Sciences	55
2.5 Structures as Modes	68
2.6 Conservative Identity and Ontological Reductionism	75
3 The Theory of Evolution and Causal Structures in Biology	**85**
3.0 Introduction to Chapter 3	85
3.1 Evolution, Fitness and Adaptationism	92
3.2 The Relevance of the Environment	102
3.3 The Criterion for Causal Biological Structures	107
3.4 Biological Functions and Functional Explanations	111

vi   *Contents*

4   Case Study: Classical and Molecular Genetics   116
    4.0 Introduction to Chapter 4   116
    4.1 Functionalization of Classical Genetics   117
    4.2 Causal mechanisms in Molecular Genetics   121
    4.3 Comparison between Both Theories   125

5   Conservative Functional Reduction   140
    5.0 Introduction to Chapter 5   140
    5.1 Functional and Reductive Explanations   142
    5.2 Functional Sub-types and the Link between the Special
        Sciences and Physics   148
    5.3 Conservative Theory Reduction and the Scientific Quality
        of the Special Sciences   158

    Conclusion   169

Summary of the Sub-chapters   173
Bibliography   177
Index of Names   197
Index of Subjects   201

Figures

1.1	Microphysical duplicate of the world.	6
1.2	Systematic overdetermination.	18
2.1	Overview of the possible positions with respect to the fundamental physical properties.	47
3.1	Galápagos Islands.	89
4.1	Classical genetics and its developments.	118
4.2	Functional definition of a gene type.	120
4.3	Translation and transcription.	123
4.4.	Relative completeness.	125
4.5	Multiple reference (realization).	128
4.6	Deduction in the case of unique realization.	129
4.7	Multiple reference and explanation.	130
4.8	Fitness differences due to multiple realization.	134
4.9	Sub-types.	135
4.10	Sub-type laws.	138
5.1	Deduction and reductive explanation.	150
5.2	Multiple reference (realization).	151
5.3	Extreme situations at the edge of normal conditions.	152
5.4	Extreme situations within normal conditions.	153
5.5	Normal conditions.	156

viii *Figures*

5.6	Construction of sub-types.	157
5.7	Sub-type laws.	158
5.8	Difference between law and sub-type laws.	159
5.9	Conservative reduction.	162

Introduction

What is the relationship between the fundamental physical theories, which apply to the whole universe, and the theories of the special sciences, such as chemistry, biology, psychology or sociology, which have a limited domain of application each? Why are there theories of the special sciences in addition to the universal theories of physics? Do these theories make a contribution to the scientific understanding of what there is in the world that physics is in principle not able to make? Or do they have only a heuristic and pragmatic value, providing for predictions in certain domains that are sufficient for all practical purposes? Until the beginning of the 20th century, modern science has been the triumph of physics, giving rise to philosophical programmes of a physicalist unity of nature and of science. However, until today, these programmes have not been worked out in detail. Moreover, the special sciences have made progress independently of physics. Against that background, philosophical theories are popular that grant autonomy to the special sciences.

We therefore still face the issue of the unity of nature and the unity of science today. On the one hand, the universal theories of physics exclude that there are, in addition to the properties that fall within their scope, emergent chemical, biological or psychological properties that produce effects of their own in the physical domain. All causal interactions that there are in the world completely come under the laws of fundamental physics. On the other hand, there are strong reservations against an eliminativist physicalism, which recognizes only physics as a scientific description of the world—in the spirit in which Ernest Rutherford is said to have claimed, "All science is either physics or stamp collecting" (reported in Blackett 1962, p. 108).

Since the 1970s, functionalism has been the mainstream philosophical reply to the question of the unity of nature and the unity of science. Functionalism is attractive because it seems to provide for an answer to that question that does justice to both sides—to the unity of nature as well as to its variety, and to the universal theories of physics as well as to the scientific quality of the theories of the special sciences. In a nutshell, that answer consists in claiming that all the properties that there are in the world are physically realized, but that the properties that define the domain of the

2 Conservative Reductionism

one or the other of the special sciences can be multiply realized. Multiple realization is the reason why the theories of the special sciences are indispensable for a scientific account of what there is in the world, without these theories referring to emergent properties in the mentioned sense.

However, since the 1990s, serious doubts have been cast on that answer. If the properties that fall within the domain of the special sciences are physically realized without being identical with physical properties, then it seems that these properties, insofar as they are not identical with physical properties, cannot cause anything so that they are epiphenomenal. This problem is a direct consequence of the concept of multiple realization, which is to ground the non-reductionist character of mainstream functionalism. How can the theories and the laws of the special sciences contribute to a scientific account of what there is in the world, given that all causal interactions are physical interactions, which in consequence can be completely described and explained in terms of the universal and fundamental physical theories? The versions of functionalism that have been developed since the 1970s risk to end up in epiphenomenalism as regards the functional properties in the domain of the special sciences, and in eliminativism as regards the scientific quality of the theories and the laws of the special sciences.

Nonetheless, we believe in the future of functionalism. It still is the only game in town that provides for an explanation of why there are in the world the properties which constitute the subject matter of the special sciences— without eliminating these properties in favour of purely physical properties, or declaring them to be unexplainable, emergent phenomena. However, functionalism has to be conceived in another manner than the usual ones, which rely on the concepts of realization and multiple realization. It is those philosophical terms of art that create the mentioned problem.

This book develops two ideas, a metaphysical one and an epistemological one. Both these ideas are reductionist, but conservative instead of eliminativist. That is why they enable us to pay heed to the unity of nature and the unity of science as well as to their variety. We argue in favour of a metaphysics of properties that conceives all properties in the world, including the fundamental physical ones, as functional properties in a large sense, namely as causal properties. More precisely, they are causal structures in the first place. We present arguments from physics and metaphysics for this theory of properties that are independent of functionalism. We then show how this theory of properties puts us in the position to defend a conservative identity of all properties in the world with physical properties, avoiding the problems of multiple realization and steering clear of the Skylla of epiphenomenalism and the Charybdis of eliminativism.

We then build a theory of the division of scientific labour between the universal theories of physics and the theories of the special sciences on this metaphysics of properties. When it comes to complex configurations of fundamental physical properties—in other words, complex causal structures—the vocabulary proper to physics describes their composition, and it is the task of the special sciences to describe their function in the sense of the salient effects that these configurations produce as a whole in a given environment. Configurations that are composed in different physical manners can nevertheless produce the same salient effects under certain environmental conditions. This is all there is as regards the significance attributed to multiple realization.

The second idea of this book, the epistemological one, is that it is nevertheless possible to establish a systematic link between the physical descriptions of such complex configurations and the descriptions of the special sciences. By means of conceiving functional sub-types, it turns out to be possible to make the functional descriptions of the special sciences in their own vocabulary so precise that they are coextensive with the physical descriptions of the composition of the configurations in question. It is thus in principle possible to derive the functional descriptions of the special sciences from physical descriptions. This principled possibility of their derivation from physics vindicates their scientific quality instead of calling it into question. It is a mistake to build up an opposition between the scientific quality of the special sciences and their reducibility to physics. If one establishes such an opposition, clinging to the idea of the irreducibility of the special sciences, it is the special sciences that are going to lose, since their scientific quality then becomes doubtful in confrontation with the universal and fundamental theories of physics. Against the background of the metaphysics of causal properties, taking the special sciences to be reducible to physics by no means prevents them from possessing a scientific quality, providing for a contribution to a scientific account of the world that physics is in principle not able to make.

Chapter 1 describes the state of the art and exposes the dilemma into which the main versions of functionalism run. Chapter 2 sets out the metaphysics of causal structures, invoking metaphysical as well as physical arguments for that metaphysics, and treating the transition from physical structures to those structures on which the special sciences focus. Against the background of the theory of evolution, Chapter 3 applies the metaphysics of causal structures to the functional properties in which biology trades. We employ biology as paradigmatic example of a special science. On the one hand, biology, in distinction from chemistry, clearly focuses on structures that are defined causally through their function instead of their physical composition. On the other hand, biology is not haunted by the additional problems that turn the philosophy of psychology into a minefield.

Chapter 4 elaborates on the relationship between classical and molecular genetics as a case study of the application of the metaphysics of causal structures and shows how a functional reduction of classical to molecular genetics is possible, vindicating the knowledge claims of the former. Against this background, chapter 5 develops a general conception of conservative reduction by means of functional sub-types, replying to the challenge from multiple realization and, in general, setting out a theory of the unity and

4 *Conservative Reductionism*

the variety of the natural sciences. The book terminates with a conclusion that summarizes the main results and lists the open issues.

This book is the English version of the German book *Kausale Strukturen: Einheit und Vielfalt in der Natur und den Naturwissenschaften*, published by Suhrkamp (Berlin 2010). We are grateful to Eva Gilmer, Jan-Erik Strasser and Nora Mercurio from Suhrkamp Verlag for leaving us the right to publish an English version of that book, and we would like to thank Erica Wetter from Routledge for the competent and cooperative way in which she handled our book proposal. In working out the English version, we have profited from helpful comments by three anonymous referees solicited for Routledge.

1 The Dilemma of Functionalism

1.0 INTRODUCTION TO CHAPTER 1

Suppose that it is possible to define the microphysical domain of the world unambiguously: let it consist in all and only those physical properties that occur at space-time points. Nothing physical can be smaller than a space-time point. In order to obtain a complete microphysical description of the world, one would thus have to quantify over all space-time points and specify which physical properties occur at these points. This idea is based on classical physics. It does not apply in that manner to contemporary physics (although it may still be possible to define the microphysical domain in an unambiguous manner). However, these complications are immaterial to present purposes.

Suppose now that the whole microphysical domain of the world is duplicated (see Figure 1.1). In other words, an operation takes place that duplicates the whole space-time including all and only those physical properties that occur at space-time points. The world w^* thus created hence is microphysically identical with the real world w. Does w^* contain all that there is in w, that is to say, all the organisms, all the biological, psychological, social, etc., properties that there are in w, including a double of this book and the ideas that are expressed in it? In other words, is w^* a duplicate *simpliciter* of w?

Our intuition is to answer this question in the affirmative. We know that all objects that exist in the real world have developed from microphysical objects and are composed exclusively of microphysical objects. There can hence be no objects that exist in w, but that miss in w^*. However, do complex, macroscopic objects possess in w^* all the qualitative properties that they possess in w? In other words, is the operation that consists in projecting the whole domain of microphysical properties from w to w^* sufficient to guarantee that all the biological, psychological, social, etc. properties that there are in w exist also in w^*? Note that there is no question of a deterministic dynamics here: we stipulate that all the microphysical properties in the *whole* space-time of w be copied to w^*. The issue of what the development of the world w in time is like, whether it is deterministic or not, has therefore no bearing on this question.

6 *Conservative Reductionism*

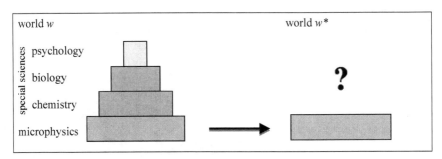

Figure 1.1 Microphysical duplicate of the world.

If a certain biological, psychological, social, etc., property existed in w, but missed in w^*, we would search for a reason for this difference. That search would take us beyond the domains of biological, psychological, social, etc., properties: according to all what we know about the world, it is not possible that a duplicate of the world lacks only one phenotypic property—say, the yellow colour of the petals of a certain individual plant, these petals being red instead of yellow in w^*—without there being also a genetic or an environmental difference between the duplicate of the world (w^*) and the world (w). However, if there is such a difference, there also is some molecular and consequently some microphysical difference between w^* and w. Hence, in this case, w^* would not be an exact microphysical duplicate of w but would differ from w in some microphysical detail.

By the same token, according to all that we know about the world, it is not possible that a duplicate of the world lacks only one psychological property—say, the thought of Barack Obama on 11 September 2010 that the war against terrorism is far from being won. If this psychological property were absent in w^*, there would be further psychological differences between Barack Obama in w^* and Barack Obama in w, since any thought is linked up with further thoughts, as well as with emotions and finally with actions. Consequently, there would be some neurobiological difference or other between w^* and w in the brain state of Barack Obama at the indicated time as well as some behavioural difference and thus some molecular and finally some microphysical difference. Again, according to all what we know about the world, it is not possible that a duplicate of the world lacks only one economic property—say, that the Dow Jones Index slightly rises on 17 September 2010. If this economic property were absent in w^*—in other words, if the Dow Jones Index developed in a different manner in w^* on that day—there would be some difference in the intentional attitudes and actions of persons between w^* and w, and thus some neurobiological and behavioural difference and hence finally some molecular including some microphysical difference. Consequently, in this case, w^*

would again not be an exact microphysical duplicate of w. Why is this so? Why are there strong reasons for taking a microphysical duplicate of the world to be a duplicate *simpliciter* of the world?

We will answer these questions in the following section and show how that answer motivates functionalism (1.1). We will then discuss the two main versions of functionalism—role functionalism (1.2) and realizer functionalism (1.3)—and point out that these versions lead into a dilemma, the dilemma of epiphenomenalism and eliminativism. Finally, we indicate the main building blocks for developing a position that leads a way out of that dilemma.

1.1 THE MOTIVATION FOR FUNCTIONALISM

In order to answer the mentioned questions, we have to consider modern physics. Since the advent of Newtonian mechanics, we have physical theories at our disposal that are *universal*, claiming to apply to everything that there is in the world, and that are *fundamental*, not depending on any other scientific theories. Being fundamental means that their laws are strict: these laws do not admit of any exceptions that cannot be described in terms of the theory in question. If the laws are deterministic, they indicate together with the specification of an initial situation complete conditions for the occurrence of the phenomena in question that are such that these phenomena cannot fail to obtain. If the phenomena nonetheless fail to obtain, the laws in question are falsified. However, it is not necessary that strict laws be deterministic laws. They can also be probabilistic. But they are exceptionless in this case as well. In other words, they indicate together with the specification of an initial situation the complete probabilities for the occurrence of the phenomena in question.

By contrast to the universal and fundamental theories of physics, the theories of the special sciences have only a limited domain of applicability each—for instance, biology considers only organisms—and they depend on the theories of physics. They are not in a position to describe their domain completely in their own concepts, but have finally to draw on the concepts of the fundamental physical theories. Their laws are not strict, but they admit of exceptions that cannot be described in their own vocabulary. The laws are so-called ceteris paribus laws. That is to say, they are valid only under normal conditions, and it cannot be defined within the vocabulary of the special science theory in question alone what exactly are the normal conditions and what exactly are the exceptions to them.

For instance, an important research topic in biology is the link between genetic causes and phenotypic effects, which are brought about by means of the production of certain proteins. However, any such link obtains only against the background of normal physical conditions. If the phenotypic effect does not come into existence, although the genetic cause is present, this does not necessarily imply that the law in question is falsified, but it may simply indicate that there are no normal physical conditions. There

8   Conservative Reductionism

always are physical factors in the organism or in its environment that can interfere with the causal chain from genetic cause to phenotypic effect and that cannot be described in the vocabulary of biology, but finally only in a fundamental physical vocabulary.

Consider a type of genes whose characteristic effect consists in producing proteins of a certain type. Such proteins may play an important role for example in determining the colour of the skin and the hair of an organism. One can describe the causal chain in question in a simplified manner as follows: a gene consists in a certain sequence of bases among other things. Replications of this sequence can be made that serve as templates for the production of sequences of amino acids. Such sequences of amino acids are then transformed into certain proteins that assume certain tasks in the cell or the organism. In this sense, there are genes whose products (the proteins) have more or less direct effects on the cell and in that way on the organism as a whole—such as, for instance, determining the colour of the skin and the hair. (In order to keep the example simple, we do not consider here genes that have phenotypic effects on the cell and the whole organism without coding for certain proteins.)

The sketched causal chain from the gene to the production of certain proteins becomes effective only under certain conditions. Such conditions are for example the presence of enough amino acids in order to build up the proteins in question. Furthermore, genetics has gained important insights in the manner in which the causal activity of genes is turned on and off. However detailed such a biological description of normal conditions may be, it finally has to refer to the fundamental physical theories. The reason is that factors that fall only within the scope of the fundamental physical theories can always interfere with the causal chain from gene to protein.

Let us now consider the main developments within modern physics in order to make the idea of the completeness of physics in contrast to the special sciences more precise. Newtonian mechanics and classical electrodynamics have been superseded by the theories of special and general relativity as well as by quantum theory in the 20th century. These theories will certainly not be the last word on the matter of fundamental physical theories either. However, whatever may be the future development of fundamental physics, considerations that stem from sciences whose theories are neither universal nor fundamental will be of no importance for that development. Classical mechanics, Newton's theory of gravitation and classical electromagnetism have not been superseded by general relativity and quantum field theory because there have been objections from chemistry, biology or psychology against their laying claim to being universal and fundamental theories, but because the objects and the properties that can be described by the laws of these theories have turned out to be not really fundamental. For instance, it has been shown that Newtonian mechanics is about classical properties that depend on quantum properties. By the same token, scientists will not achieve the unification of quantum field theory

The Dilemma of Functionalism   9

and general relativity theory in a new fundamental and universal physical theory on the basis of considerations applying to phenomena in the domain of the one or the other of the special sciences, but by throwing present presuppositions with respect to the fundamental physical objects into question (such as the presupposition of a passive background space-time in current quantum field theory, or the presupposition of a dynamical, but classical space-time in general relativity theory).

When it comes to considering the relationship between fundamental physics and the special sciences, we face since the advent of Newtonian mechanics the fact that there are fundamental and universal laws of physics that also apply to all the phenomena that fall within the domain of a special science. Even if the hypotheses about these fundamental and universal laws change consequent upon progress in physical research, such changes depend exclusively upon limits that these hypotheses meet within the domain of fundamental physics. As far as the relationship between physics and the special sciences is concerned, we have to take the fact of there being fundamental and universal physical theories and laws into account, and we cannot but base ourselves on the current best candidates for such theories and laws. In other words, the laws of quantum theory and general relativity theory may in the future be transferred to new fundamental and universal laws due to limits that these laws confront in the fundamental physical domain. However, the prospect of such a future development does not hinder that we have to consider these laws as fundamental and universally valid with respect to those phenomena that are treated by the special sciences.

The fact that there are fundamental and universal laws of physics does not exclude that the special sciences may refer to non-physical properties and thus to properties that are emergent with respect to the physical properties. When we use the term "emergent properties," we always mean the idea of properties that are not physical and that are not realized by physical properties, although they may have developed from physical properties during the temporal development of the universe. There may be special laws applying to these properties that are independent of the physical laws. However, such properties could not have any effects in the physical domain for which there are not also complete physical causes (insofar as there are causes at all—cf. the remark above about the issue of determinism). Consequently, such special laws could not be causal laws that refer to physical effects that are not completely covered by physical laws as well (insofar as they are covered by laws at all).

This is a decisive limitation: any change within an organism that can be described in terms of a biological theory always includes a microphysical change within that organism, which can only be described in terms of the concepts and laws of fundamental physics. Consequently, for any microphysical change, there are complete microphysical causes and laws (insofar as there are causes and laws at all). Any behaviour that has mental causes such as beliefs and desires always includes a microphysical change

10 Conservative Reductionism

within the body of the person. If, for instance, a person raises her left arm because she has the intention to raise her left arm, this movement includes a change of position down to the smallest microphysical particles in the arm. Their movement, however, is described only by fundamental physical laws. Consequently, for any change in the position of these particles, there are complete microphysical causes and laws (insofar as there are causes and laws at all).

The fundamental physical laws in question may be probabilistic instead of deterministic. As already mentioned, this difference is immaterial to present purposes. Even if the laws in question are probabilistic, they indicate the complete probabilities for the occurrence of the microphysical phenomena in question. No non-physical properties could influence the microphysical probabilities. This follows from the fact that the laws in question, even if they are probabilistic laws, are laws that belong to a fundamental theory. If one were to maintain that biological or mental causes exert an influence on microphysical probabilities that is not already included in the microphysical laws, one would be committed to drawing the consequence that the theories of biology or psychology which include such laws falsify the fundamental physical theories in question; for in this case, these fundamental physical theories would not indicate the correct probabilities for the occurrence of certain microphysical phenomena (see Loewer 1996 and Esfeld 2000). In other words, one would have to maintain that as soon as there are organisms or persons, the microphysical properties of organisms or persons do not behave in accordance with the microphysical theories and laws, so that the mere existence of organisms or persons would falsify these theories and laws.

Indeed, in order to refute the fundamental character of the physical theories and the principle of the completeness of physics, one would have to show that non-physical properties, falling within the range of a special science, are causally efficacious within the domain of the physical properties. In other words, there would have to be gaps in physical causation and in the laws of physics that could be filled by causes and laws from the domain of the special sciences. However, there is not the slightest indication of any such gaps. In particular, there is not the slightest hint that physical causation could leave gaps in the brain that could be filled by non-physical, mental causes. Quite to the contrary, neurobiological research bases itself on the laws of physics, notably the laws of mechanics, electromagnetism and gravitation. Descartes advanced the hypothesis of such a gap in the context of the physics known at his time, but this hypothesis is with good reason considered to be refuted since the time of Leibniz (see Leibniz, *Monadology* § 80, and P. McLaughlin 1993).

Nonetheless, the principle of the completeness of physics is a contingent fact about the world. This principle could be refuted empirically by discovering limits to the validity of the fundamental physical laws that could not be repaired by replacing one fundamental and universal physical theory

The Dilemma of Functionalism   11

with a new such theory (as Newtonian mechanics has been replaced with quantum mechanics), but that would call for the construction of specific bio-physical or psycho-physical theories with specific laws, since as soon as there are organisms or persons, the general laws of physics turn out not to be valid for the physical properties of organisms or persons.

Although the fact of there being fundamental and universal physical theories does hence not exclude that non-physical, emergent properties may exist, that fact implies that such emergent properties could only be epiphenomenal, not being able to cause any effects whose existence is not already brought about by physical causes alone. This consequence constitutes an impasse: there is no reason to suppose that there are epiphenomena. There are without doubt biological and psychological properties, but the rationale to admit their existence is just that they produce certain specific effects.

By indicating complete causes and laws for everything in the physical domain (insofar as there are causes and laws at all), the physical theories are able to explain everything in the physical domain (insofar as explanations are possible at all). Every scientific explanation draws on laws (or some law-like factors), and the laws are about properties that are causally efficacious in the situation in question. If the causal efficacy of the properties that fall within the domain of the special sciences always includes changes in microphysical properties, for which there are complete microphysical causes, laws and explanations, it is questionable what the contribution of the special sciences to the account of what there is in the world could be, a contribution that could in principle not be made by the universal and fundamental theories of physics alone.

We hence face the following situation: the fundamental theories of physics—and the domain of properties that are exclusively accounted for by these theories—are complete as regards causation, laws and explanations. Moreover, any change that has prima facie non-physical causes includes a change in the domain of microphysical properties, that is, a change that is accounted for exclusively by fundamental physical theories. We can capture this situation by employing the concept of supervenience, thereby also coming back to the starting point of this chapter. The form of supervenience that is at issue here is *global supervenience*. In the terms of Frank Jackson (1998, p. 8), global supervenience means that a minimal physical duplicate of the world is a duplicate simpliciter of the world—that is to say, contains everything that there is in the world. One conceives a minimal physical duplicate of the world if and only if one considers the domain of the world that is accounted for exclusively by the fundamental physical theories to be duplicated. Thus, the fact of there being fundamental and universal theories of physics, which are complete in the mentioned causal, nomological and explanatory sense, is the reason why an exact microphysical duplicate of the world would contain everything that there is in the world.

Applied to the descriptions that one can give of the world, supervenience is to say the following: the truth value of all propositions that refer

12 *Conservative Reductionism*

to something in the world supervenes on a complete description of the domain of those properties in the world that are treated exclusively by the fundamental physical theories. Such a complete description fixes the truth value of all other propositions about the world. In other words, the microphysical domain, which is described exclusively by the fundamental physical theories, is sufficient as truthmaker for all descriptions that refer to something in the world. Considering the consequences of global supervenience thus highlights the problem what the contribution of the special sciences to the scientific account of what there is in the world could be, a contribution that is not already covered by the fundamental and universal theories of physics.

The heuristic and pragmatic value of the special sciences is beyond dispute. As regards the phenomena in their domain, one can as a general rule presuppose that normal physical conditions hold and get to predictions and explanations of the phenomena in question in a much easier way than by employing the fundamental and universal laws of physics. However, it is questionable whether the special sciences have a cognitive value of their own, making a contribution to the scientific account of what there is in the world, which the fundamental and universal theories of physics are not able to make. Alexander Rosenberg (1994), for one, adopts an instrumentalist attitude towards biology based on a realist attitude towards physics. In sum, the fact of there being universal and fundamental laws of physics is not innocent at all in bearing only upon physics, but raises the question whether in the last resort the special sciences are dispensable when it comes to a scientific account of what there is in the world.

Nonetheless, the history of modern science since Newton is not the history of the triumph of a universal physics, offering an explanation for everything. The special sciences have developed in an autonomous manner—first chemistry, then in the 19th and the early 20th century the consolidation and new formation of many branches of biology, and finally, in the second half of the 20th century, cognitive science and neuroscience, to mention but a few central examples. Their historical development, however, does in itself not tell us anything about the systematic relationship between these sciences and physics. Nevertheless, the establishment of chemistry, biology, neuroscience and cognitive science as mature sciences of their own apart from physics entitles them prima facie to the claim of making their own contribution to the scientific account of what there is in the world. By the scientific quality of the special sciences, we mean that at least some of the properties in which they trade are natural kinds, support laws or lawlike generalizations and are causally efficacious. Accordingly, at least some of the concepts that are proper to the special sciences figure in law-like generalizations that are projectible, support counterfactuals and provide causal explanations. Highlighting merely the theoretical consequences of the completeness of physics is not sufficient to undermine the knowledge claims of the special sciences in particular, since no one has succeeded in

The Dilemma of Functionalism   13

carrying out the programme of a unified science that bases itself exclusively on physics.

We can therefore characterize the situation in the following manner: YES, of course, there are the fundamental and universal theories of physics; given these theories, one would end up in an impasse if one were to conceive the domain of the special sciences as consisting in non-physical, emergent properties. BUT nonetheless, the well-confirmed theories of the mature special sciences have not only a heuristic and pragmatic, but also a cognitive, scientific value, making a contribution of their own to the scientific account of what there is in the world, a contribution that cannot be replaced by physics. The task for the philosophical reflection on nature and the natural sciences thus is to work out a position that does justice to both these aspects—the unity of nature and the unity of science, as expressed in the knowledge claims contained in the universal and fundamental theories of physics, as well as its "plurality", as manifested in the contribution to the scientific understanding of the world that the special sciences make.

There seems to be an obvious solution to this problem: *functionalism.* This is the standard position since the 1970s not only in philosophy of mind and cognitive science, but also as regards the relationship between the special sciences and physics in general. The idea of functionalism can be summed up in the following three claims:

(1) *The properties that constitute the domain of the special sciences are functional properties.* These are causal properties: they consist in having certain specific effects, given normal conditions, and possibly also in having certain specific causes.

(2) *The functional properties that constitute the domain of the special sciences are realized by physical properties.* There is in each case a configuration of physical objects whose physical relations among themselves are such that, given normal conditions, they bring about qua configuration those effects that characterize a functional property of the special sciences. That is why they realize the functional property in question (see Melnyk 2003 for a detailed study of realization).

(3) *The functional properties that constitute the domain of the special sciences can be multiply realized by different physical properties.* Configurations of physical objects that are composed in different manners and that therefore come under different physical types (classifications) can nevertheless all realize a functional property of the same type of a special science, since they all bring about the same salient effects qua configurations under normal conditions.

The first step is by and large neutral: whatever philosophical theory one endorses, one can take up from the practices of the special sciences that they define the properties which they consider in a functional manner

14   *Conservative Reductionism*

by indicating the salient effects that these properties have under normal conditions (and possibly by including the usual causes of these properties as well). The philosophical theory that functionalism proposes consists in the second and the third step—in conceiving the functional properties that constitute the domain of the special sciences as being realized by physical properties and as being physically realized in multiple manners.

Let us come back to the mentioned example from genetics in this context: the property of being a certain gene is a functional and thus a causal property. It consists in bringing about certain phenotypic effects under normal conditions, which are, simplifying a complex story, the consequences of producing a protein of a certain type (1). Genes are realized by certain configurations of molecules. These are often DNA sequences in a certain molecular context of the cell. A detailed consideration of these matters will follow in section 4.2. These configurations of molecules are such that the manner in which the individual molecules are arranged leads to the configuration as a whole having under normal conditions the phenotypic effects that characterize the mentioned functional property. That is why the configuration realizes the gene in question (2). Molecular configurations (DNA sequences) that are composed in different physical manners can all produce qua configurations under normal conditions those phenotypic effects that characterize a gene of a certain type. That is why they can all realize the same type of gene, despite their physical differences. Thus, different molecular configurations (DNA sequences) can all code for sequences of amino acids of the same type, which then form a protein of a certain type. That is why scientists talk in terms of the redundancy of the genetic code: which amino sequence is employed to form a certain protein coded for by a triplet of bases. However, since the possible number of triplets of bases is higher than the possible number of amino sequences, one and the same type of amino sequence can be coded for by triplets of bases of different types. In other words, differently composed molecular configurations can lead to proteins of the same type (3).

In that manner, functional properties are conceived as being distinct from physical properties without being non-physical, emergent properties for they are realized by physical properties. Physical realization ties them to the physical domain, whereas multiple realizability excludes them so that they can be reduced to physical properties by being identical with them. The scientific quality of the special sciences thus consists in their classifications seizing something that is objectively there in the world without these classifications being identical with or reducible to physical classifications.

Consider again the mentioned example. One of the central concepts of biology is the one of selection. Certain configurations of molecules are selected because they have certain salient effects in certain environments. As regards selection, it is only these effects that the configurations have as a whole that count, whatever the physical composition of these configurations may be. That is why the biological classifications, which focus on these effects, seize something objectively relevant and have a scientific value that cannot be matched by physical classifications. The latter ones concentrate on the different physical compositions of these configurations. Due to multiple realization, the salient effects that all these configurations have in common despite their differences in molecular composition do not fall within the direct scope of physics. In that sense, it is biology that reveals what differently composed configurations of molecules functionally have in common—such as, for instance, producing a protein of a certain type, and it is only that functional effect of the gene that is pertinent to selection.

The multiple realizability of the properties in the domain of the special sciences hence establishes the scientific value of these sciences. That is why it seems that functionalism succeeds in doing justice to both aspects—the unity of nature and the unity of science, as expressed in the idea of the physical realization of the properties in the domain of the special sciences, as well as their variety, resulting from the fact that due to the multiple realizability of these properties, the classifications of the special sciences cannot be reduced to physical classifications.

1.2 ROLE FUNCTIONALISM

The dominant version of functionalism, which goes back mainly to Hilary Putnam (1967/1975) and Jerry Fodor (1974), regards the functional properties that are the subject of the special sciences as *causal roles*. That is why it is known as *role functionalism*. The role consists in producing certain specific effects given certain conditions. For, instance, being a gene is a causal role that consists in producing certain proteins and thereby certain phenotypic effects under certain conditions in the organism and its environment. Thus, there are, to mention but one example, genes for the colour of the skin and the hair. Oversimplifying, one can say that the production of the proteins which regulate the colour of the skin and the hair is activated only in cells of the skin and the hair.

According to role functionalism, any causal role is realized by configurations of physical objects whose physical relations are such that, given normal conditions, they bring about qua configurations those effects that characterize the role in question. Thus, genes are realized by certain molecular configurations (DNA sequences) which are such that, due to the way in which the molecules are arranged, they produce qua configurations under normal conditions the effects that characterize the gene in question. Any such role can be multiply realized. Configurations of molecules in the DNA that are composed in different manners can nevertheless have the same salient effects qua configurations. Thus, for instance, different

16 Conservative Reductionism

sequences of bases can code for the proteins that regulate the colour of the skin and the hair.

Role functionalism maintains that the role properties are not identical with the realizer properties. The reason is multiple realization. If there were no multiple realization, the distinction between role and realizer properties would break down. There would then be no rationale for considering the functional properties which constitute the subject of the special sciences as role properties and to contrast them with physical properties qua realizer properties.

By conceiving the functional properties in the domain of the special sciences as role properties, role functionalism takes them to be second-order properties. If an object has a role property, it automatically has other properties as well that realize the role in question. Possessing functional role properties consists in possessing other, physical properties that carry out the role in question. These are first-order properties. An object can have physical properties without these physical properties realizing a functional role property. By contrast, an object cannot have functional role properties without having physical properties that realize these role properties. The functional properties with which the special sciences are concerned exist in the world because during the temporal development of the universe, configurations of physical objects came into existence whose physical relations are such that these configurations produce effects due to which they realize functional role properties that are the subject of the special sciences. That is why the physical properties are first-order properties, whereas the functional properties that constitute the domain of the special sciences are second-order properties.

By requiring a physical realization, the functional role properties are tied to physical properties instead of being non-physical, emergent properties. Nonetheless, role functionalism faces the same problem as the theory of non-physical, emergent properties, namely that it is not intelligible how the role properties can be causally efficacious. According to role functionalism, the functional properties that are the subject matter of the special sciences are causal roles, defined by a characteristic pattern of effects each. However, the role properties as such are not causally efficacious. It is the properties that carry out the role, the physical properties, that bring about the effects in question. In other words, the presence of functional role properties indicates that there are other properties, the physical realizer properties, that produce certain effects. Nonetheless, citing the role properties may be relevant to causal explanations because these properties are indicators of the presence of certain causally efficacious realizer properties; what exactly these realizer properties are may not be important for certain explanatory purposes (cf. the so-called programme explanation of Jackson and Pettit 1990). Hence, if one conceives the functional properties that are the subject matter of the special sciences as role properties, being distinct from realizer properties, one faces the consequence that these functional properties

The Dilemma of Functionalism 17

are epiphenomena. Only the physical realizer properties are causally efficacious (cf. Block 1990).

To come back to genetics, if the property of being a gene is a functional role property, then not the genes, but the molecular configurations that realize genes in certain situations and that are not identical with them are causally efficacious. The genes indicate that there is something that is causally efficacious in producing certain phenotypic effects, but they do not themselves bring about these effects. It is the molecular sequences of bases, coding for certain proteins—such as those ones that regulate the colour of the skin and the hair—that are causally efficacious, and not the genes themselves.

One may attempt to avoid the consequence of epiphenomenalism by invoking systematic overdetermination (see notably Bennett 2003 and Loewer 2007). The idea is that both the role properties and the realizer properties figure in the relevant causal relations so that one and the same effect—such as the production of certain proteins—is overdetermined by two causes that are not identical with one another, such as genes and molecular sequences of bases. There is systematic overdetermination because any physical effect of a role property is caused at the same time by the realizer property in question—and given supervenience, there is a sufficient physical cause for any effect whatsoever that a role property causes. The proponents of this idea maintain that such systematic overdetermination is acceptable since the role properties strongly supervene on the realizer properties. Strong supervenience is to say that the existence of the physical realizer properties is a metaphysically sufficient condition for the existence of the functional role properties in question.

Strong supervenience is sufficient to make certain counterfactual propositions true. Suppose that in the situation represented by figure 1.2, the proposition "If p_1 had not occurred, p_2 would not have occurred either" is a true counterfactual. Then, by strong supervenience, the proposition "If b_1 had not occurred, p_2 would not have occurred either" is a true counterfactual as well, since there is no possible world in which there is a counterpart of p_1 without there being also a counterpart of b_1. However, we need an argument why that latter counterfactual should express a causal relation. In other words, we need an argument why strong supervenience on its own should exclude epiphenomenalism, that is to say, should exclude that a property which strongly supervenes on another property can be epiphenomenal. The mere fact of a property strongly supervening on another property cannot constitute a sufficient reason for claiming that the supervenient property also causes—some—of the effects that the subvenient property has so that these effects are overdetermined. Such a claim would amount to simply stipulating that properties which strongly supervene on other properties cannot be epiphenomenal, without offering any argument. The criticism that Marras (2007, pp. 318–319) voices against Kim (1998) ends up de facto in such a stipulation, as do the propositions of Harbecke (2008, chapter 4) and Kroedel (2008).

18 Conservative Reductionism

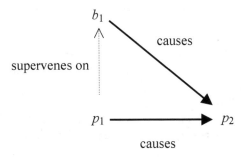

Figure 1.2 Systematic overdetermination.

This result is independent of the theory of causation to which one subscribes (for a contrary view see Ladyman 2008). The problem of epiphenomenalism arises in this context because the situation is not symmetric: supervenience is non-symmetric dependence of the supervening properties on the subvenient ones, and there is no symmetry in the causal relations into which these properties are supposed to enter either. For all physical property tokens, there are complete physical causes (insofar as there are causes at all). The laws in which types of physical properties figure are strict laws. The laws of the special sciences, by contrast, are never strict. Even if one endorses a theory of causation according to which causal relations are completely captured by counterfactual propositions, there is the mentioned failure of symmetry, since the laws of nature figure prominently among the truth conditions of the counterfactual propositions in question. That is to say, the counterfactual propositions that are about causal relations among physical property tokens have a privileged status, since they are backed up by strict laws. As already mentioned, there are of course also true counterfactual propositions linking supervenient property tokens with subsequent physical property tokens. However, there is no argument visible why these propositions should express a causal relationship—on pain of simply stipulating that supervenient properties cannot be epiphenomenal. For these reasons, we maintain that invoking the logical possibility of systematic overdetermination does not succeed in rebutting the epiphenomenalism objection against role functionalism (see Esfeld 2010 for that argument).

We hence reach the following conclusion: if one conceives multiple realization in an ontological manner as dualism of role and realizer properties, one vindicates an autonomous ontological status for the functional properties that are the subject of the special sciences and one establishes a link with the physical properties by means of the notion of realization. However, that link is too weak in order to avoid the epiphenomenalism problem into which the conception of non-physical, emergent properties obviously runs. In a nutshell, *multiple realization ontologically conceived leads to epiphenomenalism with respect to the properties that are the subject matter of*

The Dilemma of Functionalism 19

the special sciences. That is the one horn of the dilemma of functionalism. We shall introduce the other horn in the next section.

Before doing so, let us consider the idea of multiple realization, ontologically conceived, in more detail, for this very idea includes already a dilemma. Being aware of this dilemma is important in order to motivate the view of the relationship between property types and property tokens that enters into the position that we shall set out. Talking in terms of the multiple realization of functional properties is ambiguous: this talk may mean that functional property *types* are multiply realized, but also that functional property *tokens* are multiply realized. More precisely, if functional property tokens are multiply realized, then functional property types are also multiply realized, but not vice versa.

The idea of multiple realization, set out as an anti-reductionist argument, has been applied to property tokens—in contrast to property types—only since the beginning of the 1990s, in a context that we shall consider in section 2.5 (see notably Yablo 1992). To illustrate the claim at issue by drawing on our example from genetics, the idea is that one and the same gene token of a certain gene type could have produced the same protein token of a certain type even if that gene token had been realized by another molecular configuration than the one that in fact realizes it; that other molecular configuration comes under another physical type. Multiple realization can in this case not describe anything that occurs in the real world, but only relate to the comparison with other possible worlds: in another possible world, there is the same gene token, but in that other possible world, it is realized by a molecular configuration of another physical type.

There is an intuitive reservation against applying the idea of multiple realization to property tokens. Consider an analogy: Carmen, in Bizet's famous opera bearing that name, is a role for a mezzo-soprano voice. A performance is announced for a particular evening with Denyce Graves singing the role of the mezzo-soprano voice. In another possible world, Denyce Graves suffers a sudden bout of illness. The performance nevertheless takes place, but with Marta Senn singing the role of the mezzo-soprano voice. Since the person that realizes the mezzo-soprano voice has been exchanged, there is another token of the role of the mezzo-soprano voice (and not the same *token* being realized differently). In the same vein, it seems obvious that there is another gene token of the same gene type, if the molecular configuration that realizes the gene changes from one world to another world.

We can corroborate the intuitive reservation against applying the idea of multiple realization to property tokens by means of the following argument: if one endorses this idea, one is committed to the position that each token of a functional property possesses a primitive thisness, since its being is independent of the physical configuration that realizes it in a given world. In this case, there are two property tokens a and b of the same property type in the domain of a special science, in the world w_1, a is realized by a

20   Conservative Reductionism

physical configuration of type P_1, and b is realized by a physical configuration of type P_2. In the world w_2, by contrast, it is a that is realized by a physical configuration of type P_2, and it is b that is realized by a physical configuration of type P_1. The only difference between these two worlds is a swap of a and b. Such a position is known as haecceitism: worlds are recognized as being different whose only difference consists in a swap of individuals, without there being any qualitative difference between them. Haecceitism is widely considered to be an implausible position for this reason (see notably Lewis 1986b, chapter 4.4, and 2009, section 4). Applying the idea of multiple realization to property tokens thus ends up in an impasse (see also Sparber 2009, chapter 1.4.5).

Since the beginning of functionalism in the 1960s, the concept of physical realization has been applied to functional property types (see notably Putnam 1967/1975 and Fodor 1974). The idea is that properties of one and the same functional type of a special science can be realized by configurations of physical property tokens that are composed in different manners and that therefore come under different physical types. Realization thus is a relationship between a functional property *type* of a special science and physical property *tokens*. For instance, a certain gene in the sense of a certain gene type can be realized by tokens of molecular configurations that are composed in various physical manners and that hence belong to different physical types.

Realization, thus conceived, is compatible with each functional property token being identical with a configuration of physical property tokens. Realization applies to functional property types, and there is no identity between functional property types and physical property types, since any functional property type can be realized by configurations of various physical types. As multiple realization is, in the framework of functionalism, the only reason that prevents identity, one can go as far as maintaining the following: if only types, and not tokens, are multiply realized, it then follows in this context that any functional property token is identical with a configuration of physical property tokens.

Once we have reached that conclusion, however, it turns out to be questionable what the functional types could be ontologically over and above the tokens—in other words, what they could be as existing objectively in the world and not being identical with something physical. If any functional property token is identical with a configuration of physical property tokens, then some configurations of physical property tokens are functional property tokens. Token identity rules out that there is any sort of an ontological difference between the tokens in question.

It is of course possible to classify one and the same property token in different manners—according to its physical composition, as well as according to its function in the sense of its salient effects in a given environment. These classifications may of course be divergent. Not everything that comes in the same class on the criterion of function comes in that class on the criterion of physical composition as well. However, such classes are nothing that exists in the world over and above the property tokens, being somehow ontologically distinct from them. Scientists classify the tokens that they find in the world by building certain concepts—concepts for functions in the sense of salient effects in a given environment, as well as concepts for physical compositions. These concepts are different, but they can nonetheless apply to the same property tokens in the world.

The upshot of these considerations is this one: if property tokens are not multiply realized and if, consequently, the functional property tokens to which the special sciences refer are identical with configurations of physical property tokens, then the functional and physical types, being not identical with each other, cannot be anything that is ontologically out there in the natural world over and above the property tokens. The types then are concepts that classify the property tokens in the world according to different criteria (but see MacDonald and MacDonald 1986 against this conclusion). Nonetheless, all these different concepts can seize natural kinds (we shall elaborate on that point in section 5.3, and we shall consider the issue of property types as universals in section 2.5). Multiple realization of types hence boils down to multiple reference: one and the same functional *concept* of a special science refers to tokens that are composed in different physical manners and that are therefore referred to by different physical *concepts*. This result, however, amounts to a breakdown of role functionalism: we have de facto ended up in realizer functionalism now. The dilemma of the very idea of multiple realization, ontologically conceived, thus is this one: if that idea is applied to types and tokens, we are committed to a primitive thisness of the tokens (haecceitism). If that idea is applied only to types, it boils down to the multiple reference of concepts, instead of being about an ontological multiple realization.

Let us sum up. Role functionalism bases itself on a distinction between the functional properties that constitute the subject matter of the special sciences and the physical properties. The former are role properties; the latter are realizer properties. This difference exists because the functional properties can be multiply realized by physical properties. However, insofar as the functional properties are not identical with physical properties, they are epiphenomena. This is the first horn of the dilemma that functionalism faces. Moreover, if we go into the notion of multiple realization in a more detailed manner, we come to the conclusion that it is unclear how multiple realization could ground an ontological difference between functional and physical properties: if functional property *tokens* are multiply realized, one ends up in the impasse of being committed to acknowledging a primitive thisness (haecceity) of these property tokens. If the functional property *tokens* are not multiply realized, then they are identical with configurations of physical property tokens. It is then only functional *types* that are multiply realized. However, given token identity, types cannot be anything ontological that exists out there in the natural

22 *Conservative Reductionism*

world over and above the tokens and that is not identical with something physical. Types then are concepts that classify one and the same tokens in the world according to different criteria.

1.3 REALIZER FUNCTIONALISM

The position known as realizer functionalism is as old as role functionalism but used to be a minority position. It has been developed since the late 1960s notably by David Lewis and David Armstrong (see in particular Lewis 1966, 1970, 1972, 1994 as well as Armstrong 1968). We shall focus on Lewis' position in this section and not go into the differences between Lewis' and Armstrong's views. Like role functionalism, realizer functionalism starts from the functional descriptions that the special sciences use. However, whereas role functionalism conceives these descriptions as being about causal role properties, realizer functionalism takes them to refer to the physical realizer properties. That is why this position is known as realizer functionalism.

Consequently, there is no need to differentiate between functional properties as second-order properties and physical properties as first-order properties. There is only one sort of properties, namely the physical properties. Some configurations of physical objects are such that, due to the physical relations among these objects, they bring about effects that are those effects on which the functional descriptions of the special sciences focus. That is why these configurations make those descriptions true. In short, there are only physical property tokens and their configurations, but some of these configurations make not only physical descriptions true, but also functional descriptions of the special sciences. Multiple realization is to say that functional descriptions of the same type are made true by configurations of different physical types because these configurations differ in composition. It is therefore more precise to talk in terms of multiple reference: functional descriptions of one and the same type refer to configurations of different physical types.

According to David Lewis's famous thesis of Humean supervenience, the world consists in the distribution of the fundamental physical properties in space-time. The fundamental properties occur at space-time points. Mass, charge, spin, velocity, and the like are candidates for such properties. Lewis takes these properties to be categorical and intrinsic (see in particular Lewis 1986a, introduction). *Categorical properties* are pure qualities, not being causal as such: what these properties are, their essence, is independent of the causal and the nomological relations in general in which they figure. In other words, these properties are purely qualitative only, without their qualitative essence including the power or the disposition to cause certain effects. Intrinsic properties are such that objects can have these properties independently of being alone or being accompanied by other objects (see

The Dilemma of Functionalism 23

Langton and Lewis 1998 as well as Hoffmann 2010, part 1, for a detailed study about intrinsic properties).

Lewis accepts the whole distribution of the categorical and intrinsic properties at the points of space-time—in other words, the whole fundamental physical domain—as a starting point. The laws of nature supervene on this distribution as a whole. The laws therefore vary from one world to another possible world, depending on what the distribution of the fundamental physical properties at the space-time points of the world in question is like. Causal relations, in turn, depend on the laws of nature. Consequently, whether or not there is a relationship of cause and effect between two given property tokens depends on what the distribution of the fundamental physical properties as a whole is like.

According to a simple regularity theory of causation, such as the one set out by David Hume, whether or not there is a causal relationship between two spatio-temporally contiguous property tokens a and b depends on whether or not tokens of the same type as b regularly follow tokens of the same type as a (see notably Hume, *Treatise of human nature* (1739), book I, part III, and *Enquiries concerning human understanding* (1748), section VII). According to a sophisticated regularity theory of causation in terms of counterfactual dependence between property tokens, causal relationships again essentially depend on the laws of nature, because the laws of nature are a crucial element of the truth conditions of the counterfactual propositions in question, and the laws of nature supervene on the distribution of the fundamental physical properties as a whole (see notably Lewis 1973). In short, by being the supervenience basis for laws of nature and thereby for causal relations, the distribution of the categorical and intrinsic properties at space-time points over the whole of space-time makes true not only fundamental physical, but also causal, functional and dispositional descriptions of what there is in the world.

Nonetheless, it is not necessary in the framework of Lewis's position to maintain that any proposition about a causal relationship immediately refers to the world as a whole. It is possible to uphold in this framework the view that a configuration of physical objects, which consists in the last resort of particles located at space-time points, has certain effects due to its physical composition. That is to say, it has certain effects due to the physical relations that obtain among the objects which make up the configuration in question and that, apart from the spatio-temporal relations, supervene on the categorical and intrinsic properties of these objects. However, any such configuration has certain effects only against the background of there being certain laws of nature, which supervene on the distribution of the fundamental physical properties as a whole. Nothing in Lewis's position thus prevents one from maintaining that, for instance, a certain configuration of molecules has certain phenotypic effects due to its physical composition and therefore makes true a certain description in terms of classical genetics, although there is a causal

24 Conservative Reductionism

relation between the configuration of molecules and the phenotypic effect only because certain laws of nature obtain in the world.

Since certain configurations of physical objects assume in this way certain functional roles—namely by producing certain effects due to their composition against the background of the whole distribution of the fundamental physical properties—it is possible to talk in terms of functional properties in a vague sense. But this way of talking is not exact: to be precise, the functional roles are role descriptions, and the properties are not functional properties, because it is not essential to them to cause certain effects—what they are is independent of any causal dispositions. Thus, the physical configurations that make true certain functional role descriptions in the real world may assume another functional role—or no functional role at all—in other possible worlds, depending on what the distribution of the fundamental physical, purely qualitative (categorical) properties is like in the world in question.

To come back to the example from genetics, a certain molecular configuration makes a certain functional description in terms of classical genetics true, not because the properties which constitute the configuration in question are functional properties—they are purely qualitative properties; it is the occurrence of a certain configuration of categorical properties against the background of the whole distribution of the fundamental categorical properties in the world that makes the functional description in terms of classical genetics true. In a nutshell, there are no functional properties of the special sciences, but only categorical properties of physics. Nonetheless, the functional descriptions of the special sciences are true. The distribution of the categorical properties in space-time makes them true. Realizer functionalism thus provides for truthmakers of the functional descriptions of the special sciences without being committed to recognizing functional properties that exist in the world.

Multiple realization means according to realizer functionalism that the functional descriptions of the special sciences refer multiply in the following sense: descriptions of one and the same type of a special science refer to physical configurations that come under different physical types due to their differences in composition. In other words, these configurations of categorical, physical properties all make true descriptions of a certain functional type, without having something physical in common that distinguishes them from all the other physical configurations that do not make a functional description of the type in question true.

By way of consequence, it is questionable how these functional descriptions can have a scientific quality. All the effects that the physical configurations that make these descriptions true can have possess complete physical causes and can therefore be explained exclusively in physical terms. If the functional descriptions of the special sciences are not about genuinely functional properties, but refer to configurations of categorical, physical properties and if these configurations do not have anything physical in common

The Dilemma of Functionalism 25

that distinguishes them from all the other configurations, then it is not intelligible what contribution to a scientific account of the world the functional descriptions of the special sciences could make that is not already provided for by physics.

There is, however, a strategy available within realizer functionalism that seeks to link the functional descriptions of the special sciences up with physical descriptions and explanations despite multiple realization or multiple reference. This strategy supposes that multiple realization (multiple reference) does not occur within one and the same species. In other words, within a given species, a functional description of a certain type always refers to physical configurations that come under one and the same physical type. Thus, functional and physical descriptions are coextensive within a given species.

Consider an artificial example that used to be common in the literature on the philosophy of mind. Suppose that if and only if a human being suffers pain, c-fibres in the brain are stimulated. Suppose furthermore that if and only if an octopus suffers pain, b-fibres in the brain are stimulated. In this case, as far as the human species is concerned, the functional description "suffers pain" is coextensive with the physical description "c-fibres are stimulated." Furthermore, as far as the species octopus is concerned, the functional description "suffers pain" is coextensive with the physical description "b-fibres are stimulated." Consequently, the functional theory about pain can be reduced to the physical theory about c-fibres in the case of the human species, and it can be reduced to the physical theory about b-fibres in the case of the species octopus.

Coming back to the previously mentioned example from genetics, suppose for the sake of the argument that there are no significant physical differences among the genes that code for the production of proteins that regulate the colour of the skin and the hair in the human species. Suppose that in dogs, by contrast, the genes for the colour of the skin and the hair are realized in another physical manner, but again without significant physical differences within that species. In this case, the functional description of the gene for the colour of the skin and the hair can be reduced to a molecular description, but to a molecular description that changes if one passes from one species to another species.

It is not important for this strategy whether the functional concepts of the special sciences really refer uniformly within a given species. The group with respect to which there is uniform reference may be a sub-species or another group. Furthermore, the laws in question are of course only ceteris paribus laws, which admit of exceptions. The essential point of this strategy is to find for any type of a functional description of a special science groups that are physically homogeneous and with respect to which the functional description in question refers uniformly. This strategy goes back to David Lewis (1969, 1980) and has since been taken up notably by Jaegwon Kim (1998, in particular pp. 93–95, and 2005, in particular p. 25).

26   Conservative Reductionism

However, this strategy does not reply to the objection according to which the scientific quality of the special sciences gets lost in realizer functionalism due to multiple reference. This strategy is not in the position to vindicate a scientific quality for functional classifications such as "gene for the regulation of the colour of the skin and the hair" or "pain" (which takes in the mentioned artificial example the place of a functional concept of psychology). What this strategy can achieve is to vindicate a scientific quality for classifications such as "gene for the regulation of the colour of the skin and the hair in humans" or "pain in humans," insofar as these classifications group physical configurations together that come under the same physical type. However, concepts such as "gene for the regulation of the colour of the skin and the hair in humans" or "pain in humans" are not functional concepts, construed in the vocabulary of the special science in question, but hybrid functional-cum-physical concepts. The criterion that secures the uniform reference of these concepts is not a functional one of the special sciences, but a physical one. One searches for physical groups with respect to which the reference of the functional concept of the special science in question is uniform and one then defines hybrid functional-cum-physical concepts for these groups. These functional-cum-physical concepts relativize the functional concepts of the special sciences to a certain group in each case that is defined only according to physical criteria. Consequently, there is no significant common functional meaning of these concepts left. In other words, there is no space in this strategy for the functional concepts of the special sciences such as "gene for the regulation of the colour of the skin and the hair" or "pain" and the descriptions, laws and explanations that are couched in terms of these concepts. These concepts are eliminated in favour of the mentioned hybrid functional-cum-physical concepts, which apply to a certain group each that is defined according to physical criteria only.

This strategy does hence not attain a stable position which secures the scientific quality of the special sciences with respect to the challenge that they face from physics. There is no obstacle to developing this strategy into an eliminativist reductionism, such as the contemporary position known as new wave reductionism. In order to reduce the theories of the special sciences to physical theories, this position also searches for physically defined groups with respect to which the concepts of a given theory of the special sciences refer uniformly. Reduction then is achieved in the following manner: one constructs within the vocabulary of an encompassing physical theory an image of the theory of the special science in question such that the concepts of the latter theory, insofar as they are applied to specific groups, can be uniformly correlated with physical concepts. Thus, concepts such as "gene for the regulation of the colour of the skin and the hair in humans" or "pain in humans" are uniformly correlated with physical concepts. These mixed functional-cum-physical concepts are then eliminated in favour of the coextensive physical concepts of the reducing theory; for these functional-cum-physical concepts do not contain anything that could

The Dilemma of Functionalism 27

not be expressed by using the corresponding physical concepts alone. In that manner, a single theory of a special science is replaced with several group-specific physical theories that are constructed in the vocabulary of one encompassing physical theory. This conception goes back to Clifford Hooker (1981, in particular p. 49). It has been developed by John Bickle (1998, 2003) into the current known as new wave reductionism.

Let us sum up. Realizer functionalism adopts an eliminativist attitude with respect to the functional properties in which the special sciences deal. Their descriptions are nevertheless true, being made true by physical configurations. However, this eliminativist attitude with respect to the functional properties leads to the consequence that—due to multiple realization or, more precisely, multiple reference—the scientific quality of the special sciences is also eliminated. Only purely physical descriptions and theories that apply to particular, physically defined groups and that are integrated into an encompassing physical theory belong in the last resort to a scientific account of the world.

1.4 THE FUTURE OF FUNCTIONALISM

Although functionalism looks promising at first glance, its two standard versions run into a dilemma: role functionalism, which bases itself on a distinction between functional role and physical realizer properties, faces the consequence that the functional properties are epiphenomenal. Realizer functionalism eliminates not only the functional properties but also the scientific quality of the functional concepts, laws and explanations of the special sciences. We are thus confronted with a dilemma whose one horn is epiphenomenalism and whose other horn is eliminativism. Nonetheless, there is no other position visible that could take the place of functionalism. The two main non-functionalist alternative positions of either admitting non-physical emergent properties or of retreating to a physicalism that recognizes only physics obviously run into the mentioned dilemma as well—epiphenomenalism in the first case, eliminativism in the second one.

Functionalism is the only position that offers an explanation of why there are the properties in the world that make up the subject matter of the special sciences. These properties exist in the world because during the temporal development of the universe, stable configurations of microphysical objects have developed that are arranged in such a manner that they bring about qua configurations under certain environmental conditions the effects of which characterize the functional properties of the special sciences. This type of explanation is known as functional reduction. We shall consider it in detail in section 5.1.

This analysis suggests the following conclusion: functionalism still is an attractive position. The arguments that motivate it and that we have sketched out in section 1.1 have by no means lost their force. We still

28   *Conservative Reductionism*

need a middle way between emergentist dualism on the one hand and eliminativist physicalism on the other, doing justice to both the unity of nature, expressed in the principle of the completeness of physics, and to its plurality, expressed by the scientific quality of the special sciences. Functionalism is the only option available to construct such a middle way. However, functionalism has to be spelled out in another manner than in the standard versions of role and realizer functionalism, which run into exactly the same dilemma that emergentist dualism and eliminativist physicalism face.

We take the analysis of the roots of that dilemma as a motivation for drawing the following two conclusions:

(1) It is wrong-headed to conceive an opposition between functional and physical properties (or functional and physical descriptions, respectively).
(2) It is wrong-headed to build an anti-reductionist argument on multiple realization.

If one sets out to secure the domain and the scientific quality of the special sciences by distinguishing functional from physical properties and by employing multiple realization as an anti-reductionist argument, the special sciences will not win, but lose (see also P. Smith 1992, in particular p. 25). For in that case, the properties that are the subject of the special sciences can only be epiphenomenal, and, given the principle of the completeness of physics, it is not intelligible what the scientific quality of the special sciences could be, making a contribution to a scientific account of the world that is not already made by physics alone.

However, how can one avoid eliminativism, if one is not prepared to accept a contrast between functional and physical properties and if one does not conceive multiple realization, or the multiple reference of the functional descriptions of the special sciences, as an anti-reductionist argument? The considerations in the subsequent chapters of this book build on the following two theses:

(1) All properties that there are in the world, including the physical ones, are functional properties in the sense of being causal properties.
(2) All true descriptions (laws, theories) that the special sciences propose can in principle be reduced to physical descriptions (laws, theories) by means of functional reduction, despite multiple realization.

Adding a further premise about the nature of properties, the first thesis opens up the way for holding that the functional properties on which the special sciences focus are identical with physical properties without ending up in an eliminativist position; for the physical properties are themselves functional—in the sense of being causal properties—and endorsing the

The Dilemma of Functionalism 29

claim of the properties of the special sciences being identical with physical properties is the only way open to vindicate their causal efficacy, given the causal completeness of the physical domain. By pleading for identity, we abandon the claim that functional properties are—physically—realized. There is no question of realization, but simply identity. What characterizes instead our position as a version of functionalism is that we take all properties to be functional in the sense of being causal properties. It goes without saying that we have to explain this thesis and have to set out arguments for it that are independent of the debate about the mentioned dilemma of functionalism. We shall do so in the next chapter in this volume.

The second thesis ties the descriptions, laws and theories of the special sciences to physical descriptions, laws and theories. More precisely, only by providing for the principled possibility of reducing the descriptions, laws and theories of the special sciences to physical descriptions, laws and theories are we in a position to argue that these descriptions, laws and theories possess a scientific quality, making a contribution to the account of what there is in the world, without its being possible to replace them with physical descriptions, laws and theories. In a nutshell, we need reduction, since opposing the special sciences to physics will end up in the special sciences losing that competition, but a reduction that is not open to replacement. We shall show in chapter 5 in this volume how this result can be achieved.

The position to which these two theses point is a *conservative reductionism*. A reductionism—ontological as well as epistemological—is conservative if and only if it is able to show why it does not pave the way for drawing eliminativist consequences. Our task thus is to develop a reductionist, but anti-eliminativist position. The key for accomplishing that task is the conception of all properties as functional properties, more precisely causal properties in the sense of causal structures.

2 The Metaphysics of Causal Structures

2.0 INTRODUCTION TO CHAPTER 2

Let us come back to the thought experiment developed at the beginning of the first chapter. Let us now sharpen that thought experiment in the following manner: suppose that one can define an initial state of the world in time unambiguously. In this state, there are only microphysical properties, which can be described by a fundamental physical, cosmological theory. Suppose now that this initial state is copied in the sense that one creates a duplicate w^* of the real world w whose initial state is identical with the initial state of w. Is in this case the whole development in time of w^* also identical with the development in time of w, so that—against the background of the answer to the thought experiment at the beginning of the first chapter—w^* is a duplicate *simpliciter* of w?

We have no clear intuition to answer this question. On the one hand, answering this question in the affirmative means to maintain an encompassing determinism: together with the properties at the initial state of nature, there are certain laws, and these laws and the conditions at the initial state determine the whole development of the world. One would need strong arguments to establish such an encompassing determinism, and such arguments are not simply provided by the current physical theories or general philosophical considerations.

On the other hand, simply rejecting the idea expressed in this thought experiment is not plausible either. Our intuitions are not such that we think that given identical initial states in w and w^*, the further development of both these worlds could be completely divergent, such that w^* could turn out to be entirely different from w: the only thing that they have in common is their identical initial states, but there then develop entirely different properties and objects in w^*. If this were so, then for any point of time t_n, there could be a world w^* that is up to t_n identical with w, but completely diverges from w after t_n. Let us suppose that the time indication 20 September 2010 5.30 p.m. can be translated into an unequivocal global time indication. There then could be a world w^* that

The Metaphysics of Casual Structures 31

is up to that time identical with w, but completely diverges from w after that time in that there are properties in w^* that are alien to w.

Our intuition is to maintain the following: with the properties that occur at the initial state of the world, certain laws of nature are determined for the world, and there therefore are certain tendencies for the future of the world, which can be expressed in terms of probabilities. It is not the case that everything is fixed at the beginning of the world, but it is also not the case that just anything can happen. This intuition is sufficient to water down the distinction between functional and physical properties and to introduce the causal theory of properties.

In this chapter, we shall pursue this intuition by setting out a philosophical argumentation. In the first place, we introduce the philosophical argument for the causal theory of properties (section 2.1). This argument tacitly assumes that the fundamental properties are intrinsic properties. However, according to today's fundamental physical theories, the fundamental properties are in the first place relations or structures rather than intrinsic properties (section 2.2). Against this background—philosophical argument for causal properties, physical argument for structures—we build up a theory of causal structures (section 2.3) and reconstruct the transition from the fundamental physical structures to local, complex structures that constitute the domain of the one or the other of the special sciences (section 2.4). We develop the metaphysics of causal structures to show a way out of the mentioned dilemma of epiphenomenalism and eliminativism. In order to be in the position to do so, we first have to set out arguments in favour of this metaphysics that are independent of the debate about functionalism and the relationship between physics and the special sciences. By the same token, we first have to give reasons for our view of properties as ways (modes) in which the objects are that are independent of this debate (section 2.5). Having established the metaphysics of causal structures as the ways (modes) in which the objects are, we can then work out a conservative ontological reductionism that avoids the dilemma of epiphenomenalism and eliminativism at the end of this chapter (section 2.6).

2.1 THE PHILOSOPHICAL ARGUMENT FOR CAUSAL PROPERTIES

When considering the two standard versions of functionalism in chapter 1, this volume, we have taken for granted that there is a clear distinction between functional and physical properties, as well as between functional and physical descriptions. The latter realize the former or make the former descriptions true. However, this distinction is by no means unambiguous. Mental properties are considered to be a paradigmatic example of functional properties. It is assumed that mental properties are realized

32 Conservative Reductionism

by neurobiological properties. The latter hence are non-functional, physical properties with respect to mental properties. However, neurobiological properties are themselves properties within the domain of a special science, by contrast to those properties that fundamental physics considers. In comparison to the fundamental physical properties, neurobiological properties are seen as functional properties that are multiply realized by physical properties. One and the same properties can hence be physical realizer properties with respect to other functional properties in the domain of a special science and multiply realizable functional properties with respect to the fundamental physical properties.

A consideration in this vein applies even if one supposes that the properties which realize mental properties are molecular biological properties—instead of neurobiological properties, which can themselves be realized in multiple molecular manners. One can maintain that even the molecular biological properties are functional properties in comparison with the fundamental physical properties (see Rosenberg 1994, pp. 24–25; cf. also the position that Gillet 2007 describes as continuity functionalism). Only the fundamental physical properties, whose configurations realize in the last resort all the functional properties that there are in the world, would thus be non-functional, physical properties.

However, the problem that the mentioned reflection highlights cannot be solved in that way. For the descriptions of the fundamental physical properties are also functional descriptions. Consider what Frank Jackson says about this matter:

> When physicists tell us about the properties they take to be fundamental, they tell us what these properties *do*. This is no accident. We know about what things are like essentially through the way they impinge on us and our measuring instruments. . . . it does suggest the possibility that (i) there are two quite different intrinsic properties, P and P^*, which are exactly alike in the causal relations they enter into, (ii) sometimes one is possessed and sometimes the other, and (iii) we mistakenly think that there is just one property because the difference does not make a difference (. . .). An obvious extension of this possibility leads to the uncomfortable idea that we may know next to nothing about the intrinsic nature of the world. We know only its causal cum relational nature. (Jackson 1998, pp. 23–24; see also Blackburn 1990)

We can know the properties of the objects that there are in the world only insofar as these properties display causal relations. In order for us to gain knowledge of something, there has to be a causal relation with our cognitive apparatus, however indirect that relation may be. This fact neither implies any relativism nor any limitations of our cognitive capacities. We can put forward universal physical theories that claim to apply to everything in the world, and we may have good reasons to regard these theories as true; they may in fact be true. However, in order to distinguish these theories as empirical theories about the real world in contrast to simple models of possible worlds, it has to be possible to build up a causal relation between the objects that these theories admit and our cognitive apparatus, however indirect that causal relation may be.

This argument implies that there is no separation between functional and physical descriptions. The physical descriptions are also functional descriptions, since they describe the properties to which they refer in terms of certain relations among these properties, notably causal relations. These causal relations include, via experimental arrangements, in the last resort relations with our cognitive apparatus. These latter relations do not have any particular status. The propositions that express laws of nature indicate relations among properties, and the relations with our cognitive apparatus simply are some such relations. As mentioned, this fact does not imply any limitations of our cognitive capacities.

A limitation of our cognitive capacities follows if—and only if—one maintains, as Jackson does in the citation above, that at least some of the properties to which the functional descriptions refer are intrinsic and categorical properties. In other words, they are properties whose essence is not given by the causal relations which they display or can display. They are pure qualities. Only under this presupposition does it follow that there is an essence of these properties which is independent of the relations in which they manifest themselves and of which we can consequently not gain any knowledge. The reason for maintaining that at least some of the fundamental physical properties are intrinsic and categorical properties cannot stem from any scientific description of these properties. Science limits itself to indicating relations. It is simply a metaphysical assumption to postulate that there is a purely qualitative essence of these properties underlying the relations in which they are engaged.

The limitation of our cognitive capacities that Jackson considers in the quotation above hence is a consequence of a metaphysical assumption about the essence of the properties: their essence is purely qualitative, being a primitive suchness, known as *quiddity* (that term has been introduced in the contemporary debate by Black 2000). That quiddity or pure quality is primitive, since it is independent of all causal and nomological relations in which the properties figure. We thus face a gap between metaphysics and epistemology: according to the metaphysics under consideration, the essence of properties is a primitive suchness. It is in principle not possible to gain knowledge of it. This latter consequence is known as *humility* in the literature. The concept of humility is employed in this context to express the idea that a cognitive access to the essence of the properties is impossible for metaphysical reasons (see Langton 1998 for an elaborate treatment).

When discussing the idea of the multiple realizability of property tokens in section 1.2, we encountered—and criticized—the idea of a haecceitistic difference between possible worlds. That is a difference between worlds

34 *Conservative Reductionism*

which consists only in the fact that there are different individuals in two worlds, without there being any qualitative difference between the worlds in question. In other words, a haecceitistic difference is a difference between individuals which has the consequence that worlds have to be recognized as different, although they are indiscernible. If one maintains that the essence of properties is a primitive suchness (a quiddity), a similar consequence ensues: one is in this case committed to recognizing worlds as different that are identical with respect to all causal and nomological relations, but that differ in the purely qualitative essence of the properties that exist in them. It is a difference that does not make a difference, as Jackson puts it in the quotation above. *A quidditistic difference thus is a qualitative difference between worlds due to which worlds have to be recognized as different, although they are indiscernible.*

Let us come back to David Lewis in order to illustrate how one can elaborate on this position. Following Lewis, all scientific descriptions of the world are descriptions of a functional role that refer to the properties that realize the role in question. However, we cannot know these properties (the realizer properties). They possess according to Lewis a purely qualitative essence (a primitive suchness or quiddity) (see Lewis 2009). Consider one of the examples discussed in section 1.3: following Lewis's conception of reduction, we can reduce the description "suffers pain" in the case of the human species to the description "c-fibres are stimulated." The latter one, however, also is a functional description. One can further reduce the description "c-fibres are stimulated," possibly with further restrictions to specific groups, until one gets to a fundamental physical description. The same applies to the description "gene for the regulation of the colour of the skin and the hair." Suppose that we can reduce this description in the case of the human species to exactly one type of a molecular description and that latter description to a fundamental physical description. However, the fundamental physical description also is a functional description, indicating relations, notably causal relations.

All these descriptions refer to the realizer properties, that is, the properties which display the relations in question against the background of the whole distribution of the fundamental physical properties in the world. However, these descriptions do not reveal the essence of these properties. Lewis presupposes that the properties which fulfil the role descriptions are intrinsic and categorical properties. They possess a qualitative essence, a primitive suchness (quiddity) that is independent of the relations which they display. Ann Whittle (2006, pp. 469–472) and Alyssa Ney (2007, pp. 50–53) are right in highlighting that our descriptions refer nonetheless to the fundamental properties. But these descriptions cannot disclose what the properties they refer to are, since what these properties are is independent of the causal roles they play in a given world (see also Locke 2009, pp. 227–228). Properties of the same type whose essence is a primitive suchness can display entirely different causal and nomological relations in different possible worlds, depending

The Metaphysics of Casual Structures   35

on what the distribution of the intrinsic and categorical properties as a whole is like in the world in question.

Consequently, there always automatically is multiple realizability or the possibility of multiple reference. Functional descriptions of one and the same type can be made true by configurations of intrinsic properties whose primitive suchness is entirely different, as long as the relations among these properties are such that they fulfil the functional descriptions in question against the background of the whole distribution of intrinsic and categorical properties in the world in question. Thus, for instance, the intrinsic properties that make true the fundamental physical description "negative elementary charge" in the real world can make true the fundamental physical description "mass x" in another possible world, and vice versa. In other words, properties of one and the same type—having the same primitive suchness—can in one world fulfil the charge role and in another world the mass role. That is why one cannot deduce the nature of the realizer from the role.

In that manner, all our descriptions including the fundamental physical ones can automatically refer multiply. Jackson speaks in the quotation above of two types of intrinsic properties P and P^* whose occurrences display exactly the same causal relations so that it is in principle impossible to gain knowledge of the difference between these properties. This is a case of multiple realization: exactly the same causal, functional relations or descriptions can be realized by properties of the type P, but also by properties of the type P^*.

We can sum up the result of these considerations in the following manner:

(1) There is no principled difference between functional and physical descriptions. The physical descriptions are also functional ones, since they indicate relations, notably causal relations.

(2) If one maintains that there is a principled difference between functional and physical properties or that the properties in the world are physical in contrast to functional ones, one is committed to the view that the essence of the physical properties consists in a primitive suchness (quiddity). Consequently, we cannot know the essence of these properties; for our descriptions, being functional ones, can only capture the relations into which these properties enter, but not their intrinsic, qualitative nature. This consequence is known as humility.

(3) If one maintains that the physical properties have an intrinsic, purely qualitative essence, it follows that the functional properties are always automatically multiply realizable and that the functional descriptions can always automatically refer multiply; for properties whose purely qualitative essences are entirely different can nevertheless display the same causal, functional relations (fulfil the same role).

Why should one endorse the view that the essence of the properties that there are in the world is a primitive suchness (a quiddity) so that we can

36 *Conservative Reductionism*

in principle not know that essence? Recognizing a primitive suchness is a strong metaphysical commitment: the qualitative nature of the properties is supposed to be something primitive that is independent of all causal and nomological relations. Consequently, the difference between two types of fundamental properties is a primitive one—a difference that does not make a difference as Jackson puts it in the quotation above. As mentioned above, we are hence committed to recognizing worlds as different, although they are indiscernible. Considering these consequences, one may very well come to the conclusion that the argumentation has ended in an impasse by contrast to a reasonable metaphysical position (see already Black 2000; for a contrary view see Noonan 2010).

Instead of maintaining, as does Jackson in the quotation above, that there are intrinsic and categorical properties (pure qualities) underlying the causal relations, one can propose a metaphysics of properties according to which the properties are causal in themselves. In other words, instead of the essence of a property being a primitive suchness, the essence of a property is the power to enter into certain causal relations. Consequently, what the properties are manifests itself in the causal relations in which they figure, or in which objects stand in virtue of the properties that they have. It is not possible to separate the properties from the causal relations. Sydney Shoemaker (1980), for instance, draws from considerations that are similar to the one of Jackson in the quotation above the consequence of a causal theory of properties.

The causal view of properties has become a strong contender in the metaphysics of properties since the 1980s. In addition to Sydney Shoemaker (1980) and Rom Harré and E. H. Madden (1975), versions of this view are developed today mainly by Stephen Mumford (1998, chapter 9) and Alexander Bird (2007a) as well as C. B. Martin (1997) and John Heil (2003, chapter 11) (see also Hawthorne 2001, who characterizes this view as "causal structuralism" and Chakravartty 2007, chapter 3– 5, as well as Strawson 2008). We propose to spell this view out in the following manner: *in being certain qualities, properties are causal, namely powers to produce certain specific effects.*

Take charge for example. This is a fundamental physical property that can occur at space-time points. Charge is a certain quality that is distinct from, for instance, mass. There are fundamental physical objects which have the same charge, but different rest mass and vice versa (electrons and myons, and electrons and positrons). In being a certain qualitative property, charge is a power that manifests itself in certain causal relations, namely the power to generate an electromagnetic field, resulting in the attraction of opposite-charged and the repulsion of like-charged objects. These causal relations are described by the physical field theory of electromagnetism (much more precision would of course be needed for an adequate discussion of electromagnetism; the example is only meant as an illustration of the view of properties that we defend).

The Metaphysics of Casual Structures 37

This view of properties is only coherent on the condition that one considers the qualitative and the causal character of properties as identical. These are not even different aspects of properties, but exactly one and the same. The position of C. B. Martin (1997) and John Heil (2003, chapter 11) is often read as a double aspect theory of properties—properties having a qualitative and a causal aspect—and is thus seen as standing in opposition to the position of Sydney Shoemaker (1980) and Alexander Bird (2007a). However, Heil (2009, p. 178) says with respect to Martin's last position that he finally conceived properties as "powerful qualities". Against that background, there is no substantial disagreement between the views of Martin and Heil on the one hand and Shoemaker (1980) and Bird (2007a) on the other.

If, by contrast, one interprets Martin and Heil as holding a double aspect theory, there are two obvious objections: what is the relationship between the qualitative and the causal aspect of a property? How can the objection of quidditism be avoided as regards the purely qualitative aspect of properties? There is only one reasonable position in this context, namely the one that conceives properties as being causal in being certain qualities: properties that are purely causal without being certain qualities would be pure potentialities instead of being real, actual properties (cf. the objection of Armstrong 1999, section 4). And properties that are certain qualities without these qualities being certain causal powers would be quiddities, committing us to recognize worlds that are indiscernible as being qualitatively different nonetheless.

Properties that are causal powers in being certain qualities are dispositions. If this theory applies to all properties, the fundamental physical properties are dispositions as well. This view therefore implies that dispositions do not presuppose a categorical basis. However, if one conceives dispositional properties as being certain actual qualities, it is no problem that there are no underlying categorical bases. One would run into a problem if and only if one conceived dispositions as pure potentialities, which are not actual properties as such, but presuppose a categorical basis (cf. Bird 2007b, pp. 519–523). The intuition which drives the view that one obtains a coherent position if and only if one maintains that there are intrinsic properties underlying the causal relations loses its appeal if—and only if—one regards the qualitative nature of properties as being a causal nature.

This conception implies the view that the fundamental dispositions do not depend on triggering conditions for bringing about effects. On the contrary, the fundamental physical properties produce effects spontaneously. If the fundamental physical properties, being dispositions, were dependent on external triggering conditions, then their qualitative nature would again be hidden. There could then be a possible world in which the triggering conditions in question are absent. Consequently, there could again be two types of properties P and P^* without the difference between them leading

38 *Conservative Reductionism*

to different effects anywhere in the world. In other words, there could again be a difference that does not make a difference.

Take again charge for example. Charge is qualitatively distinct from mass and other fundamental physical properties by being the power to attract and repulse objects in certain manners. Even if there are no objects that are attracted or repulsed in a given situation, the disposition in question exists. But it is not a pure disposition being based upon an intrinsic and categorical suchness. The power that charge is produces in any case an effect, namely the effect of generating an electromagnetic field spontaneously. By the same token, mass is tied to gravitational interaction according to general relativity theory.

Not only do the fundamental physical properties produce effects spontaneously, but they also exist only in producing effects. Bringing about effects is what their being consists in. The question of what powers do when they are not manifested (Psillos 2006b)—that is, when they do not produce any effects—does not arise in a position that conceives powers as real properties and that considers the qualitative and the causal nature of properties to be identical. One may therefore go as far as saying that properties are producing certain effects in being certain qualities.

If one regards properties as causal in being certain qualities, one can nevertheless maintain that properties are in a certain sense intrinsic. It is a fact about an object in itself, independently of other objects, that it has certain powers in having certain qualities. This fact is independent of whether the object in question is alone or accompanied by other objects (cf. the definition of intrinsic properties by Langton and Lewis 1998). Charge, for instance, may be an intrinsic and qualitative property inhering in an object and at the same time a causal property, since the qualitative nature of this property consists in generating an electromagnetic field, resulting in the attraction of opposite-charged and the repulsion of like-charged objects.

Furthermore, the effects that an object produces in virtue of having certain properties can in a certain sense be intrinsic properties as well: the properties that are such effects exist in the real world only because they are caused by other properties. Nonetheless, in another possible world, it may be the case that properties of the same types as those ones that exist in the real world only as effects of other properties occur at the initial state of that other world. To put it differently, properties whose existence in the real world is brought about by other properties may nevertheless be intrinsic properties, because properties of the same types occur uncaused in other possible worlds. The causal dependence that there is in the real world does not imply any ontological dependence of the properties of the types in question on other properties. That is why causal relations, even if they are conceived in the framework of the causal theory of properties, are not sufficient to justifying speaking of holism in a substantial sense (see Esfeld 1998).

Even if properties are causal, the relata of causal relations can be objects or events. Causal relations obtain between objects or events in virtue of

The Metaphysics of Casual Structures   39

their properties. That the properties are causal is to say the following: insofar as an object or event has certain properties, it has certain powers. As regards the fundamental physical properties, objects or events produce spontaneously the effects that they can bring about in virtue of having certain properties. The causal relations that consist in the production of these effects are metaphysically necessary in the following sense: in any possible world in which there are properties of the types in question, there are also causal relations of these types. Thus, in any possible world in which there is charge, charged objects generate an electromagnetic field, resulting in the attraction of opposite-charged and the repulsion of like-charged objects.

In recent literature, doubts are expressed as to whether in case one conceives the fundamental properties as dispositions and thus in a causal manner, one inevitably is committed to recognizing necessary connections in the world, thereby contradicting Humean metaphysics (see Handfield 2008). Nonetheless, there is a clear contrast between the Humean metaphysics of categorical properties and the metaphysics of properties as dispositions. According to Humean metaphysics, property tokens of the same type can fulfil very different causal roles in different possible worlds. By contrast, according to the metaphysics of properties as dispositions, the qualitative character of a property type determines the causal role that the property type in question plays and hence determines the causal relations into which the tokens of the property type in question enter. That is why the metaphysics of properties as dispositions is a causal theory of properties, and the Humean metaphysics of categorical properties is not a causal theory of properties.

Rani Lill Anjum and Stephen Mumford (2010) accept this type of necessity—in the sense of the causal role being essential to a property—but deny that the conception of such a necessity commits one to recognizing necessary connections in nature. However, in order to be in a position to distinguish between necessity in the sense of the causal role being essential to a property and necessity in the sense of the connection between cause and effect being necessary, one has to make the following two presuppositions: (a) the exercise of the power (disposition) that a property is always dependent on contingent external triggering conditions, even in the case of fundamental physical properties; (b) there can be factors that interfere with the connection between the power and its effect even in the case of fundamental physical properties.

There is a metaphysical and a physical objection against these presuppositions. We have argued above in favour of the claim that the consequence of being committed to a primitive suchness is avoided if and only if one conceives the fundamental physical properties as spontaneously producing effects. The example of charge was meant to suggest that such a conception is also reasonable from a physical point of view (although, of course, an adequate discussion of electromagnetism would require much more space). Further examples will follow in the next sections. Moreover, no time elapses

40 *Conservative Reductionism*

between the exercise of the powers that the fundamental physical properties are and their immediate effects in the sense that something could interfere with the connection between cause and effect, preventing the effect from coming into being. Thus, the immediate effect of a point-like charge is not the attraction of opposite-charged and the repulsion of like-charged objects, but generating an electromagnetic field in its immediate environment (by means of which other objects are then attracted or repulsed if they are present). Nothing can interfere with the charge generating an electromagnetic field. The way in which objects then move in this field obviously depends on further, contingent factors. Hence, if one sets out to measure an electromagnetic field, one needs test particles; for that reason, test particles are an inevitable triggering condition in order to be in the position to measure the effects of charge or gravitational mass and the like. If by the manifestation of a disposition, one means its measured or observed effects, there is no necessary connection between the disposition and its manifestation; for in order to obtain measured or observed effects, more is necessary than the disposition producing an effect, namely the presence of test bodies or measuring instruments, and external factors can interfere as far as the interaction with test bodies or measuring instruments is concerned. But this fact does not speak against the claim that the disposition always spontaneously exercises the power that it is—for instance, in generating an electromagnetic field (charge) or a gravitational field (mass).

To take another example, the process of quantum physical state reductions from superpositions to classical properties (e.g., decay of a radioactive atom) is not such that contingent external factors could interfere with that process. That process occurs spontaneously and it is not extended in time. In a nutshell, since following the metaphysics of properties as dispositions, it is the nature of properties to bring about certain effects, the connection between cause and effect is a necessary one: if there is the property in question, the effect cannot fail to come about as well, at least as far as fundamental properties are concerned.

By the same token, the laws of nature are not contingent (in that they supervene on the distribution of the fundamental physical properties as a whole that there happens to be in a world) but are metaphysically necessary: the laws of nature describe the effects that objects can produce in virtue of their properties. When talking about laws in physics and in the special sciences in the following, we have this view of laws in mind, according to which the laws of nature tell us what the properties to which they refer can cause. In other words, not laws as such, but properties qua causal powers are metaphysically fundamental (cf. as regards this view of laws for instance Cartwright 1989, Hüttemann 1998 and Dorato 2005, chapter 4). Since properties are powers to produce certain effects, the laws of nature are the same in all possible worlds, given that the identity of the properties consists in the disposition or power to bring about certain effects. If it is a law of nature that all *F*s are followed by *G*s, because *F*s are the power to

The Metaphysics of Casual Structures 41

bring about Gs, then in any possible world in which there are Fs, these are followed by Gs. Of course, our hypotheses about the laws of nature may be false and are subject to change. However, what the laws are does not depend on these hypotheses, but only on the nature of the properties.

At first glance, it may seem to be a heavy metaphysical burden to countenance necessary connections in nature, and such connections are sometimes regarded as mysterious. However, that first impression is fallacious: the existence of metaphysically necessary connections in nature simply is a consequence of the causal essence of properties. The argument for the causal theory of properties is to avoid the commitment to a primitive suchness (quiddity) and its consequence, namely that it is in principle not possible to gain knowledge of the essence of properties (humility). In short, what is mysterious and ontologically inflationary is the commitment to a primitive qualitative essence of properties and its consequence to have to recognize worlds that are indiscernible as being qualitatively different nonetheless. One avoids these commitments by conceiving the essence of properties as being tied to the causal relations in which they figure, and it then follows in a clear and transparent manner in what sense there are necessary connections in nature.

2.2 PHYSICS AND STRUCTURAL REALISM

It would not be reasonable to set out a metaphysics of properties that is intended to apply to the real world without taking into account what physics says about the properties that there are in the world. The argument presented in section 2.1 is an a priori argument that is valid whatever may be the properties in the world. Nonetheless, this argument tacitly assumes that the fundamental properties in the world are intrinsic properties in the first place. However, as regards this assumption, physics is relevant. We can answer the question whether or not the fundamental properties are intrinsic only by paying heed to what our physical theories say about the properties that they take to be fundamental. We have considered above charge as an example in order to illustrate how it is possible for a property to be qualitative and causal in one. One may indeed regard charge as an intrinsic property.

However, charge does not occur in isolation. If an object in the domain of fundamental physics is charged, it also has properties such as mass in the sense of rest mass, position, momentum, and spin in a given direction. Among these properties, only charge and mass are properties that can be conceived as falling within the position sketched out in section 2.1, namely as causal and intrinsic properties (as regards mass, however, it is in dispute whether it is an intrinsic property, since in general relativity theory, mass is tied to gravitational interaction and thus tied to the metrical field; see Lehmkuhl 2010). In any case, properties such as charge and mass occur only

42 *Conservative Reductionism*

together with properties that one cannot conceive as intrinsic properties in the framework of contemporary physics. That is why we have to consider in this section in what manner today's physics conceives central fundamental properties as relations instead of intrinsic properties. As regards spin, which is a sort of angular momentum peculiar to quantum objects, we always mean in the following the components of spin in a given direction, and not the spin as such. The latter is a determinable property that fixes which determinate values of spin an object can take in a given direction.

Charge falls within the scope of quantum theory (more precisely, quantum electrodynamics, which is a quantum field theory; for the following considerations in this book, it is, however, sufficient to limit ourselves to non-relativistic quantum mechanics). In quantum mechanics, charge is represented by an operator that commutes with all other operators. That is to say, any definite numerical value of charge can coexist with all other possible definite numerical values of any other property of a quantum object. The same applies to rest mass and all the other state-independent properties of quantum objects—that is properties whose value does not change during the existence of the object.

The state-dependent properties of quantum objects—properties such as position, momentum, and spin in a given direction, whose values change during the existence of the object—by contrast, are represented by operators that do not commute with all the other operators. The physical meaning of this fact is that these properties are subject to the principle of superpositions: a quantum object usually is not in a state in which it has one definite numerical value of these properties, but it is in a state that is a superposition of all the possible values of these properties. Even if the object is in a state in which it has a definite numerical value of one of these properties, it is excluded that it also has a definite numerical value of those properties whose operators do not commute with the operator that represents the property in question.

Thus, for instance, it is not possible that a quantum object is in a state in which it has a definite numerical value of both position and momentum. This is what the famous Heisenberg indeterminacy relation says. By the same token, a quantum object cannot be in a state in which it has a definite numerical value of spin in more than one of the three orthogonal spatial directions. Electrons, for instance, are quantum objects of spin 1/2. That is to say, there are only two possible values of spin in each of the three orthogonal spatial directions, spin up and spin down. If such an object has a definite numerical value in one direction, say spin minus the direction of the x axis, its state is a superposition of the possible values spin plus and spin minus in the direction of the y axis and in the direction of the z axis, both these possible values having the same weight in this superposition in this case. Operationally speaking, this is to say that if a measurement of spin y or a measurement of spin z is made, the results spin up and spin down are equiprobable (probability 0.5 each).

The superposition principle is not limited to the states of single quantum objects taken in isolation. Whenever one considers an object that is composed of two or more quantum objects (for instance, two or more electrons), the superposition principle applies to the states of these objects taken together. The state of the whole object usually is a superposition of all the possible ways in which the states of the single quantum objects that are its parts can be related with each other. Such a state of the whole object is known as an *entangled state*. That is to say that the state is a superposition of all the possible correlations between the state-dependent properties of the quantum objects in question. However, none of these objects is in a state in which it possesses a definite numerical value of any of these properties. These correlations are known as Einstein–Podolsky–Rosen correlations (EPR), since Einstein and these two other physicists were the first to draw attention to them in a famous paper in 1935.

The simplest example of entanglement is a whole that is composed of two electrons whose states are entangled with respect to the spin in each spatial direction (this example goes back to Bohm 1951, pp. 611–622). This state is known as singlet state. Electrons are, as mentioned, quantum objects of spin 1/2, and they are fermions. That is to say, as mentioned, there are only two possible values of spin in each of the three orthogonal spatial directions (spin up and spin down), and, furthermore, electrons are anti-correlated with respect to spin. If in this case one electron possesses the value spin up in a given direction, the other electron possesses the value spin down in that direction, and vice versa. The state of the whole—the singlet state—thus is a superposition of first electron spin up and second electron spin down minus first electron spin down and second electron spin up in any spatial direction.

Entanglement hence means that there are only certain *relations* among the quantum objects in question, namely correlations between all the possible definite numerical values of the state-dependent properties of these objects, without any of these objects being in a state in which it has a definite numerical value of any of these properties. There are no intrinsic properties of quantum objects that ground these relations in the sense that these relations supervene on them. If one maintained that there are such intrinsic properties—and be it so-called hidden variables whose values we ignore—then one could not reproduce the correlations that quantum theory postulates. This is the result of the famous theorem that John Bell proved in 1964. A metaphysical hypothesis—possibly unknowable, intrinsic properties that constitute a supervenience basis for the relations of entanglement—thus has in this case mathematically calculable consequences that are refuted empirically by quantum theory and the experiments that confirm quantum theory (see Esfeld 2001, chapters 7 and 8, for details).

Nonetheless, the state-independent properties of quantum objects—such as charge and mass—are not subject to superpositions and entanglement. They always have a definite numerical value, which does not change. Thus,

44 *Conservative Reductionism*

electrons always have an elementary negative charge and a rest mass of 0.51 MeV (whereby 1 MeV = 1,782 × 10^{-27} g). It is therefore possible to consider them as intrinsic properties of quantum objects. However, these properties cannot constitute a supervenience basis for the relations of entanglement. These properties do not determine whether or not quantum objects stand in a relation of entanglement and what that relation is like. Furthermore, one cannot distinguish one quantum object from other quantum objects of the same kind on the basis of the state-independent properties such as charge and rest mass. All electrons for instance have the same value of charge and rest mass. The state-dependent properties, being subject to entanglement, are not able to establish a distinction among quantum objects either. In the mentioned example of the singlet state, there is no spin property whatsoever, not even a value- or a probability distribution of a spin property, that could distinguish the one electron from the other one. The same applies to all the other state-dependent properties of any quantum objects that are involved in an entangled state, including position and momentum. Insofar as one can say something about the positions of quantum objects whose states are entangled, the same propositions about position apply to all the quantum objects in question.

Quantum objects whose states are entangled thus are numerically distinct, since quantum mechanics indicates a definite number of them; but there are no properties whatsoever that establish a distinction among these objects. The relation of entanglement, being a symmetric, but irreflexive relation (nothing can be entangled with itself) brings out that there is a numerical plurality of objects (at least two). However, it does not distinguish between these objects: these objects can have all their intrinsic properties and relations in common (see, as regards this point, the discussion between Saunders 2006, F. Muller and Saunders 2008 and F. Muller and Seevinck 2009 on the one hand and Dieks and Versteegh 2008 and Ladyman and Bigaj 2010 on the other hand; see Esfeld and Lam 2011 for more details as regards objects in entangled states).

The relations of entanglement among quantum objects give rise to one of the central physical arguments for the metaphysical position of *structural realism*. Instead of intrinsic properties, certain relations—namely the relations of entanglement—are characteristic of quantum objects. A *structure* can be conceived in this context as a *network of concrete, qualitative physical relations among objects that do not possess an identity independently of the relations in which they stand.* They do hence not possess an intrinsic identity. Of course, if there is a network of relations, there are also relata—that is objects which stand in the relations. Recognizing objects as relata characterizes the position that we propose as *moderate structural realism* (see Esfeld 2004 as well as Esfeld and Lam 2008 and 2011). This position is thereby distinct from the radical ontic structural realism that Steven French and James Ladyman have developed and according to which there are no objects at all—or if there are a objects, they are derived from the relations,

The Metaphysics of Casual Structures   45

being knots of relations (see French and Ladyman 2003 and 2010 as well as Ladyman and Ross 2007, chapter 3, and Ainsworth 2010 and furthermore French 2010, section 7, for a discussion of the different versions of ontic structural realism). It would be a mistake to describe the moderate version of structural realism as recognizing relations and over and above that objects, relations and objects being different entities that are ontologically dependent on one another. On the contrary, the central claim of moderate structural realism is this one: *the relations are the ways (môdes) in which the objects are* (see Esfeld and Lam 2011). There thus are objects, but what these objects are, their being, may entirely consist in the relations that exist among them. In other words, the objects do not have any intrinsic properties that ground the relations and that constitute their identity. As far as structural realism is concerned, it is even possible that the objects which stand in the relations do not have any intrinsic properties at all.

There is a clear example of this latter case, namely space-time points. According to the standard geometric formulation of general relativity theory, space-time consists in relations among physical points, these relations being determined by the metrical field. The metrical properties are not intrinsic properties, but relational ones, since the metrical properties of each point depend on its—infinitesimal—environment. If one maintained that these points possess intrinsic properties or a primitive thisness (haecceity) that constitutes their identity over and above the metrical properties, one would enter into a conflict with general relativity theory. There would then be situations that have to be regarded as different, but that are distinct only in that different points of space-time bear the metrical field properties. These situations are physically indiscernible. One would thus again have to recognize worlds as being different—namely different as regards the individuals that bear the metrical field properties—although they are indiscernible. Furthermore, the determinism that general relativity theory implies would in this case break down (this is shown by the so-called hole argument; see Earman and Norton 1987 and for instance Stachel 2002 for a good discussion). That is why the assumption of an intrinsic identity of the space-time points leads to a consequence that is unacceptable within general relativity theory. Consequently, general relativity theory also supports structural realism, more precisely the moderate version of structural realism (see Esfeld and Lam 2008).

Nonetheless, the way in which general relativity theory speaks in favour of structural realism is different from the way in which quantum theory suggests this position. In the case of quantum theory, the crucial point is the non-separability of quantum objects, consisting in the relations of entanglement, that is, superpositions of correlations. There is nothing like non-separability in the domain of general relativity theory. On the contrary, Einstein said that general relativity theory carries out the principle of separability to the extreme in localizing the physical properties at space-time points (Einstein 1948, p. 321; English translation in Howard 1985,

46   *Conservative Reductionism*

p. 188). General relativity theory supports structural realism only in that the properties of the fundamental objects to which it is committed according to the standard geometric formulation—space-time points—are relational instead of intrinsic properties (namely metrical relations).

It may at first glance seem trivial that structural realism applies to space-time: space-time points are far from being a natural candidate for physical objects of which it is generally assumed that they possess an intrinsic identity, which is constituted by intrinsic properties (or a primitive thisness). It may therefore seem evident even without invoking such sophisticated arguments as the hole argument in general relativity theory that space-time is a physical structure, namely a network of concrete metrical relations among points that are nothing but what stands in these relations (that much of ungrounded structure would fit even into David Lewis's famous thesis of Humean supervenience; see Lewis 1986a, pp. ix–x). However, according to general relativity theory, the metrical relations are not purely spatio-temporal, geometric relations in distinction to material relations, since they bring about the gravitational interaction. The metrical relations depend on the distribution of the non-gravitational energy-matter in space-time (space-time being curved). General relativity theory treats the metrical field on a par with the fields of non-gravitational energy-matter. Furthermore, the Einstein field equations admit so-called empty solutions, that is, solutions without fields of non-gravitational energy-matter, in which there consequently is only the metrical field, containing the gravitational energy. The existence of these solutions is a weighty argument in favour of recognizing the space-time points as genuine physical objects.

Moreover, it is far from trivial that structural realism applies not only to space-time, but also to the central material properties, as shown by the relations of quantum entanglement. In sum, one can therefore maintain that the contemporary fundamental physical theories describe the world as consisting in the first place in structures, that is networks of concrete physical relations among objects that do not possess an identity independently of the relations in which they stand (no intrinsic identity). These structures are all material in that they contain all energy, including the metrical relations constituting space-time.

2.3   THE ARGUMENT FOR CAUSAL STRUCTURES

Let us now consider the relationship between the argument for the causal theory of properties, set out in section 2.1 within the framework of intrinsic properties, and structural realism as supported by the current fundamental physical theories. The question is whether or not the structures that these theories consider are causal structures. Are they such that in being certain qualitative physical structures, they are the power to bring about certain effects? Or are they purely qualitative structures, that is, categorical structures?

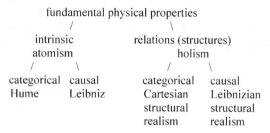

Figure 2.1 Overview of the possible positions with respect to the fundamental physical properties.

The logical space of possible positions with respect to the fundamental physical properties consequently is built up by four positions that can be represented as shown in figure 2.1.

The first distinction is the one between intrinsic properties and relations, marking the contrast between atomism and holism. If the fundamental physical properties are intrinsic properties, objects possess these properties independently of whether they are alone or accompanied by other objects. By contrast, if the fundamental properties are relations, the objects are tied together by these relations instead of existing independently of each other. The second distinction is the one between categorical and causal properties. This distinction applies to atomism as well as to holism. We thus get to four different positions.

The position on the left in figure 2.1, intrinsic and categorical properties, is classical atomism. It is associated with Hume and with what is today considered as Humean metaphysics. One can link the position next to it, intrinsic and causal properties, with Leibniz who considers—in opposition to Descartes—the fundamental physical properties as forces. The position of categorical structures is close to Descartes because Descartes can be read as envisaging to trace all physical properties back to spatio-temporal, geometric properties. Spatio-temporal structures are the paradigmatic example of categorical structures in classical physics. One can therefore characterize this position as Cartesian structural realism. It falls within in the framework of what is considered Humean metaphysics in today's philosophy because it does not recognize any necessary connections in nature; however, the term "Cartesian structural realism" seems to us to characterize this position better than "Humean structural realism" (see Sparber 2009, chapter 5, as regards this position).

The position on the right in figure 2.1 becomes available only consequent upon the physics of the 20th century. The dualism of dynamical, material properties and space-time as a passive background structure into which matter is inserted is abandoned only in the physical theory of general relativity. (Valtteri Viljanen 2007, however, regards Spinoza as a precursor of that position. According to Viljanen, Spinoza considers space itself as a force.) One can talk in terms of a Leibnizian structural realism with respect

48 *Conservative Reductionism*

to this position: the fundamental physical properties are causal properties, but they are structures in the first place instead of intrinsic properties.

These are four pure positions, which taken together build up the logical space of possible positions. Combinations between these positions are of course possible or even inevitable. Thus, one cannot maintain the metaphysics of intrinsic and categorical properties as a pure position, because one cannot trace spatio-temporal relations back to intrinsic and categorical properties. Even David Lewis recognizes structures under the guise of spatio-temporal relations as that what holds the world together (Lewis 1986b, chapter 1.6). Furthermore, structural realism can admit intrinsic properties, provided that they do not constitute identity conditions for the fundamental physical objects. However, structural realism is not forced to recognize such intrinsic properties (space-time points do not possess any intrinsic properties, whereas in the case of quantum objects, properties such as charge and rest mass can be considered as intrinsic properties).

As regards the distinction between categorical and causal properties, it is much more difficult to argue in favour of combined positions. If one maintains that there are both categorical and causal properties in the world, one has to put forward convincing reasons why some qualitative, physical properties are purely categorical properties, whereas others are the power to produce certain effects in being certain qualities. If one accepts the consequences of quidditism and humility for some fundamental physical properties, why not endorse these consequences for all fundamental physical properties? And if one accepts that some fundamental physical properties are powers in being certain qualities, why should one not maintain that all fundamental physical properties are causal properties? As already indicated, consequent upon the physical theory of general relativity, it is no longer possible to take a dualism of spatio-temporal relations as categorical background structure and material properties as causal properties for granted.

Today's fundamental physical theories shift the focus from atomism to holism, from a metaphysics of intrinsic properties to a metaphysics of relations (structural realism). As mentioned in section 2.2, there are strong arguments from general relativity theory as well as from quantum theory which show that the metaphysics of intrinsic properties is committed to consequences that are unacceptable within these theories. Consequently, only the holistic positions on the right of figure 2.1 are coherent with today's scientific knowledge in the domain of fundamental physics. However, the fundamental physical theories do not tell us without further interpretative moves whether the structures are categorical or causal. If one sets out to make a case for the one or the other of these two options, one has to take the debate in the metaphysics of properties into account that we have presented in section 2.1 and that is worked out well with respect to intrinsic properties. What happens with the arguments in this debate if one replaces the metaphysics of intrinsic properties with structural realism? In order to ground the metaphysics

The Metaphysics of Casual Structures   49

of causal structures, which we shall employ in the following to conceive a way out of the dilemma of epiphenomenalism and eliminativism in the form of a conservative reductionism, we have to answer this question in this section.

At first glance, it seems that the realism of categorical structures is able to reply to the objection that we have introduced in section 2.1 on the basis of the quotation from Jackson, without committing itself to quidditism and humility and without endorsing the causal theory of properties: what there is in the world are in the first place not categorical intrinsic properties, but categorical structures. Since these are structures and thus relations instead of intrinsic properties, they are not unknowable: they are as described by the fundamental physical theories. They are qualitative structures, which are not causal, but there is no question of an intrinsic, primitive suchness (quiddity).

One can draw on the original programme of geometrodynamics of John A. Wheeler in order to illustrate this position. According to this programme, the physical world is identical with space-time, which can be considered as a categorical structure. Not only gravitation, but all material properties and interactions are included in space-time: they are ways in which space-time is curved (see Wheeler 1962a and for a summary Wheeler 1962b). One can take this programme as the attempt to work out Descartes' philosophy of nature in the framework of general relativity theory, since Descartes regards the physical world as being identical with space-time (see Graves 1971, pp. 79–101). In a nutshell, what there is in the world are categorical structures, and physics is able to describe these structures, since their essence consists in being geometric structures. Hence, it seems that by shifting from a metaphysics of intrinsic properties to a metaphysics of structures, one can avoid the objections of quidditism and humility, without having to subscribe to the causal theory of properties.

However, on a close regard, it turns out that these objections cannot be dispelled that easily. The argument for the causal theory of properties presented in section 2.1 says that if and only if one conceives the qualitative essence of properties as a causal essence (a power to produce certain effects) one avoids having to recognize quidditistic differences, that is, purely qualitative differences between worlds that are indiscernible. Simply shifting the focus from categorical intrinsic properties to categorical structures is neither necessary nor sufficient to avoid the commitments to quidditism and humility.

The structures in the world to which the fundamental physical theories refer cannot stand in a direct causal relation to our cognitive apparatus. They are theoretical entities, because they are not directly observable. The quantum relations of entanglement are not observable. What is observed are certain correlations among measurement outcomes (but no superpositions of such correlations, that is, no entanglement). One recognizes the existence of superpositions including entanglement in order to explain the measurement outcomes and the correlations between them. By the same

50 Conservative Reductionism

token, the spatio-temporal, gravitational relations that the theory of general relativity acknowledges and that show that space-time is curved are not observable as such. A local observer cannot determine whether or not space-time is curved, for she can always choose a coordinate system that represents space-time as flat where she is located. It is only when one takes the various local observations together in order to form a representation of space-time as a whole that one gets to regard space-time as curved. In short, the fundamental physical structures are theoretical entities, and we recognize them because they explain the observed phenomena. The explanation in question is a causal one: these structures are the causal origin of the observed phenomena.

However, we have already mentioned in section 2.1 a fact than can also be expressed in the following manner: if the causal relations in the world supervene on fundamental physical properties that are intrinsic and categorical properties, then there always is the possibility of multiple realizations of those causal relations—and consequently of the observable phenomena—by fundamental intrinsic and categorical properties of different types. Hence, it is in principle not possible to gain knowledge of these intrinsic and categorical properties. This matter does not change if one shifts the focus from intrinsic and categorical properties to categorical structures. The essence of categorical properties including categorical structures is independent of the causal relations that there are in the world. By way of consequence, it is possible to hold fixed all the causal relations and to change the underlying categorical properties, independently of whether these properties are intrinsic categorical properties or categorical structures.

Any set of causal relations can thus be multiply realized by different types of arrangements of fundamental and categorical structures. The possibilities of combination are certainly restricted if one shifts from intrinsic categorical properties to categorical structures. Nonetheless, there always are two possible worlds w and w^*, these worlds are indiscernible as regards the causal relations that obtain in them, but they are distinct in that different underlying fundamental physical categorical structures realize these causal relations. One thus is again committed to a sort of quidditism: there is a qualitative difference between worlds so that these worlds have to be recognized as being different worlds, although they are indiscernible.

Hence, if one conceives properties as categorical, one is committed to acknowledging purely qualitative differences between properties that do not make a difference because they do not entail any causal or nomological difference (quidditism). Consequently, it is in principle not possible to gain knowledge of the qualitative essence of properties (humility). These commitments are independent of whether one conceives the properties as intrinsic or as structures. If the fundamental physical properties are categorical and intrinsic, we cannot have any idea of what they are. If the fundamental properties are categorical and structures, one can regard the fundamental physical theories as putting forward conjectures as to what they are

The Metaphysics of Casual Structures 51

by employing mathematical structures. However, we cannot be justified in adopting a realist attitude towards the fundamental structures that any version of the current fundamental physical theories or any successors of them posits, since the whole domain of the causal relations of the actual world can be realized by different types of arrangements of fundamental physical structures. Consequently, we can in principle not know what the fundamental physical structures of the actual world are. Shifting from a metaphysics of categorical and intrinsic properties to a metaphysics of categorical structures hence does not provide for a solution to the problem of the following metaphysical underdetermination: different types of arrangements of fundamental categorical properties including structures can be correlated with identical arrangements of causal relations. Consequently, worlds have to be recognized as different, although their only difference concerns the purely qualitative essence of the intrinsic properties or structures in them so that such worlds are indiscernible (see Esfeld 2009 for a detailed argument).

If, by contrast, the fundamental physical properties are causal properties, then their essence is to produce certain effects, and to do so spontaneously. Consequently, differences in the fundamental properties always automatically imply causal differences. Hence, if the fundamental properties are causal properties, it is not the case that there are differences between possible worlds that do not make a difference, that is to say, that do not imply a causal difference. In other words, if—and only if—the fundamental properties are causal properties, there is not multiple realization, but a biconditional link between the fundamental properties and the causal relations: if there is a certain arrangement of fundamental properties, there are certain causal relations, and if there are these causal relations, there is also that arrangement of fundamental properties. The gap between metaphysics and epistemology that arises in the metaphysics of categorical properties including categorical structures disappears as soon as one shifts to a metaphysics of causal properties including causal structures: the qualitative essence of properties is a causal essence, namely the power to produce certain effects. Consequently, qualitative differences between properties always entail causal differences and thus discernible differences.

In section 2.2, we have briefly rehearsed the arguments which suggest that the fundamental physical theories commit us in the first place to structures rather than intrinsic properties. We have now seen that the shift to structures cannot remove the argument against categorical properties. That argument, however, is a philosophical one. That is why we have said at the beginning of this section that the fundamental physical theories do not tell us without further interpretative moves whether the structures are categorical or causal. Nonetheless, physics does not remain neutral with respect to the philosophical debate about properties being categorical or causal. There are strong arguments from physics in

52 *Conservative Reductionism*

favour of the metaphysics of causal properties. It is not the objective of this book to dwell into the interpretation of the fundamental physical theories. Nonetheless, it is important to mention these arguments here in order to point out that the case for causal structures can be built on arguments that are independent of the debate about the mentioned dilemma of functionalism.

An important question in the philosophy of physics is this one: What distinguishes real physical from mere mathematical structures? The fundamental physical theories employ mathematical structures, such as geometric or algebraic structures, in order to represent physical reality and to predict observable phenomena. However, not all the mathematical structures that physical theories employ refer to physical structures and represent their constitution. We therefore need a criterion that distinguishes real physical from mathematical structures.

Let us come back to Cartesian structural realism in the literal sense, as worked out for instance in Wheeler's original programme of geometrodynamics. According to this position, the fundamental physical structures are geometric structures. One can try to refuse to answer the question what makes it that a geometric structure is a real physical by contrast to a mere mathematical structure, claiming that it is a fundamental fact that spatio-temporal, geometric relations are physical relations. Nonetheless, it is true also of the spatio-temporal relations in the physical world that we obtain knowledge of them only through causal relations. That is one of the reasons why Leibniz maintains that the network of spatio-temporal relations as such is not a physical entity, being a purely mathematical in distinction to a real physical structure.

More importantly, Wheeler's original programme of geometrodynamics failed, notably because it could not take the particularities of quantum physics into account (see Misner, Thorne and Wheeler 1973, § 44.3–4, in particular p. 1205). It is not possible to consider the quantum structures of entanglement as spatio-temporal, geometric structures, since these structures are independent of relations of spatio-temporal distance. If one sets out to conceive the quantum structures as categorical structures, the only option is to regard them as structures defined on a mathematical space, notably algebraic structures (cf. the algebraic formulation of quantum field theory, in particular Haag 1992, and see Kuhlmann 2010, chapters 5–6, for an assessment of its philosophical importance). General relativity theory also admits of an algebraic formulation (see Bain 2006 and Lam 2007, chapter 6.5). Consequently, one can also regard general relativity theory as being committed to algebraic structures. In any case, given that general relativity theory abandons the commitment to a background space-time, there is no question of its being interpretable in terms of there being primitive, geometric structures of spatio-temporal extension. In short, today's fundamental physical theories represent the world by employing abstract mathematical structures (geometric or algebraic

The Metaphysics of Casual Structures 53

ones), and if these are to be real physical in contrast to mere mathematical structures, their physical nature can by no means be a primitive fact.

The metaphysics of causal structures provides for a clear answer to this question. Mathematical structures, whatever they may be, are not causally efficacious. The use that persons make of mathematical structures in building physical theories is of course causally efficacious, but these structures do not have any causal power themselves. Real physical distinguish themselves from mere mathematical structures by being causally efficacious. More precisely, applying the causal theory of properties to structures, we come to the conclusion that a structure is physically real if and only if it is causally efficacious (causal criterion of existence, ontologically necessary and sufficient condition). Structures are causally efficacious in exactly the same sense as intrinsic properties: an intrinsic property is causally efficacious by enabling the object or event that has the property in question to produce certain specific effects. A structure is causally efficacious by enabling the objects or events that stand in the relations in question to produce taken together—that is, as a whole—certain specific effects. In other words, in virtue of standing in certain relations, the objects or events in question produce certain specific effects, the relations thus being the power to produce certain effects. Consequently, two structures are physically different if and only if they differ in the effects they bring about. If there is no causal difference, we deal only with different mathematical representations of the same physical reality.

However, these considerations do not imply that epistemologically we always are in the position to detect the causal differences in question experimentally. That is why, epistemologically speaking, it is only a necessary but not also a sufficient condition for a description in terms of mathematical structures to refer to real physical structures and to reveal their constitution that these structures can be conceived as being causally efficacious. There can be situations in which two different theories of the same domain (or two different models or interpretations of a given theory) recognize different structures as physically real and indicate causal differences between these structures, but we are currently not in the position to perform a laboratory experiment to detect these differences. If one seeks to uphold scientific realism in such a situation of contingent empirical underdetermination, one needs further criteria than the causal one (such as, for instance, a coherence criterion).

In defending a causal theory of physical existence, our view agrees with the current known as entity realism. In today's philosophy of science, entity realism is a position that proposes to recognize something as a real physical entity—in contrast to a mere mathematical description tool—if and only if it is possible to manipulate the entity in question, that is, to attribute causal properties to it and to employ these causal properties in laboratory experiments. Ian Hacking, for one, replies to the question whether electrons are real by saying, "If you can spray them, they are real" (Hacking 1983,

54   *Conservative Reductionism*

pp. 22–23; see as regards entity realism in particular Hacking 1983, chapters 1, 5, 6, 10 and 16, as well as Cartwright 1983, 1989; see furthermore Suárez 2008 and Psillos 2008 with the replies by Cartwright 2008a and 2008b). Entity realism is by no means committed to an ontology of individual particles in fundamental physics; instead of being individual particles, the entities in question can also be objects that are essentially related to each other in certain ways, that is, structures. Structural realism, in conceiving the structures to which it is committed as causal, can join entity realism, and vice versa.

Entity realism sees itself as standing in contrast to theory realism. Entity realism claims to adopt a direct realist attitude to entities, without having to interpret the theories in which the entities in question figure in a realist manner. However, we are not convinced that there is such a contrast. The objects of the fundamental physical theories are theoretical entities. We have an access to these entities only through theories. For instance, one cannot manipulate electrons directly, but only by relying on theories that tell us something about their causal powers. For this reason, we are open-minded with respect to theory realism, but agree with entity realism in adopting a causal criterion for recognizing something as a physical entity. We reject a theory realism that considers a description in terms of mathematical structures to be sufficient for a realism with respect to physical entities. We interpret theories in a realist manner only insofar as they attribute causal properties to physical entities (necessary condition, see the remark above). But we adopt a realist attitude to causal properties independently of whether or not scientists are in a position to manipulate these properties. Consequently, we are prepared to endorse realism also with respect to cosmology (see by contrast Hacking 1989). In short, also in the domain of fundamental physics including cosmology the answer to the question of whether or not objects or structures are real is this one: "If they are causally efficacious, they are real."

Let us pursue the contrast between the metaphysics of causal and the metaphysics of categorical structures one further step. Another argument against the latter position is that it does not seize the role that laws of nature play in scientific explanations. Humean metaphysics conceives the properties in the world as categorical so that what these properties are is independent of the laws of nature. The laws supervene on the distribution of the fundamental physical properties as a whole, because this distribution contingently exhibits certain regularities. Consequently, the laws of nature are fixed only once the whole distribution of fundamental physical properties is given. The laws are hence not in a position to explain anything in this distribution. Shifting from categorical intrinsic properties to categorical structures does not change that matter. The laws supervene in this case on the whole distribution of the fundamental categorical structures and are hence not in a position to explain anything in this distribution. Thus, the metaphysics of categorical properties has to accept the whole distribution of fundamental physical properties including structures as primitive. It is not able to explain anything in the domain of fundamental physics. By contrast, if the properties including the structures are causal, the laws of nature follow from the qualitative, causal character of the properties including the structures. In accordance with scientific practice, one can therefore employ the laws of nature in order to explain why the distribution of the fundamental physical properties, including the fundamental physical structures in the world, develops in that particular manner in that it in fact develops—without having to accept these laws as primitive (see Maudlin 2007 for a primitivism about physical laws).

In sum, the fundamental physical theories do not commit us in the same manner to causal by contrast to categorical structures in which they commit us to there being structures rather than intrinsic properties in the first place in the fundamental physical domain. However, these theories do not remain neutral with respect to the question of whether the structures are categorical or causal. Only the metaphysics of causal structures amounts to a structural *realism* with respect to the fundamental physical structures. It is in the position to distinguish real physical from mere mathematical structures, and it does justice to the role that laws of nature play in scientific explanations.

2.4 CAUSAL STRUCTURES IN PHYSICS AND THE TRANSITION TO THE SPECIAL SCIENCES

Up to now, we have elaborated on a philosophical argument for the metaphysics of causal properties—the argument against quidditism and thus against purely qualitative differences between worlds that are indiscernible—and we have shown that this argument applies not only to intrinsic properties but also to structures. Furthermore, we have indicated general physical arguments in favour of conceiving the fundamental physical structures as causal structures. We will pursue this thread in this section. On the one hand, by going into the interpretation of quantum theory—and briefly into the interpretation of general relativity theory—we will set out in concrete terms how one can conceive the fundamental physical structures as causal structures; before employing the metaphysics of causal structures to build up a theory of the relationship between the special sciences and physics in the sense of a conservative reductionism, we wish to indicate how that metaphysics can be grounded in physics. On the other hand, we seek to sketch out at the same time a theory of the transition from the fundamental physical structures to the classical structures on which the special sciences focus.

Steven French and James Ladyman were the first in the contemporary discussion to put structural realism forward as a metaphysical position that makes a claim about the foundations of nature (Ladyman 1998, French

56   Conservative Reductionism

and Ladyman 2003). They always conceived the structures to which the fundamental physical theories are committed in a modal manner: these structures are not categorical, but contain a primitive modality. However, they do not commit themselves to spelling out the modal character of the structures as causal character (French 2006, pp. 181–182, and 2010, sections 4 and 5, expresses a positive attitude towards this possibility, whereas Ladyman and Ross 2007, chapter 2 to 5, are sceptical about a causal conception of the fundamental structures). Stathis Psillos (2006a, pp. 567–570) objects that structural realism does not take causation into account. Anjan Chakravartty (2007, chapter 3–5) replies to this objection by maintaining that the physical structures are brought about by underlying causal properties. By contrast, we submit that the structures are causal as such: their modal character is a causal character. Insofar as there are certain qualitative, physical structures in the world, these are powers to produce certain specific effects. In that manner, as mentioned above, there also is a clear distinction between physical and mathematical structures, so that the stock objection against structural realism, namely that it blurs the distinction between physical and mathematical entities (see e.g. Cao 2003), does not apply to this position.

Consider quantum physics. The central problem in the interpretation of quantum theory is the so-called measurement problem, that is, the question how superpositions including entangled states can develop into states in which objects have definite numerical values of their properties (instead of their state being a superposition of all the possible values of the property in question). This problem is known as the measurement problem because one takes for granted that when a quantum object is measured, it acquires a definite numerical value of the measured property as a result of the measurement process. However, it is entirely unacceptable to simply postulate that whenever there is an interaction between a quantum object and a measurement device, the Schrödinger dynamics, which leads to ever more entanglement, is no longer valid and a reduction of entanglement to classical properties with definite numerical values occurs.

Measurement processes and measurement devices are not natural kinds, but human beings employ various physical systems as measurement devices if they suit their interests. It is impossible to give a precise physical definition of a measurement process and a measurement apparatus, since there is no physical difference that distinguishes a measurement process from other physical interactions. Measurement devices are an invention of human beings that presupposes the existence of macroscopic systems which are not subject to quantum entanglement. Taking cosmology into account, it is evident that there have been processes of the dissolution of quantum entanglement (state reductions) in the temporal development of the universe independently of humans for us to be able to use certain physical systems as measurement devices. Such

The Metaphysics of Casual Structures 57

processes were the basis on which classical physical systems such as molecules, organisms and finally humans developed. The measurement problem thus is not about measurement in particular. It is a placeholder for the general problem how to understand the transition from quantum systems in entangled states to systems that possess classical properties. It is this problem that the thought experiment of Schrödinger's cat highlights: Schrödinger considers a small quantity of a radioactive substance coupled to a mechanism such that if one radioactive atom decays, a mechanism is triggered in which a hammer destroys a bottle containing a poison and a cat next to the bottle is instantly killed by inhaling the poison. According to the Schrödinger dynamics, this whole set-up rapidly develops into an entangled state, the radioactive substance being in a superposition of an atom having decayed and no atom having decayed and the cat accordingly in a superposition of being dead and being alive. However, one can countenance atoms being in superposed and entangled states, but apparently not cats.

If one recognizes that there is both the quantum domain as characterized by superpositions and entangled states as well as classical properties with definite numerical values, one is committed to searching for a dynamics that amends the Schrödinger equation in such a way that the transition from entanglement to classical properties is included. The only elaborate physical proposal for such a dynamics goes back to the Italian physicists Gian Carlo Ghirardi, Alberto Rimini and Tullio Weber (1986) (GRW) (forerunners of this proposal include notably Pearle 1976 and Gisin 1984). GRW add a stochastic term to the linear Schrödinger equation such that this equation contains probabilities for state reductions in the form of spontaneous localizations. The more quantum objects a structure of entanglement includes, the higher is the probability for a state reduction through spontaneous localization. Since macroscopic objects consist of very many quantum objects, they are no longer subject to entanglement, but possess de facto always classical, definite numerical values of their properties. Nonetheless, spontaneous localization in GRW does not amount to microscopic quantum objects having exactly one definite numerical value of position: the stochastic term that GRW add to the Schrödinger equation leads to the consequence that the quantum state is represented as a Gaussian as a result of spontaneous localization, being concentrated around a peak in configuration space, but not entirely disappearing outside that peak. The philosophical consequence of this mathematical fact is that the definite numerical values that are the result of state reductions are objectively there, but slightly vague or fuzzy (see Albert and Loewer 1996; the discussion on this problem focused in recent years on the counting anomaly raised by P. Lewis 1997 and Clifton and Monton 1999; but the reply to that objection by Bassi and Ghirardi 1999 and 2001 seems to us to be entirely convincing; see also Wallace 2008, pp. 58–61).

58 Conservative Reductionism

The versions of quantum theory that, like GRW, include a dynamics for state reductions are the primary object of a philosophical interpretation in terms of causal structures: the structures of quantum entanglement are the power or disposition to bring about classical properties with definite numerical values through state reductions. In other words, *in being certain qualities, the quantum structures of entanglement are causal structures, namely the power or disposition to produce as a whole classical properties* (see Dorato 2007, Suárez 2007, pp. 426–433, and Dorato and Esfeld 2010). These dispositions are fundamental. They do not have an underlying categorical basis. They are real and actual properties, by contrast to mere potentialities. They do not depend on external triggering or manifestation conditions. According to GRW, these are dispositions for *spontaneous* localization. Since the entangled states are not separable and not localized in space-time, it is no problem to regard the disposition for spontaneous localization as characterizing the entangled state as such: a quantum structure of entanglement just *is* the power or disposition for spontaneous localization of the objects that stand in this structure taken together. When this disposition manifests itself, all the objects that stand in the structure of entanglement in question automatically become localized.

There are several arguments in favour of this interpretation that can be summed up as follows (see Dorato and Esfeld 2010 for details).

(1) First of all, this interpretation gives a clear answer to the question what the properties of quantum objects are when there are no state-dependent properties with definite numerical values. Saying that there are no state-dependent properties at all if there are no definite numerical values is entirely absurd, since a physical object cannot exist without possessing physical properties, and properties with definite numerical values cannot develop out of nothing. And saying that there simply is the wave function or state vector begs the question, since the wave function or state vector is a mathematical tool to represent physical reality, but not itself physical reality. In other words, one has to spell out an account of what the physical reality as represented by the wave function or state vector is. Conceiving the quantum structures of entanglement in terms of dispositions provides for such an account: the properties that there are in entangled states when there are no definite values are dispositions to develop such values, and the causal theory of properties makes clear how such dispositions can be real and actual properties.

(2) Secondly, this interpretation amounts to a clear solution to the measurement problem that recognizes the existence of both entangled states and classical properties without invoking observers and without smuggling the notion of measurement into a fundamental physical theory. There is a power for spontaneous localization in the form

The Metaphysics of Casual Structures   59

of entangled states. The manifestation of this power occurs spontaneously, not requiring interactions and thus being independent of interactions with measurement devices. Measurements are simply one type of interactions among others, which do not call for a special treatment in a fundamental physical theory.

(3) Thirdly, this interpretation takes objective probabilities for single cases into account. It is not in dispute that the quantum probabilities are objective probabilities, applying to single cases, and that they cannot be understood in terms of simple frequencies. Nonetheless, Frigg and Hoefer (2007) prefer a Humean account of probabilities in the context of GRW. In order to get beyond an analysis in terms of simple frequencies, they rely on the parameters of simplicity and strength and the best balance between them, which characterize the Humean best system analysis. But these are epistemic parameters. It is therefore doubtful whether such an approach can really yield objective, single case probabilities. By contrast, conceiving entangled states as dispositions in the form of causal powers implies, when it comes to probabilities, that the powers that the entangled states are amount to *propensities*. They are dispositions that have a certain quantifiable strength for spontaneous manifestation in a certain manner, that is, producing a certain numerical value at the exclusion of other values. That strength is expressed in the form of probabilities. In other words, in this framework, we are committed to applying the propensity theory of probabilities to the quantum probabilities. The advantage of doing so is that we clearly get the account of probabilities that is needed for the quantum probabilities, namely objective single case probabilities (see Popper 1959 and then in particular the papers of Suárez 2004a, 2004b and 2007 as well as Gisin 1991 and Dorato 2007).

The Schrödinger equation is deterministic. The modification of the Schrödinger equation that GRW propose takes the transition to classical properties into account by including irreducible, objective single case probabilities. The GRW modification of the Schrödinger equation thus is a candidate for a fundamental law of nature that is probabilistic. Nonetheless, in the framework of the causal theory of properties, probabilistic laws are metaphysically necessary like deterministic laws (see section 2.1).

(4) Fourthly, this interpretation has the means to include the state-independent properties of quantum objects such as charge and mass. One may consider these within quantum theory as intrinsic properties, although they are not able to provide for identity conditions of quantum objects. In this framework, we can conceive properties such as charge and mass as dispositions as well—charge as the disposition to generate an electromagnetic field, mass as the disposition for gravitational interaction (that latter conception raises, however,

60   *Conservative Reductionism*

the question whether mass really is an intrinsic property; cf. Lehmkuhl 2010). Only by conceiving these properties in a causal manner, that is, as dispositions or powers, can we avoid the commitment to a primitive suchness (quiddity). Hence, the causal theory of properties is able to seize all the properties of quantum objects: they are causal structures to which intrinsic causal properties are tied.

(5) Furthermore, this interpretation is in the position to explain the origin of the direction of time. Amending the Schrödinger equation with a stochastic term as GRW do in order to account for state reductions has not only the consequence that the dynamics is indeterministic, but also that it is not time-reversal invariant. In other words, the GRW equation is a candidate for a fundamental *law of nature that is not time-reversal invariant*. Quantum objects that have undergone a spontaneous localization may of course again enter into entangled states, but conceiving a process that runs from a spontaneous localization back to the entangled state that existed before that localization would contradict the GRW law, more precisely the stochastic term that GRW add to the Schrödinger equation. As Albert (2000, chapter 7) has shown, the GRW processes of spontaneous localization are not only irreversible, thus singling out a direction of time, but they can also serve as the origin of all time-asymmetric phenomena. Conceiving entangled states in terms of dispositions or powers leads to an explanation of this lack of time-reversal invariance: the production of an effect by a cause is the paradigmatic example of an irreversible process. Consequently, if spontaneous localization is the manifestation of a disposition, it is evident why processes of state reduction can in principle not be reversed and why they are the foundation of the direction of time.

(6) Last but not least, this interpretation shows how a version of quantum theory that includes state reductions can amount to a candidate for a fundamental theory of nature. The GRW version of quantum theory is not limited to being a phenomenological theory for calculating probabilities for state reductions (see, by contrast, Allori et al. 2008, who regard the classical properties localized in spacetime, which are the result of state reductions, as the primitive ontology of GRW). GRW explain the existence of classical properties in the world on the basis of adopting a realist attitude to the quantum state vector (wave function): the state vector describes structures of entanglement that are objectively there in the world, and the causal interpretation of these structures in terms of dispositions for spontaneous localization explains the transition to classical properties. The benefit that we get from this view is unification: this position puts forward a unified ontology that includes both the domain of quantum superpositions and entanglement and the domain of

classical properties. It thus enables us to adopt a realist attitude to both these domains, because it accounts for the transition between them in terms of a single, unified dynamics.

Quantum entanglement is independent of spatio-temporal distances. That is why one can take the quantum structures of entanglement to be more fundamental than the metrical structures of space-time. One important current in the search for a quantum theory of gravitation, which unifies quantum field theory with general relativity theory, indeed makes the assumption that classical space-time is not fundamental (see, for instance, Kiefer 2004, in particular chapter 10). But what then is fundamental and how does what is physically fundamental distinguish itself from a mere mathematical entity? As we have claimed in section 2.3, if one does not take it to be a primitive fact that physical reality is spatio-temporal, there only is a causal criterion available to distinguish physical from mathematical existence. By showing how one can conceive the structures of quantum entanglement as causal structures, the GRW version of quantum theory opens up the way to be developed into a fundamental theory of causal physical structures. It goes without saying that such a theory has to be compatible with general relativity theory in order to be able to tackle that task. First results of current research as regards that matter suggest that it is possible to conceive in the framework of GRW a dynamics of state reductions without being committed to acknowledge the existence of a globally preferred reference frame or coordinate system, thus respecting the principle of general covariance that is central to general relativity theory (see Tumulka 2006 as well as the discussion of Tumulka's proposition by Maudlin 2008).

These six arguments underline that the idea of causal properties including causal structures in particular can be employed in the philosophy of quantum physics and leads to an interpretation of quantum theory that achieves two things: a proposition about what is fundamental in nature, and a proposition about the transition to classical properties including the observable phenomena. The mentioned six arguments concern only the interpretation of quantum theory, being independent of general philosophical and metaphysical considerations.

Interpreting what quantum theory tells us about the world in terms of causal properties, more precisely causal structures, is usually seen as being tied to those versions of quantum theory that admit state reductions, GRW being the most elaborate of these versions. However, since Everett (1957), versions of quantum theory have been set out that do not include state reductions and that take the Schrödinger dynamics to be the complete dynamics of quantum objects. One is in this case committed to regarding the quantum structures of entanglement as being universal: they encompass all the objects in the world and all their dynamical properties, including all the macroscopic objects and in the last resort also the

62 *Conservative Reductionism*

consciousness of observers. According to the main version of this view, the world splits into infinitely many branches that exist in parallel so that all the objects in the world including the consciousness of each observer are infinitely many times duplicated, existing in infinitely many branches of the universe, and having one of the possible dynamical values of their properties in each of these branches. In other words, all the possible definite numerical values of a property that enter into the superpositions and entanglement do in fact exist, but are distributed among infinitely many branches of the universe.

The observation of classical properties is usually accounted for in this framework in the following manner: the structures of entanglement develop into a process that is known as decoherence. Decoherence is a process leading in a very short time to the different terms of an entangled state no longer interfering with each other. A local observer who stands within such a structure of entanglement therefore has in her observations no access to the other terms of the superposition, which exist in other branches of the universe. In a nutshell, the world appears classically to us, because being local observers, we cannot observe the structures of entanglement as a whole (which nevertheless really exist) (see Wallace 2008, section 2.4, as well as the papers in Saunders et al. 2010 for a detailed assessment of the contemporary discussion about the interpretation of quantum theory that goes back to Everett).

It is also possible in this interpretative framework to consider the quantum structures of entanglement as causal structures. The Everett interpretation has to answer notably the following two questions:

(1) What does the physical reality of the quantum structures of entanglement consist in, so that these structures can develop through decoherence into a splitting of the world in infinitely many branches? A clear answer to this question that recognizes the physical reality of the structures of quantum entanglement without confusing that physical reality with the mathematical reality of the state vector (wave function) consists in saying the following: the quantum structures of entanglement are causal structures, being the power or disposition to produce through decoherence infinitely many branches of the universe, which do not interfere with one another and which contain definite numerical values of quantum properties each. On this reading, decoherence is a causal process, consisting in the manifestation of causal structures in the form of the structures of entanglement.

(2) How can decoherence be the key to irreversibility? Although decoherence is situated entirely within the Schrödinger dynamics, one has to vindicate decoherence as an irreversible process if one sets out to employ decoherence in order to explain how it comes about that the world appears classically to us. One would miss such an explanation

The Metaphysics of Casual Structures   63

if the process of the splitting of the world in infinitely many branches that contain definite numerical values of quantum properties each were reversible so that it could run from these non-interfering branches back to interference (or if the process of the splitting of the world in different branches could from a given point of time run not only into the future of that point, but also into its past). If one conceives decoherence and the splitting of the world in a causal manner as the manifestation of the dispositions that the quantum structures of entanglement are, one is in the position to account for the direction of time and thus for irreversible processes (see argument (5) above).

In sum, there are weighty arguments speaking in favour of conceiving the quantum structures of entanglement as causal structures.

By contrast, the spatio-temporal relations are widely seen as the paradigmatic example of categorical structures. It is true that we gain knowledge of spatio-temporal relations between material objects only through causal relations that these objects entertain, but it seems evident that the spatio-temporal relations themselves are by no means dispositions or powers. In classical physics up to and including special relativity, space-time is indeed conceived as a passive background structure in which material objects and their properties are embedded. However, general relativity theory abandons this conception of space-time. According to general relativity theory, the metrical field contains itself energy, namely the gravitational energy. Hence, general relativity theory excludes a dualism between space-time as a passive background arena and matter as that which is inserted into this arena. Space-time, as constituted by the metrical field, is itself a dynamical entity and interacts with non-gravitational energy-matter as well as with itself.

For this reason, the metrical field can be conceived as a material entity on a par with all the other physical fields. In this vein, one can regard gravitation as a fundamental physical interaction on a par with the other fundamental physical interactions—the fact that gravitation is universal and includes all physical objects notwithstanding (whereas the electromagnetic interaction, for instance, concerns only all charged objects) (see in particular Rovelli 2007, section 4). On this view, in short, the fact that space-time is no passive background structure in general relativity signifies that the spatio-temporal, gravitational structures are material structures as well. On this basis, it is therefore possible to conceive the spatio-temporal, gravitational relations as a causal structure on a par with the other material, causal structures: in being qualitative, metrical properties of the points of space-time, these are the power or disposition to produce the gravitational effects, which are in principle observable (such as, e.g., tidal effects) (see Bartels 1996, pp. 37–38, Bartels 2010 and Bird 2009, section 2.3; see Livanios 2008 against this position—however, simply pointing out the fact that the metrical structures are geometrical structures begs the question, since they contain the gravitational energy).

64   *Conservative Reductionism*

Nonetheless, the metrical relations and the quantum relations of entanglement are different kinds of concrete, qualitative physical relations. There is in the domain of the metrical structures nothing like non-separability, which characterizes the quantum structures of entanglement (cf. Einstein 1948, p. 321, English translation in Howard 1985, p. 188). Accordingly, the manner in which the quantum structures and the metrical structures are causally efficacious qua structures is different. The quantum structures of entanglement can be causally efficacious qua structures without violating the principle of local action according to which effects propagate at most with the velocity of light in space-time, just because they are non-separable so that the objects that stand in these structures are not localized at points in space-time. By contrast, the metrical structures are causally efficacious by being metrical properties of space-time points. Since the metrical properties of space-time points are not intrinsic properties, but consist in relations (the metrical, gravitational relations), what is at issue in this case is a causal efficacy of structures as well. A space-time point brings gravitational effects about in virtue of the metrical relations in which it stands. Again, the metrical properties produce their effects spontaneously (gravitational effects that exist also in so-called vacuum solutions of the Einstein field equations in which there are no fields of non-gravitational energy-matter and thus no test particles).

Conceiving the metrical structures as causal structures as well does not commit us to the view of there being an objective temporal order of all events in the universe and thus a globally privileged reference frame or coordinate system. That view is already incompatible with special relativity theory, and it is at odds with general relativity theory by contradicting the principle of general covariance. It is possible to consider the metrical structures as causal structures and to maintain that existence is not tied to a certain tense (past, present, future), but that everything that there is in four-dimensional space-time simply exists. The causal conception of the metrical structures requires only that it is possible to define locally for each point of space-time a past and a future light cone and that causal processes are directed from the past to the future light cone. These assumptions are sufficient for being in a position to maintain that there is an objective temporal order in space-time of all those events that are related with each other as cause and immediate effect of a given cause. Independently of which reference frame or coordinate system one chooses, the effects always occur later than their causes.

These assumptions are sufficient in order to be able to hold that the events that are effects depend for their existence on the events that are their causes: these events exist at a certain point or region in space-time only because there are in their past other events that are their causes, and the reason for this existential dependence is that the latter events produce the former ones, bringing them into existence. In order for this position

The Metaphysics of Casual Structures   65

to be available, the temporal order that is provided by the past and the future light cones that can be locally defined for each space-time point is sufficient. From the perspective of a point in space-time, one cannot claim that the events in its future light cone exist *already*. It is not admissible to confuse the language of timeless predicates, which applies to the description of four-dimensional space-time as a whole, with the language of time-dependent predicates, which refers to the temporal order of events at a given point in space-time. Even if everything that there is in four-dimensional space-time simply exists, the events that exist in the future light cone of a given point in space-time may causally depend on what there is at the point in question, in the sense of causation being a real connection of production in the world.

In making these claims, we put ourselves in opposition to the tradition going back to the criticism that Bertrand Russell (1912) voices against the notion of causation as production. In today's philosophy of physics, the papers of John Norton (2007a and 2007b) against causation in fundamental physics are representative of this tradition. By contrast to what this tradition suggests, it is not only possible to interpret today's fundamental physical theories in a causal manner, but there are a number of arguments for doing so: general philosophical arguments (that is, the arguments from the metaphysics of properties), the requirement to be able to distinguish real physical from mere mathematical structures, the requirement to take the role of the laws of nature in scientific explanations into account, and a whole bunch of concrete arguments in the interpretation of quantum theory and the interpretation of general relativity theory. It goes without saying that one has to base oneself on such concrete arguments in making a case for causal structures, instead of imposing an a priori principle of causation on the metaphysics of science (see also Frisch 2009 contra Norton in this vein).

In the following, we base ourselves on a version of quantum theory that recognizes state reductions, GRW being the most elaborate physical proposal for such a version. There are good reasons for maintaining that the quantum domain exists as described by quantum theory, namely as characterized by entanglement, and there are good reasons for maintaining that there really are classical properties in the world. If we subscribed only to the former, but not to the latter assumption, we would moreover be committed to an inflationary ontology of there being infinitely many branches of the universe that exist in parallel and in which all the objects in the universe including the consciousness of each person exist infinitely many times duplicated. Endorsing state reductions, by contrast, we get to a parsimonious ontology of a causal transition from fundamental physical structures to the observed phenomena, enabling us to adopt a realist attitude with respect to the quantum structures of entanglement as well as with respect to classical properties. Nonetheless, the following considerations in this book are not tied to adopting this position in the philosophy of quantum

66   Conservative Reductionism

physics: if one is not a friend of state reductions, one can read all the following statements about classical properties in this book as referring to specific branches of the universe.

According to this position, classical properties enter into the world as a result of state reductions in the form of spontaneous localizations of quantum objects. On the basis of these classical properties then develop those complex properties that constitute the domain of the one or the other of the special sciences. Are these latter ones intrinsic properties? Is the view this one: the quantum structures of entanglement are fundamental; as a result of the events of state reduction, classical properties come into existence, so that from this stage on the world can be described in the framework of the classical atomist metaphysics of intrinsic properties? The error of this metaphysics would thus consist only in that it takes the domain of properties that are in fact the result of state reductions to be fundamental.

The quantum structures of entanglement are superpositions of correlations. The simplest example of entanglement, the singlet state mentioned in section 2.2, is a superposition of the correlations "first object spin plus and second object spin minus" and "first object spin minus and second object spin plus". As a result of a state reduction, this superposition is reduced to one of these correlations, that is either "first object spin plus and second object spin minus" or "first object spin minus and second object spin plus". Correlations are not intrinsic properties. In this case, subsequent upon the state reduction, each of the two objects has a definite numerical value of spin in a given direction (the state of the whole system is a product state, that is, the product of the states of the two objects); however, one object has a definite numerical value of spin in a given direction only relative to the other object having the opposite definite numerical value of spin in the same direction. In general, insofar as objects acquire definite numerical values of properties through state reductions, these are values that exist only relative to definite numerical values of properties of other objects.

The singlet state is a specially conceived example in order to conceptually and experimentally vindicate the mentioned correlations independent of spatio-temporal distances. In any real situation in nature, a structure of entanglement contains not only two quantum objects in isolation, but a vast number of quantum objects. The structures of entanglement are global by contrast to local structures. Consequently, a state reduction in nature always concerns a vast number of quantum objects and thus leads to a spatio-temporally more or less contiguous localization of such objects. Against the background of the GRW dynamics, John Bell (1987, p. 45/p. 204 in the reprint) describes macroscopic objects as galaxies of such quantum events of spontaneous localization.

Hence, what we get through state reductions in the form of spontaneous localizations are not intrinsic properties, but local structures. State reductions are the transition from global structures of entanglement to

The Metaphysics of Casual Structures 67

local classical structures. The states of the quantum objects that stand in these structures continue of course to develop according to the one fundamental dynamics (such as the GRW dynamics). Nonetheless, these local structures—and with them the macroscopic objects that consist in these structures—can be stable structures with stable classical properties; for due to the vast number of quantum objects that stand in any such local structure, new entanglements dissolve in a very short time. A paradigmatic example of such stable local structures are molecules and configurations of molecules. All further macroscopic objects are composed of molecules and their configurations: they all develop out of molecules on the basis of quantum events of spontaneous localizations.

It is not a philosophical problem that the spontaneous localizations are events and that, accordingly, the mentioned local structures are configurations of events. Such a view fits into special and general relativity theory—which are classical physical theories in contrast to quantum theory, but which conceive space and time as being united in a four-dimensional space-time. Since there is no globally privileged reference frame or coordinate system, these theories commit us to the view of the world as a four-dimensional block universe, consisting in events and processes in the sense of spatio-temporally contiguous sequences of events, instead of containing substances that persist as a whole for a certain time (see for instance Balashov 2010 for a detailed argumentation in favour of these claims). Even if the quantum structures of entanglement were to turn out to be more fundamental than the spatio-temporal structures, there is nothing about the quantum structures of entanglement that would suggest a commitment to substances in the mentioned sense—on the contrary, quantum objects do not possess an identity in time. In the form of state reductions, there are events of spontaneous localizations, and these are events in the sense of the conception of events of the metaphysics of the block universe. In that respect, quantum physics and relativity physics are coherent with one another. It is furthermore possible to conceive macroscopic objects as well as spatio-temporally contiguous sequences of such four-dimensional events (see for instance Reydon 2008 as regards biological objects).

We have argued at the beginning of this section in favour of conceiving the quantum structures of entanglement as causal structures. If these quantum structures are causal structures and if they develop through state reductions into local structures, then those local structures are of course causal structures as well. However, they are classical physical structures in contrast to quantum structures of entanglement. That is to say, the objects that stand in these structures possess a quite definite spatio-temporal localization and in general properties with definite numerical values each. Nonetheless, these are structures, since, as mentioned above, these properties are relational instead of intrinsic ones—any of the objects in question possesses a definite numerical value of any such property only relative to the

68 *Conservative Reductionism*

other objects possessing certain definite numerical values of properties of the same type.

All these properties are causal. That is to say, in being certain qualities, they are powers to produce certain effects. The causal properties that the objects which stand in such a local structure have relative to each other open up the possibility that such a structure as a whole is the power to produce certain significant effects. In other words, the properties that the objects standing in such a structure have relative to each other enable the objects in question to produce certain significant effects taken together. Thus, molecules produce as a whole certain significant effects by means of which they distinguish themselves from their environment. Some of these effects are those effects on which the special sciences focus by conceiving such local structures as functional structures. The effects that these local structures produce as a whole derive from the manner in which the fundamental objects that stand in these structures are arranged, since these effects are the result of the causal properties that these objects have relative to each other. We shall explain notably in section 3.3 how one can conceive in this framework the causal-functional structures on which the special sciences and biology in particular focus on the basis of the fundamental physical, causal structures.

2.5 STRUCTURES AS MODES

We can sum up the results obtained so far in this chapter in the following manner: The fundamental physical properties are in the first place structures instead of intrinsic properties, more precisely causal by contrast to categorical structures. The global structures of quantum entanglement develop through events of state reduction into local, macroscopic structures some of which constitute the domain of the one or the other of the special sciences. A structure is a network of concrete, qualitative physical relations among objects that do not possess an intrinsic identity independently of the relations in which they stand.

We can formulate this view also in the following manner: the structures (relations) are the ways (modes) in which the objects are. Qua ways in which the objects are, the structures are networks of concrete physical relations. In other words, they are property tokens by contrast to universals. The view of properties as ways in which the objects are is a necessary element for our solution of the dilemma of epiphenomenalism and eliminativism. We therefore present this view in this section.

Properties in the sense of particulars are often called "tropes" in the contemporary literature. The Greek term *trope* says in this context the same as the Latin term *mode*. Nonetheless, we prefer the term "mode" to the term "trope," since the view of properties as tropes is often associated with the conception of objects as bundles of tropes. Considering properties as

The Metaphysics of Casual Structures   69

the ways (modes) in which objects are, by contrast, does not invite any association with the theory of objects as bundles of properties. Apart from that, the conception of properties as modes fits into the history of modern philosophy: one can trace this conception back to Spinoza at least (see Heil 2003, chapter 13, and Strawson 2008 as regards the conception of properties as modes; cf. also Armstrong 1989, pp. 96–98).

There is a forceful objection against the view of objects as bundles of properties in our context: it is not intelligible how objects could be bundles of relations. On the contrary, relations require objects as that what stands in the relations, since any concrete physical relation obtains between two objects at least, being expressed by a two-place predicate at least. As already mentioned in section 2.2, the recognition of objects distinguishes the moderate structural realism that we maintain from the radical ontic structural realism of Steven French and James Ladyman. However, there is no need for the objects to possess an intrinsic identity independently of the relations in which they stand. That is why we propose to conceive the structures as the ways (modes) in which the objects are. On the one hand, this proposition highlights that the objects do not exist independently of the structures. On the other hand, this proposition also points out that the structures cannot exist independently of objects that stand in them. Furthermore, this proposition makes clear that it would be inappropriate to talk in terms of a mutual ontological dependence between objects and structures. There are not two ontologically distinct entities, objects and structures, that entertain a relationship of mutual ontological dependence. As far as ontology is concerned, there is only one thing—objects whose ways of being (modes) are structures.

If the properties that there are in the world are in the first place relations (structures), the objection against the bundle theory hence is that it is not intelligible how objects could be bundles of relations. This is, however, only the first step in an argumentation that seeks to establish that properties including structures (relations) are the ways (modes) in which objects are; for instead of modes, properties could be universals. Objects could instantiate relations qua universals in the same way as they could instantiate intrinsic properties qua universals.

What we observe and interact with in the world are individual tokens of properties including individual tokens of relations (structures). If one seeks to trace back these tokens to universals, one has to make the relationship of instantiation intelligible that is supposed to hold between universals and tokens. This task has not been accomplished since the days of Plato and Aristotle. If one conceives universals as something that exists beyond the empirical world, the question remains unanswered what it means that the tokens in the empirical world take part in or instantiate the universals. The problem that this question highlights has already been pointed out by Plato himself in the *Parmenides* (130e–133a), and it still is an open issue. Conceiving the universals as abstract mathematical structures that

70 *Conservative Reductionism*

are instantiated by concrete physical structures in the world does not help to make the relationship of instantiation intelligible. If one conceives, following Aristotle, the universals as being inherent in individual objects in the world, it is not intelligible how numerically one and the same universal can be instantiated in many different objects. We take this situation to suggest that there is no convincing motivation for postulating the existence of universals. This assumption raises more questions than it answers.

The stock objection against the position that refuses to recognize the existence of universals is that the individual property tokens including the individual tokens of relations (structures) exhibit significant similarities, and any similarity presupposes some qualitative identity; for similarity means qualitative identity under a certain aspect. We can accept this argument. However, it is by no means mandatory to conclude from this argument that the qualitative identity which underlies similarity consists in universals. It is possible to explain everything for which it is reasonable to demand an explanation by presupposing only the existence of property tokens in the world and of concepts (predicates) that classify these property tokens. The concepts (predicates) are universal and abstract, but they are products of our thinking, existing only in our minds and in linguistic communication.

The fundamental physical properties in the sense of modes are perfectly similar and thus qualitatively identical. This perfect similarity (qualitative identity) is the basis for all further significant, objective similarities in the world. In other words, fundamental physical modes come under one and the same fundamental physical concept if and only if they are exactly the same, that is, qualitatively identical. All modes of negative elementary charge in the world, for instance, are exactly the same, that is, qualitatively identical. By the same token, all the modes that are a certain value of rest mass are qualitatively identical. By modes, we mean here always determinate properties and not determinable ones—that is, not properties such as, for instance, elementary charge or rest mass, but e.g. negative elementary charge and rest mass 0.51 MeV. All electrons in the world constitute a natural kind, because their characteristic properties—negative elementary charge and rest mass 0.51 MeV—are exactly the same (see Busse 2008 for an elaborate position in this sense). An analogous consideration applies to structures: all modes of the type of correlation "first electron spin plus and second electron spin minus"—and thus all modes of the type singlet state of quantum objects of the same kind—are exactly the same, that is, qualitatively identical.

Fundamental physical properties in the sense of modes hence are numerically distinct, but qualitatively identical. All and only those fundamental physical modes that are qualitatively identical make true the same description (concept, predicate) that expresses what these properties are—such as "negative elementary charge" or "rest mass 0.51 MeV." There are no relations of similarity among fundamental physical modes in the sense that these modes are identical under one aspect and different under other

The Metaphysics of Casual Structures   71

aspects, but only in the sense that modes can come under the same determinable kind, but constitute different determinate values of the kind in question. For instance, all modes of elementary charge are simply different from all modes of rest mass. They do not have anything significant in common—apart from the fact that they are time-independent, fundamental physical properties that are ways of being of fundamental physical objects. All modes of negative elementary charge and all modes of positive elementary charge are similar in that they are modes of elementary charge, but differ in the determinate numerical value of elementary charge.

A determinate numerical value does not have to be a definite numerical value: the singlet state, being the superposition of the correlations "first object spin plus and second object spin minus" and "first object spin minus and second object spin plus" is a determinate numerical value of a spin-correlation, although none of the two quantum objects possesses a definite numerical value of spin in any spatial direction. Not only definite numerical values, but also value distributions that admit of a precise mathematical description can be determinate numerical values. In other words, any definite numerical value is a determinate numerical value, but not vice versa.

Determinate values of charge, rest mass, spin, and the like are the ways in which fundamental physical objects are. What makes it that *different* such modes are the ways in which *one and the same* fundamental physical object is? In other words, under which conditions do such modes belong to different fundamental physical objects, and under which conditions are they the ways in which one and the same fundamental physical object is? Leaving the quantum structures of entanglement aside, the answer to these questions is evident: modes of different kinds are the ways in which one and the same fundamental physical object is if and only if they occur at the same place, and they are ways in which different fundamental physical objects are, if and only if they occur at different places. A mode of the kind negative elementary charge and a mode of the kind rest mass 0.51 MeV, for instance, are two ways in which one and the same electron is, if and only if they occur at the same place. Fundamental physical modes are such that they can occur at space-time points.

As mentioned at the end of section 2.4, taking relativity physics into account, it is necessary to conceive objects in a four-dimensional manner as events and as spatio-temporally contiguous sequences of events (processes). Events occur at space-time points. The identity of an object in time—in the sense of a sequence of events—is weaker than the identity of an object at a time: there are no three-dimensional substances that persist as a whole for a certain time and that hence do not have temporal parts. The identity of an object at a time is constituted by its spatio-temporal localization: all and only those properties that occur at the same point in space-time are the ways of being of one and the same fundamental physical object. An object persists in time (perdures) insofar as these properties remain constant. An electron, for instance, is a spatio-temporally

72   Conservative Reductionism

contiguous sequence of events whose ways of being all include negative charge and a rest mass of 0.51 MeV.

This conception of objects and their identity does not apply to the quantum structures of entanglement, which are independent of spatio-temporal localization and spatio-temporal distances. If one endorses the interpretation of quantum physics in terms of state reductions mentioned in section 2.4, one can nevertheless say that the quantum objects are characterized by the disposition (power) to localize—and thus to localize as a certain charge and a certain rest mass, and so on. In short, what objects are derives in this case from the disposition for spontaneous localization.

As soon as events of state reduction have led to localized fundamental physical objects, we can conceive complex objects as spatio-temporally contiguous configurations of such fundamental objects. To put the matter in the language of the four-dimensional block universe, they are processes that are composed of events. If one adopts only a geometric criterion, one can regard arbitrary configurations of spatio-temporally contiguous fundamental physical objects as a complex object. The geometric criterion therefore is not suitable to define complex objects. We need a causal criterion. A configuration of spatio-temporally contiguous fundamental physical objects is a *complex* object if and only if it produces as a whole significant effects by means of which it distinguishes itself from its environment.

A molecule for instance is a complex object in this sense, because it interacts as a whole in a certain manner with its environment, including other molecules. Through these interactions, it distinguishes itself from its environment. The same applies to some spatio-temporally contiguous configurations of molecules: they produce as a whole certain significant effects by means of which they distinguish themselves from their environment. A DNA sequence, for instance, is a complex object, because it has as a whole certain phenotypic effects through which it distinguishes itself from its environment. The same goes for organisms up to and including persons. Since complex objects are characterized by producing certain significant effects as a whole through which they distinguish themselves from their environment, it is reasonable to focus scientific investigations on these objects: they constitute the domain of the one or the other of the special sciences. Which significant effects they produce as a whole fixes to which special science they belong.

Complex objects are nothing but spatio-temporally contiguous configurations of fundamental physical objects—however, configurations that have as a whole certain causal properties, producing effects through which they distinguish themselves from their environment. Nonetheless, one can explain the powers that complex objects have as a whole on the basis of the properties of the fundamental physical objects of which they are composed, as explained at the end of section 2.4. These properties are causal properties as well—including the spatio-temporal, metrical properties, being gravitational properties.

The Metaphysics of Casual Structures   73

In order to manifest the effects that are characteristic of them, complex objects often depend on certain normal physical conditions obtaining in their environment. We thus get to the following view: the fundamental physical properties are causal properties and the objects whose ways of being (modes) these properties are spontaneously produce effects that they can produce in virtue of possessing these properties. Paradigmatic examples are the electromagnetic field that a fundamental physical object generates in virtue of its charge, or the events of quantum state reductions (spontaneous localizations) that quantum objects bring about in virtue of the relations (structures) of entanglement in which they stand. Some configurations of localized, fundamental physical objects then have in virtue of the relations in which these objects stand certain causal properties as a whole—powers to produce significant effects by means of which they distinguish themselves from their environment. Because of these powers, they then come under the concepts of the one or the other of the special sciences. However, these causal powers depend on certain conditions in the environment in order to manifest themselves. We shall come back to this matter at the end of section 3.3 in particular. Not everything that enters into such normal conditions in the environment can be described in the vocabulary of the special science that focuses itself on the significant effects that some such complex objects produce as a whole given certain environmental conditions. That is why the laws of the special sciences are ceteris paribus laws, presupposing normal physical conditions that they cannot completely describe in their own vocabulary.

As regards the fundamental physical objects, what these objects are is captured by the description of the fundamental physical properties, including notably the fundamental physical structures. As regards complex objects, by contrast, there are two different manners of describing what these objects are: the description of their physical composition and the description of the significant effects that they have as a whole in certain environmental conditions. In other words, one can consider complex objects under the aspect of their composition; but one can also consider them under the aspect of the significant effects that they have as a whole. The latter one is the perspective of the special sciences that trade in functional properties.

One and the same fundamental physical concept or predicate refers to two or more fundamental physical properties in the sense of property tokens (modes) if and only if these are exactly the same, that is, qualitatively identical. By contrast, it is not necessary that the physical composition of two or more complex objects is exactly the same for them to make the same physical description focussing on their composition true. Some slight differences in composition are acceptable. The reason is a pragmatic one: if identical composition were required, we would have to deal with a vast amount of descriptions of complex objects, achieving by no means a good balance between simplicity and empirical strength. To what extent

74 *Conservative Reductionism*

differences in composition are tolerable for complex objects to come under the same physical description is again fixed by a causal criterion: as soon as the differences in composition become relevant to the effects that the complex objects in question can produce as a whole, different physical descriptions are called for. In general, the more complex the considered objects are, the more differences in composition are acceptable for these objects to come under the same physical descriptions. For instance, in the case of individual molecules of water, already the existence of an additional neutron can be sufficient for having to switch to a different physical description—in this case, chemically speaking, we no longer have simply water, but heavy water (deuterium oxide). In the case of DNA sequences that are genes, producing certain phenotypic effects, by contrast, there often are differences in atomic composition that have no effect upon the physical classification of these DNA sequences.

Even more differences are acceptable when it comes to the classifications of the special sciences that consider complex objects under the aspect of their significant effects as a whole. The purpose of the concepts, theories and laws of the special sciences just is to seize many complex objects under the aspect of significant effects that they have in common given certain environmental conditions. The point at issue is not identity of effects, but a significant similarity of effects that such complex objects have as a whole in certain environments. Complex objects that are composed in very different physical manners can have such significant similar effects in common. For instance, DNA sequences that are composed in very different molecular manners can be genes of the same type, because they produce significantly similar phenotypic effects under certain environmental conditions.

Complex objects hence admit of different types of descriptions—physical descriptions that focus on their composition, and descriptions of the special sciences that focus on significant effects that they have as a whole in certain environments. The physical description is the more fundamental one: if one knows the physical composition, one knows the causal properties of the fundamental physical objects that compose the complex object in question (and which are causal structures in the first place instead of intrinsic properties). On the basis of this description—plus the physical description of the environment—one could in principle deduce the description of the significant effects that the complex object has as whole, if one had a sufficiently large computational capacity at one's disposal. However, the opposite possibility does not obtain: having the description of the significant effects of a complex object in terms of a special science at one's disposal is not necessarily a sufficient condition to infer its physical composition, since complex objects that are composed in quite different physical manners can all have the same significant effects as a whole under certain environmental conditions. That is why the special sciences have not only a pragmatic, but also a scientific value: as regards the significant effects that complex objects that are composed in different physical manners have in

The Metaphysics of Casual Structures   75

common, there are no physical concepts that seize these effects, but only concepts of the special sciences. These latter concepts therefore enable us to formulate laws about such effects. We shall elaborate on this matter in section 5.3.

2.6 CONSERVATIVE IDENTITY AND ONTOLOGICAL REDUCTIONISM

We now have set out all the premises that are necessary in order to build up the new version of functionalism that is intended to avoid the dilemma of epiphenomenalism and eliminativism elaborated on in chapter 1, this volume. We require the following three premises:

(1) The fundamental physical properties are in the first place structures instead of intrinsic properties (arguments from physics, see section 2.2).
(2) All properties including the structures are causal properties: in being certain qualities, they are powers (dispositions) to produce certain effects (philosophical argument and arguments from physics, see sections 2.1, 2.3 and 2.4).
(3) All properties including structures that there are in the world are tokens: properties are modes, that is, the ways in which the objects are (philosophical argument, see section 2.5).

In short, what there is in the world, from fundamental physics via molecules and organisms to persons and their social institutions, are causal-functional structures. These are the ways (modes) in which the objects that exist in the world are (see as regards premises (2) and (3) also Whittle 2008, arguing for a theory of properties as being causal-functional properties and as being modes or tropes).

These premises make a conservative identity theory available: the complex objects that constitute the domain of the one or the other of the special sciences are identical with configurations of fundamental physical objects. All their properties—including notably the significant causal properties that they have as a whole—are identical with physical properties that can be described in the vocabulary of a fundamental physical theory. More precisely, they are identical with local physical structures, that is, the network of relations among the fundamental physical objects of which they are composed. As argued in section 2.4, such local structures develop out of global structures of quantum entanglement via state reductions. In identifying the causal properties that complex objects have as a whole with such local structures, we conceive these local structures as including the metrical relations (gravitation) as well as the electromagnetic relations (charge); we have

76 *Conservative Reductionism*

briefly mentioned in sections 2.2 and 2.4 (argument (4)) how one can consider charge as an intrinsic property that is tied to the quantum structures of entanglement. In other words, the causal properties that complex objects have as a whole and that are seized by the special sciences are identical with the whole network of fundamental physical relations among the fundamental physical objects of which these complex objects are composed.

There is in the first place an argument from the development of the universe in time speaking in favour of accepting this identity claim: complex objects and their properties have developed out of global structures of quantum entanglement and the local structures to which these global structures lead through state reductions. If these local structures and their environment are the same, these complex objects and their properties are also the same—and if, given the same environmental conditions, there is a difference in the properties of complex objects, there also is a difference in these local structures (supervenience of the properties of complex objects as a whole on local physical structures).

However, the argument from development and the argument from supervenience are not sufficient in order to ground the claim of identity of the properties of complex objects as a whole with the mentioned local structures. These properties could also be emergent properties (in the sense of properties that are not identical with physical properties). In order to exclude that view, we have to come back to the physical-philosophical argument set out in section 1.1: if the properties of complex objects were emergent properties, they could only be epiphenomena. These properties, however, are a paradigmatic example of properties that are causally efficacious: the only reason for recognizing the properties with which the special sciences deal is that these properties have significant effects. For instance, we admit genes, because they have certain phenotypic effects for the organism. Given the causal completeness of the domain of fundamental physical properties, these properties can only be causally efficacious by being identical with fundamental physical properties. And the only way in which causally efficacious properties that complex objects have as a whole can be identical with fundamental physical properties is that they are identical with the mentioned local structures.

Apart from laying stress on structures instead of intrinsic properties as what there is in the fundamental physical domain in the first place, this argumentation is not new. The problem into which this argumentation runs is the following one: if one maintains that the properties of complex objects on which the special sciences focus are identical with physical properties, then there is the danger of this position ending de facto up in an eliminativism with respect to these properties of complex objects, because even given the premise of identity, it is not able to show how these properties can be causally efficacious. However, this problem cannot be simply a consequence of the claim of identity: identity is a logical relation that is symmetric. If the causally efficacious properties that complex objects have as a

The Metaphysics of Casual Structures   77

whole are identical with local physical structures in the mentioned sense, then some local physical structures are causally efficacious properties of complex objects as a whole. In general, if all As are identical with Bs, then some Bs are identical with As. It does not make sense to ask whether a given complex object brings about certain effects qua its local physical structure or qua its properties as a whole, since both are the same. In general, if the property of being A is the same as the property of being B, then all the effects that an object brings about qua being A are the effects that it brings about qua being B, and vice versa.

One can thus not trace the eliminativism problem back to the identity claim as such. On the contrary, the mentioned problem is a consequence of the theory of properties against the background of which this identity claim is conceived. The claim of identity on its own does not say much. One has to show how the properties of complex objects on which the special sciences focus can be identical with physical properties. That is why the premises (2) and (3) are crucial for our argumentation. The properties of complex objects with which the special sciences deal are a paradigmatic example of causal properties. As already mentioned, the only reason why we recognize the existence of these properties is that complex objects have certain specific effects as a whole. The claim of these properties being identical with physical properties is therefore intelligible if and only if those physical properties are causal properties as well. Otherwise, one would be committed to the consequence that certain configurations of physical properties, which are not causal as such, make true certain causal descriptions of the special sciences, but that there are no causal properties of the objects to which the special sciences refer (see section 1.3). To put the matter in other terms, against the background of the causal theory of properties, the reason for this identity is that all the properties in question are causal-functional: the properties on which the special sciences focus consist in producing certain effects, and these effects are identical with the effects that certain local physical structures bring about as a whole in certain environments, the physical properties being causal properties as well. It is therefore not possible to tell them apart on a causal basis.

An eliminativist consequence hence arises if and only if one presupposes a non-causal theory of properties as pure qualities. Given such a presupposition it is indeed not intelligible how the properties on which the special sciences focus can be causal-functional properties and be identical with configurations of properties that are categorical instead of causal properties. If, by contrast, one maintains that properties are causal powers in being certain qualities, the door is open to vindicate the mentioned claim of a conservative identity: the causal properties of complex objects on which the special sciences focus exist, they are causally efficacious, and they are identical with local, causal physical structures. This position is a sort of *ontological reductionism*, since everything that there is in the world are physical structures; but it is a *conservative reductionism* that does not invite any eliminativist

78 *Conservative Reductionism*

consequences: some of these physical structures *are* the properties of complex objects as a whole on which the special sciences focus.

The nominalist premise of properties being modes (3) is as important as the premise of the causal theory of properties (2) in order to make this position available. If properties were universals, then the properties of complex objects as a whole on which the special sciences focus could not be identical with physical properties. The reason why there are special sciences that focus on these properties is that the classifications that introduce these sciences in order to seize these properties capture significant similarities that are not expressed by the physical classification of these objects according to their composition. In other words, complex objects that differ in their physical composition can have significant causal properties as a whole in common. If these properties were universals, they could therefore not be identical with physical properties (structures) qua universals.

If, by contrast, properties are not universals, but modes, it is no problem how causal properties that complex objects have as a whole can be identical with their physical structure: the manner in which a complex object is insofar as it is the power to produce certain specific effects as a whole is the manner in which it is insofar as it is a local physical structure in the mentioned sense. These are two different descriptions (concepts, predicates) of one and the same way a complex object is.

The idea of causal properties including causal structures as well as causal explanations has its origin in the everyday experience of the environment and of ourselves as acting beings. In the same vein, what we experience in the world are individual property tokens. These ideas are retained in science. On the basis of the causal theory of properties and the theory of properties as modes, we can achieve a complete and unified view of nature that includes both the fundamental physical theories and the theories of the special sciences. This coherence speaks of course in favour of this position: it is a reason for conceiving the fundamental physical properties including the structures in a causal manner that this conception enables us to understand the properties on which the special sciences focus up to the common sense experience of the world and ourselves on the basis of the fundamental physical structures. By the same token, it is a reason for endorsing the theory of properties as modes that this theory enables us to show how the properties on which the special sciences focus including the mental properties of persons can be causally efficacious given the causal completeness of the domain of the physical properties.

Nonetheless, it is crucial for our argumentation to establish these positions in the first place independently of such considerations of overall coherence, in order to avoid the suspicion of circular argumentation. Even if one limits oneself to the domain of fundamental physics, it is the best interpretation of the current fundamental physical theories to conceive the properties including notably the structures that these theories treat in a causal

The Metaphysics of Casual Structures 79

manner, as indicated in sections 2.3 and 2.4. As mentioned at the beginning of section 2.5, purely metaphysical considerations speak in favour of the theory of properties as modes.

Our position is a version of functionalism because we take all properties, including the fundamental physical ones, to be causal properties. More precisely, what there is are causal structures in the first place—from physics to the special sciences. We propose a reductionist functionalism, because we maintain that all properties that there are in the world are identical with physical structures. Nonetheless, this functionalism is conservative; for admitting identity secures the causal efficacy of the properties on which the special sciences focus. In a nutshell, the new, comprehensive functionalism that we put forward avoids the dilemma of epiphenomenalism and eliminativism into which the standard versions of functionalism run by conceiving all properties as causal-functional structures that are the ways (modes) in which the objects are.

The argumentation according to which one can vindicate the causal efficacy of the properties on which the special sciences focus if and only if one conceives these properties as being identical with physical properties is associated with the works of Jaegwon Kim in the contemporary discussion (see notably the books Kim 1998 and 2005). On the one hand, Kim tends to conceiving all properties in a causal manner (e.g., Kim 2005, p. 159), and he rejects the Humean regularity theory of causation at least as far as mental causation is concerned (see Kim 2007 and 2009); on the other hand, his position comes in the end close to the functionalism of David Lewis: Kim draws the consequence that there are in the last resort no properties that correspond to the descriptions of the special sciences; these descriptions refer to tokens of fundamental physical properties, and they do not possess a scientific quality, seizing salient objective similarities in nature, but only a pragmatic value (see in particular Kim 1998, p. 111, Kim 1999, p. 17–18, Kim 2005, pp. 26, 58, and Kim 2008, pp. 108–112). Kim adopts Lewis' conception of a local, species-specific reduction (see Kim 1998, in particular pp. 93–95, and 2005, in particular p. 25). However, in that manner, Kim's position ends up in the eliminativism horn of the dilemma of the standard versions of functionalism, as argued in section 1.3. Our position can be received as a further development of Kim's position, having the aim in view to develop a version of functionalism that avoids the mentioned dilemma by being a conservative reductionism.

Like Kim, John Heil (2003) argues against the conception of there being different ontological levels of properties out there in the world. Heil also maintains that the properties which are supposed to exist on higher levels can only be causally efficacious by being identical with physical properties. Going beyond Kim, Heil argues in favour of a version of the causal theory of properties (see section 2.1 for details of his position in that respect), and he conceives properties as modes. The

80   *Conservative Reductionism*

position developed in this book therefore is close to the one of Heil. However, paying heed to contemporary physics, we put causal structures in the first place which spontaneously produces effects, instead of intrinsic dispositional properties, whose manifestation furthermore depends on external triggering conditions. Our main criticism of Heil's ontology is that he does not develop the consequences that his premises would allow him to draw: his view finally amounts to the conclusion that the functional properties of the special sciences do not exist, there being only the fundamental physical properties (see Heil 2003, pp. 45, 153 and Heil 2006, pp. 18–21, for a clear and concise statement, as well as Esfeld 2006 on this consequence of Heil's position). Again, the threat of the dilemma between eliminativism and epiphenomenalism is obvious.

The causal theory of properties is associated in particular with Sydney Shoemaker's paper "Causality and properties" (1980). In later work, Shoemaker argues for a view according to which the properties on which the special sciences focus are realized by physical properties without being identical with them: in brief, the powers that characterize a property of the special sciences are a subset of the powers that characterize the respective physical realizer properties (see Shoemaker 2007, chapter 2, especially pp. 11–14). Following Yablo (1992), Shoemaker draws a distinction between determinable and determinate properties and takes this distinction to illustrate that view: the powers that characterize a determinable property are a subset of the powers that characterize the respective determinate realizer properties. Thus, the causal powers that characterize the property of being blue are a subset of the causal powers that characterize the property of being marine blue: marine blue has all the causal powers of blue and further powers, namely those ones that distinguish marine blue from, for instance, cobalt blue.

However, by making that ontological distinction between properties, Shoemaker runs into the same problem as the role functionalism of Putnam and Fodor (see section 1.2). As Carl Gillet and Bradley Rives (2005, section 3) point out, the determinate or realizer properties include by definition all the powers of the respective determinables. Consequently, the determinate properties are sufficient to bring about all the effects that the determinables could cause. Unless one acknowledges token identity between realized and realizer properties, one thus faces again the epiphenomenalism objection that haunts role functionalism. That objection could only be avoided by either admitting systematic overdetermination or by accepting interactionism, thus rejecting the causal completeness of the physical domain (B. McLaughlin 2007 interprets Shoemaker's position in that latter way; see also the emergentism that Gillet 2006 contemplates).

It can with reason be maintained that the differentiation between determinables and determinates is not an ontological one between properties that there are in the world, but concerns only concepts and descriptions. The predicates that we use in order to describe the properties in the world

The Metaphysics of Casual Structures   81

can be determinable or determinate, such as the predicates "blue" and "marine blue." The properties that there are in the world are all determinate ones (see Gillet and Rives 2005). Being blue and being marine blue are in no manner different properties that there are in the world. One and the same property in the sense of a way (mode) in which an object can be described in a precise manner by using the predicate "marine blue" and in a less precise manner by using the predicate "blue."

Shoemaker's claim that a physical property that realizes a property in the domain of a special science brings about the effects that characterize the latter property only in virtue of a subset of its causal powers is disputable, if one bears in mind that what is causally efficacious are property tokens, not types. The properties of the special sciences cannot be realized by single physical properties, but only by configurations of physical properties (local structures). Any property token of the special sciences can cause the effects that characterize the property type in question in the vocabulary of a special science only by bringing about the effects that a certain local physical structure produces as a whole. For instance, any gene token can produce the specific protein that it brings about in a certain situation only by having all the molecular effects that a certain DNA configuration has as a whole in that situation, for it is through those effects that the protein comes into being. To take another example, any pain token can cause the specific pain behaviour that it brings about in a certain situation only by producing the neuronal effects that a certain configuration of neurons has as a whole in that situation, because it is through those effects that the pain behaviour comes about. The properties on which the special sciences focus hence are in the same manner determinate properties as are the physical properties. It is only that their descriptions in the vocabulary of a special science are not as detailed as physical descriptions. These considerations confirm the view that the properties on which the special sciences focus can only be causally efficacious by being identical with physical properties in the sense of local physical structures.

This short discussion shows that newer version of functionalism that are proposed in the contemporary literature also run into the dilemma of epiphenomenalism and eliminativism, which the classical versions of functionalism of Putnam and Fodor on the one hand and Lewis on the other hand face. The way out of this dilemma consists in proposing a causal theory of properties together with a theory of properties as modes and to base on this view of properties the claim of the properties on which the special sciences focus being identical with configurations of physical properties (local physical structures). We have argued for such a conservative, ontological reductionism in this chapter.

Token identity in the sense of an identity of properties as tropes or modes as a proposal to resolve the problem of the causal efficacy of the properties on which the special sciences focus is not new. Notably David Robb (1997) has argued for token identity on the basis of a metaphysics

82 Conservative Reductionism

of properties as tropes. What our proposal adds to Robb is a causal-functional conception of all properties and the view of properties as structures, supported by independent arguments. Nonetheless, one may object that this move is not sufficient to solve the mentioned problem: the metaphysics of properties as particulars (modes or tropes) is employed in this context because there is no type identity between types of the special sciences—such as biological or psychological types—and physical types due to multiple realization. One can in this context object to the following: insofar as there is only a reduction of tokens, but not of types, the problem remains whether the properties on which the special sciences focus cause anything qua biological, or mental properties, and so on.

Let us briefly consider the background of that problem: Donald Davidson (1970) claims in his famous paper "Mental events" that mental events are identical with physical events. More precisely, all events admit a physical description, and some events admit also a mental description. It is not possible to reduce the mental to a physical description. This position is known as anomalous monism—monism, because all events are physical, anomalous, because there is no law-like connection between the mental and the physical description of events, which would enable a reduction of the former to the latter. This position is widely recognized to fail due to the following objection: it cannot show that events cause anything insofar as they are mental events. Fred Dretske highlights this problem by conceiving the following example: the voice of a soprano singer causes a thin glass to shatter. This effects occurs in virtue of the amplitude and frequency of the sounds. The meaning of the sounds is irrelevant to this effect (Dretske 1989, pp. 1–2). The same applies to events insofar as they are mental in Davidson's anomalous monism according to a widely recognized objection (see the papers in Heil and Mele 1993).

The position that we put forward differs from the one of Davidson in that we take what is identical not to be events, but property tokens in the sense of modes or tropes. Nonetheless, Paul Noordhof (1998) objects to Robb (1997) that in the same way as it is reasonable to ask whether a Davidsonian mental event causes anything qua mental, it is reasonable to ask whether a mental trope causes anything qua being a trope of a mental type (see, as regards this objection, also Kistler 2009, chapter 5.2). Robb (2001) retorts that if identity is applied to those entities in virtue of which an object or event causes something, namely properties in the sense of tropes, it makes no sense to raise the qua-question for these entities, since they are already the most fine-grained ones (cf. also Whittle 2007, section 4).

Even though that reply is correct, there remains a problem. If all that exists in the world are particulars (objects and their modes), then types are concepts that seize salient similarities among the ways objects are, whereby such salient similarities can amount to natural kinds. As regards the mentioned local structures that are the ways in which complex physical objects are, these modes make true descriptions in terms of physical

The Metaphysics of Casual Structures   83

concepts that focus on their composition as well as descriptions in terms of concepts of the special sciences that focus on the salient effects they bring about as a whole in a given environment. Multiple realization is the epistemological fact that modes coming under one single concept of the special sciences often come under different physical concepts; it is therefore more appropriate to talk in terms of multiple reference. Not only do the concepts of the special sciences and the corresponding physical concepts differ in meaning, but they are also not coextensive.

On the one hand, not only the physical concepts but also the concepts of the special sciences possess a scientific quality, consisting in these concepts figuring in law-like generalizations that are projectible, support counterfactuals and provide causal explanations. On the other hand, not only Davidson in his anomalous monism, but also most of the philosophers who favour token identity in the fine-grained sense of identity of properties as particulars (modes, tropes) maintain that the descriptions (laws, theories) in which concepts that are proper to the special sciences figure cannot be reduced to physical descriptions (laws, theories) (or remain at least neutral with respect to that latter point). In other words, they defend ontological reductionism combined with an epistemological anti-reductionism (or at least combined with neutrality as regards epistemological reductionism).

However, in that case, the problem that haunts Davidson and that Noordhof raises against Robb reappears: it has to be possible to relate the different descriptions in a systematic, reductive manner, if they are descriptions that are made true by one and the same way an object is and if each of them is to provide for law-like generalizations that are projectible, support counterfactuals and yield causal explanations. Otherwise, it could not be vindicated that these descriptions are about the *same* entities in the fine-grained sense of modes instead of being about *different* properties that objects have, that is, different ways in which they are. Consequently, the position would end up either in property dualism with the threat that the ways objects are insofar as they make true descriptions of the special sciences are epiphenomenal, or in eliminativism as regards the scientific quality of the descriptions in terms of the special sciences.

The argumentation set out in this chapter hence is not complete as yet. The ontological reductionism proposed in this chapter stands or falls together with an epistemological reductionism. Multiple realization prevents the types in which the special sciences trade from being identical with physical types. In other words, the concepts that are proper to the special sciences are not coextensive with physical concepts. Nonetheless, we have to achieve some sort of type reduction, that is, provide for a way that enables in principle the reduction of the descriptions (laws, theories) of the special sciences to physical descriptions (laws, theories) in order to retain the scientific quality of the former ones. We shall do so in chapter 5, this volume. Before going into that matter, we shall seek

84 *Conservative Reductionism*

to strengthen the theoretical considerations of this chapter by a concrete discussion of the philosophy of biology. The following chapter will treat evolution and biological functions. Chapter 4, this volume, then employs the relationship between classical and molecular genetics as a case study to illustrate the reduction of a theory of a special science to a more fundamental theory.

3 The Theory of Evolution and Causal Structures in Biology

3.0 INTRODUCTION TO CHAPTER 3

More than 200 years have passed since Charles Darwin's day of birth (1809–1882). His work on common ancestry and biological evolution has changed our perspective on the world and still influences our understanding of life, since "nothing in biology makes sense except in the light of evolution" (Dobzhansky 1973). In 1859, Darwin's most known publication, *The origin of the species*, revolutionized our thoughts about us and other recent or already extinct species. As Dobzhansky's dictum puts it nicely, why-questions about biological properties do not receive a satisfactory answer without reference to the evolutionary past. We cannot understand biological phenomena without paying heed to their history. And it is evolutionary biology that constitutes an encompassing causal-historical foundation for the explanation of biological properties and hence for any other biological discipline.

Even though Darwin's life, the origin of his theory, the conditions of its publication and the ensuing public and scientific discussion are of outstanding interest, we focus only on certain empirical and conceptual issues that link with the preceding chapters, consider causal-functional issues in biology and its explanations and prepare furthermore our account of conservative theory reduction (as regards Darwin, see also Kitcher 1985 or Ruse 2007). In Darwin's time, the idea of a perfect adaptation of all living beings to their environment is current. Because of this apparent design of the known organisms, a supernatural force that has intentionally created living organisms is generally taken for granted. According to this idea, any species is created to fulfil a certain role. Lions are created with the capacity, one may say, to move very fast in order to prey on zebras. Zebras in turn have their characteristic crossings in order to camouflage. In the same vein, any other species can be described in a teleological manner. Accordingly, natural theology tries to better understand the intention of the divine creation by studying the characteristic properties of species.

Keeping this idea of intentional creation and design in mind, let us consider two connected matters about which Darwin may have wondered

86 *Conservative Reductionism*

himself during his voyage on the *H.M.S. Beagle* (1831–1836). Individuals of one species are both similar to and different from one another. How can it thus come about that individuals of the same species, in spite of their apparent differences, are perfectly adapted to a certain environment and fulfil the same role they are designed to fulfil? What happens to the individuals of one species that are perfectly adapted to certain environmental conditions, if these very conditions continuously change as geology and palaeontology strongly suggest? One may add here that the geologist James Hutton (1726–1797) argued already in the 18th century that major geological changes result from accumulations of minor, gradual geological changes. Because of minor changes and processes like erosion, mountains flatten more and more, valleys come into existence due to rivers and so on. Charles Lyell (1797–1875) generalized this theory in his *Principles of geology* (1830). He argued that the actual geological processes are like the past ones (uniformitarianism). The world thus constantly changes geologically. Both gradualism and uniformitarianism influenced Darwin who studied Lyell's *Principles* during his voyage on the *Beagle* (Darwin 1859, especially chapter 4; see as well Mayr 1985 and Ruse 2007). Given the continuous geological changes, the question thus is whether species can remain perfectly adapted to their environment without any biological change taking place. And if there is biological change, maybe biological species change gradually as well in each generation, resulting in major changes in the long run.

The scepticism about any kind of fixism (the view that there is no biological evolution) increases if one compares the anatomy of fossils of extinct species to the anatomy of still living species —as Darwin did during his voyage. At the beginning of the 19th century, Georges Cuvier (1769–1832), the founder of palaeontology, established comparative anatomy as a proper branch of biological research. Since 1812, the extinction of certain species has been an accepted fact in the scientific community (Cuvier 1812, see furthermore Damuth 1992). Cuvier's field work showed that fossils of deeper and thus older sediments resemble fewer still living species than fossils that are found in higher sediments and that hence are of more recent time. The older the fossils are, the more they differ from recent species. Being conscious of these facts about certain fossils and recent species, Darwin discovered in South America fossils that belong to an extinct species there, but that resemble horses that are not extinct on other continents (Darwin 1859, chapter 11). Drawing attention to numerous such discoveries and comparisons, Darwin points out how problematic the idea of a divine creation of *unchangeable* species that are *perfectly* adapted to their environment or that are designed to fulfil a precise role is (see also Gould 1980). Instead, these discoveries suggest that there is a biological evolution that is essentially linked to geological changes. Nonetheless, to claim that there is such a biological evolution and to back this claim up with analyses of fossils is one issue; to *explain* biological evolution is, however, something different

The Theory of Evolution and Casual Structures in Biology 87

and more demanding (see Darwin's own assessment in the introduction and preface of his *Origin*).

Darwin's hypothesis is that biological evolution is linked to geological changes. The question then is how to back up, spell out and explain this link in order to reveal the essential mechanisms of biological evolution. One of the main challenges is to explain *both* aspects of evolution in a *similar* way —the extinction of species and the coming into being of new species. Since the first aspect is comparatively easy to understand (consider for instance catastrophes), it is the second one that is demanding. How may less extreme environmental changes render the emergence of new species possible?

Before going into this matter, let us add some general considerations. Firstly, in searching for an explanation of the evolution of species, Darwin is influenced by *An essay on the principle of population* of the economist Thomas Malthus (1766–1834). Having read this book in 1838, it inspired him to think of, metaphorically speaking, a selecting environment (see Darwin 1859, chapter 4; see as well M. Abrams 2009, Mayr 2002, chapters 4–6, and Stephens 2007). There is an intra- or interspecific competition for resources among individuals whenever the resources are limited and thus not sufficient for the survival and the reproduction of all the individuals in question. Secondly, one can observe that certain differences between individuals (of one or different species) constitute advantages for their survival, their access to resources and their reproduction. Thirdly, the observable similarities among parents and offspring suggest that there has to be some kind of inheritance of properties. The fact that Darwin's own conception of the inheritance mechanism is wrong does not matter here.

Darwin puts these three issues in the context of the hypothesis of a continuously changing environment and postulates that there are inherited properties that, depending on the given environmental conditions, have a positive or negative effect on the probability to survive, the battle for the resources, the number of offspring, and so on. The result thus is natural selection that leads to the disappearance of conspecific varieties: those properties that are advantageous for survival and reproduction under the given environmental conditions have a higher probability to be transmitted to the next generation than those that constitute relative disadvantages. Consequently, the former ones spread more and more within the population (species), while the latter ones disappear more and more (see Darwin 1859, chapters 3–5).

By combining these empirically well-grounded observations, it is possible to explain certain aspects of evolution. Local populations and whole species —or more general taxa —may become extinct if the environmental conditions change such that the individuals in question do not survive and reproduce sufficiently (see as well Sepkoski 2008). The reason may be a natural catastrophe like an ice age or long-lasting aridity, but it may also result from a disadvantage in some interspecific competition for resources under the given or changed environmental conditions. Extinction is an

88 *Conservative Reductionism*

extreme case within biological evolution. The general impact of natural selection is the reduction of inheritable differences. Conspecific varieties tend to disappear, since the advantageous properties are transmitted more often than those ones that do not constitute selective advantages. If no other processes intervene (see section 3.1), natural selection leads to fixation: all the individuals of a given population possess the same inheritable trait —as, for instance, all members of a certain finch population on the Galápagos Islands have beaks with the same size and shape.

If, however, natural selection generally leads to a reduction of differences or the extinction of populations and species, how is it possible to refer to it in order to explain similarly the coming into existence of new species? A full answer to this question has to take genetic knowledge into account that was not known in Darwin's time. In particular, Darwin has no knowledge of genetic mutations that are, in the long run, *the* generator of variation. Nonetheless, it is worth looking first of all at Darwin's own explanatory approach and then adding some crucial issues of genetic knowledge. Let us consider some of Darwin's observations and discoveries on the Galápagos Islands, which we represent for simplicity reasons in a modified way. Think of three islands —a, b and c. On island a, there is a population of finches of the species F, and the individual finches exhibit certain inheritable differences, for instance differences in beak size and beak shape. Due to some particular wind conditions at a certain time, let's say, a unique migration is possible such that some finches arrive at the other islands b and c.

There thus are finches of the species F on each of the islands. Assume that the three islands differ with respect to the geological and climatic conditions and with respect to the given flora and fauna as well. There are thus different environmental conditions in which different properties may constitute advantages or disadvantages for the survival and the reproduction of the finches. Suppose that on island b the finches with deep and large beaks have an advantage in the access to the resource of big seeds, which is common on that island. The individuals with such beaks thus have an advantage in comparison to those that have flatter and smaller beaks. Because of that difference in the access to resources, finches with deep and large beaks live on the average longer and have more offspring. It is therefore only a matter of time that all individuals of the population on island b have deep and large beaks (fixation of that trait) and individuals with flat and small beaks disappear.

Another evolution takes place on island c. There, the flat and small beaks constitute an advantage to pick seeds in the cactus widespread on island c. Hence, finches with deep and large beaks disappear more and more and the trait of having flat and small beaks becomes fixed in the population. In such a way, Darwin tried to explain how natural selection, leading to a reduction of differences *within* populations, can increase the differences *between* separated populations. If the increase of differences between separated populations of one species is sufficiently high, it amounts to there being two different species. It is a still open debate whether there are any general and objective differences that may account for there being different species in contrast to there being just different verities of one species (we come back to this issue in section 5.3). According to Mayr and his primary focus on zoology, two separated populations of one species have developed into two different species when the individuals of the two populations cannot have offspring together anymore (Mayr 1969, p. 26; see also 1942, p. 120, and 2002, chapters 8 and 9; see also Coyne 1994, Dobzhansky 1935, O'Malley 2010, Provine 2004 and R. A. Richards 2008).

To put it differently, as soon as natural barriers prevent migration and different environmental conditions favour different inheritable properties of the finches that are relevant to their survival and reproduction, then it is just a question of time until two different species develop out of two populations that belonged beforehand to one and the same species. Even though Darwin thought that his collected finches of the Galápagos Islands were only different varieties of one and the same species, they belonged in fact to different species as the ornithologist John Gould (1804–1881) established after detailed analysis. Figure 3.1 sums up the issue.

We can add further details in order to support Darwin's approach. Rosemary and Peter Grant began in 1973 to observe finch populations on the Galápagos Island Daphne major (P. Grant 1986, R. Grant and P. Grant 1993, Ridley 2009; see furthermore Mayr 2002, chapter 6). They discovered that the finches undergo evolutionary changes in the course of the years. These changes essentially depend on the weather conditions and thus on the given resources. For instance, the existing population of middle basic finches had to adjust to larger seeds due to drought. Individuals with larger

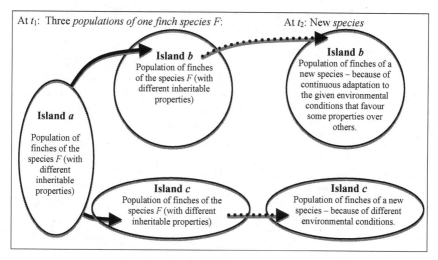

Figure 3.1   Galápagos Islands.

90 *Conservative Reductionism*

beaks were able to do so rather quickly and spread thus in the population. In addition, in 1982 the large basic finch arrived on the island and competed with the existing middle basic finches for resources. In consequence, and given a renewed drought, the middle basic finch occupied another niche where smaller beaks were advantageous. Thus, unlike before in adjusting to larger seeds during drought and leading to larger beaks in the population, the effect was that the individuals of the middle basic finches with smaller beaks spread out in the population. Rosemary and Peter Grant assume that a few of such episodes are sufficient for the development of a new species that occupies other niches than the original species (P. Grant and R. Grant 2002 and 2006; see as well regarding the genetic basis for the size and shape of the beaks Abzhanov et al. 2004 and 2006; see furthermore Griesemer 2008, Huber et al. 2007 and Forber 2009b). This assumption is supported by genetic investigations, which show that all the kinds of finches existing on the Galápagos Island possess a common descent (see for instance Sato et al. 2001).

Taking the larger framework of biological progress in the 20th century into account, we have to consider genetics in more detail, since it exerts a crucial influence on the further elaboration of the theory of evolution. As already mentioned, Darwin's theory of genetic transmission was unconvincing. Subsequent to the rediscovery and confirmation of Mendel's experiments (Mendel 1865), genetics became a biological research discipline of its own at the beginning of the 20th century. The integration of genetics into the theory of evolution in the first half of the 20th century is often called the great synthesis. This synthesis is, among others, closely connected with the works of the biologist and evolutionary theorist August Weismann (1834–1914), the theoretical biologist, geneticist and expert on statistics Ronald A. Fisher (1890–1962), the geneticist, zoologist and evolutionary theorist Theodosius Dobzhansky (1900–1975), the zoologist Ernst Mayr (1904–2005), and the geneticist Sewall Wright (1889–1988) (see among others Weismann 1895, Fisher 1930, Dobzhansky 1937, Mayr 1942, and S. Wright 1931). At that time one often speaks of Neodarwinism, which today is often referred to as the modern evolutionary synthesis, new synthesis or Neodarwinian synthesis (for further historical and conceptual details see in general Lennox 2008, Lewontin 1980, Mayr 2002, chapters 4 and 5, Sarkar 2007 and Stephens 2008; as regards Fisher in particular, see Okasha 2008a and Skipper 2007; as regards S. Wright, see Crow 1988). That synthesis enabled us to better understand the causes of inheritable differences (genmutations) among otherwise identical individuals, and it improved our comprehension of the broader genetic relations (especially classical and population genetics) that are salient for evolution.

Having this genetic knowledge in mind (which we will consider in more detail in the next chapter), let us return to our example of the finch populations on the different islands. The three finch populations on the islands

The Theory of Evolution and Casual Structures in Biology 91

a, *b* and *c* belong to the same species at the beginning (at t_1). Gene mutations, and thus inheritable differences, arise in the respective populations with a certain probability. If a gene mutation constitutes a disadvantage for survival or reproduction under the given environmental conditions on the respective island, the mutant —the individual with the gene mutation and/or the gene—disappears with a certain probability in the population. If, by contrast, the occurrence of the mutant is advantageous under the given environmental conditions, it spreads with a certain probability and beats the original one (the so-called wild type). Since the environmental conditions of the three islands differ, it is only a question of time that the three finch populations evolve differently, because different mutants and wild types prevail in each population.

We can thus suppose that, say, only on island *b* the occurrence of long legs, due to a gene mutation, constitutes a selective advantage so that individuals with short legs disappear on this island. By contrast, only the occurrence of long feathers, due to gene mutation, constitutes a selective advantage on island *c* because of other environmental conditions that have the effect that short feathers disappear on that island. In analogy to gradualism in geology, the different occurrences of gene mutations and the different retention of mutants due to the given environmental conditions have the consequence that spatially separated populations of one species become in the course of time more and more distinct from each other and constitute finally different species. The mechanism of the development of new species outlined in this example illustrates a general scheme to explain the evolution of biological properties and species.

After a more detailed consideration of Darwin's theory of evolution, we shall elaborate on the notions of fitness and adaptation in the next section, since both are essential for an adequate understanding of evolutionary biology. By means of the discussion of these notions, we shall also consider the scientific status of evolutionary biology in particular. Thus, we discuss to what extent only the principle of natural selection and to what extent also other factors are explanatory for biological evolution (section 3.1). Subsequently, we turn in more detail to Darwin's insight that biological evolution depends on the given environment, which itself continuously changes. The question is whether and how the notions of the environment, the resources and the niche can be defined in order to obtain a clear concept of a biologically *relevant* environment (section 3.2). This section then leads to an enquiry into the traits that both physical and biological causal structures have in common and their main differences. We end this discussion with an abstract approach to the transition from non-living to living structures in the world (section 3.3). Finally, we turn to a general definition of biological functions (section 3.4). We argue on the basis of biological considerations for a causal-dispositional approach that fits well with the causal theory of properties outlined in chapter 2, this volume.

92   *Conservative Reductionism*

3.1   EVOLUTION, FITNESS AND ADAPTATIONISM

Evolution is a form of change. Since the time of Darwin, the biological notion of evolution refers in general to changes of species or populations (see R. J. Richards 1992). The great synthesis of evolutionary biology and genetics links such changes up with changes of genes or alleles. Let us take a simplified definition of evolution: we speak of evolution as soon as the allele frequency changes within a population with respect to at least one gene. Our following consideration would not change substantially by another focus like that on changes of genotype frequencies since what matters here is to know more about possible explanations of biological evolution in general.

It can be observed that the number of individuals of a population or a species rises exponentially, if sufficient resources are present. Resources are for a certain individual or a population anything that potentially increases its probability to survive and reproduce. As soon as resources are limited, the result is a direct or indirect competition for the resources in question and thus a competition for survival and reproduction (see P. Abrams 1992, Fox Keller 1992, Mayr 1963, pp. 42–43, and McIntosh 1992; we shall consider resources and the environment in more detail in the next section). Furthermore, it is obvious that the individuals of a population or a species both resemble and differ from each other. Individuals vary in their phenotypes (that is, in short, observable differences due to genetic differences like different eye colours, beak sizes, leaf shapes, etc.). We can observe furthermore that parents and offspring are usually by far more similar in their phenotypes than other individuals of a given population. Therefore, Darwin, above all considering breeding results, concludes that there is a mechanism of heredity transmission (Darwin 1859, chapter 1). To take on our example, genes for the beak size are passed on from one finch generation to the next one. The relatively large similarity between parents and their respective descendants is thereby explained.

One of Darwin's great achievements is to bring the notion of competition for resources together with the idea of the transmission of characteristic traits that are pertinent for that very competition. Simplified, as soon as the resources are limited, the selection pressure in favour of advantageous properties increases. More precisely, an organism that possesses advantages in the battle for resources due to certain of its phenotypic properties that are heritable has a larger probability to survive and reproduce—and thus to pass on these very genes to the next generation. In contrast, phenotypic properties that imply a disadvantage in the battle for resources have a smaller probability to be passed on to the next generation. If not otherwise indicated, we understand probabilities in an epistemic manner, concerning our knowledge, since it is possible that the discussed genetic connections occur in each individual case according to deterministic physical laws (see also Rosenberg 1994, pp. 126–128, Sober 1999, chapter 3.2, and Weber 2001).

The Theory of Evolution and Casual Structures in Biology   93

On the assumption that the mentioned descriptive premises are fulfilled on earth, the result is biological evolution in the sense of a change in allele (or genotype) frequency, and this change is tied to (changes in the) environmental conditions. It depends on the environment which alleles amount to phenotypic effects resulting in advantages in the battle for survival and reproduction and thus have a higher probability to be passed on to the next generation. Because of the different environmental conditions on the Galápagos Islands, different characteristic traits of the finches became fixed on each island. The observable variations between the finch populations of two Galápagos Islands are a paradigm case of the so-called adaptive radiation. Due to natural selection finally different species develop that have different characteristic traits that are adaptive in their respective battles for survival and reproduction.

The notion of a species has changed since Darwin's time. Darwin himself stresses for example again and again that the difference between species and variation is only a subjective one. However, as already mentioned, there is a still ongoing debate about this point and we will take a stance on this debate at the end of the book (section 5.3), arguing for a realist position with respect to natural biological kinds (for the debate, see Mayr 1942, p. 120, Mayr 1969, p. 26, and Mayr 2002, chapters 8 and 9; see also Brigandt 2003 and 2009, Dupré 1981 and 1992, Ereshefsky 2007, 2008 and 2010, LaPorte 2004, Mallet 2010, O'Malley 2010, Pigliucci and Kaplan 2006, chapter 9, Plutynski 2008, Provine 2004, R. A. Richards 2008, Sober 1999, chapter 6, Sterelny and Griffiths 1999, chapter 9, and Stevens 1992).

Having the example of the Galápagos Islands in mind, we can link Darwin's general naturalistic explanation of biological evolution with another important concept—the one of the common ancestry of all biological species. In accordance with the theory of evolution, there is a phylogenetic tree, also called the tree of life, that represents one causal history of the origin and the evolution of life. Think of the well-known phylogenetic tree of the vertebrate animals by Ernst Haeckel (1834–1919) that reflects the morphologic, palaeontological and systematic knowledge of that time in the spirit of Darwin's theory (Haeckel 1866; see also Dawkins 1992). Closely linked to the species debate, the dichotomy structure of a tree that contains no crossing branches has been a target of many criticisms. Mainly because of possible hybridization and the so-called horizontal gene transfer across many, even eukaryotic species lineages, one may "cut down" the tree and replace it with a reticular structure as the more adequate and explanatory one to represent evolutionary history (see Andam et al. 2010, Bapteste and Burian 2010, Beiko 2010, Boto 2010, Bouchard 2010, Charlebois and Doolittle 2004, Doolittle 2010, Franklin-Hall 2010, Gogarten and Townsend 2005, Mallet 2005, Rieppel 2010, Velasco and Sober 2010). Once again, we take it that what matters here is *that* there is one causal evolutionary history and thus, at best, a possible explanation of it in terms of biology. Furthermore, the approximate universality of

94 *Conservative Reductionism*

the genetic code and other molecular similarities in all well known recent and fossil organisms suggests a common origin of all biological species. This position is falsifiable, but has not been falsified (see Dawkins 1986, chapter 10). The origin of species in the form of single-celled organisms can be dated back to approximately 3.8 billion years B.C. due to fossil records of microbes (see for example Mojzsis et al. 1996, Rosing 1999, Schopf et al. 2002; see for the philosophical discussion of this point also Mayr 2002, chapter 3).

As any evolutionary biologist admits, we do not possess a complete picture of the biological evolution—from the first organisms to the kinds living today—and we will hardly do so one day. However, the existing fossil records leave no doubt about the evolution of biological species that includes the extinction of many species. Keeping in mind that there are always knowledge gaps in the phylogenetic tree (or more adequate forms of representation), the known fossils in fact falsify any non-evolutionary position about life. On the other hand, however, they only confirm that there was evolution, whereas the exact explanation of this evolution, for instance the Darwinian, Neodarwinian or neutralist one, remains a debated question. We come back to this issue later on in this and also the next section. What matters here is that the general position —that there is evolution —is a well-confirmed, but falsifiable scientific assumption.

Let us thus continue with the great synthesis of Darwin's approach and genetics. In this theoretical framework and supported by empirical data, one can explain the manifold of life as follows: genetic differences accumulate in the course of generations within a species due to gene mutations, recombinations, and the like. Such an accumulation of differences is particularly well studied in the case of so-called model organisms, but it is also observed in any other analysed species such as the finches of the Galápagos Islands. Due to genetic differences, there are phenotypic differences between the individuals that result in (dis)advantages for survival and reproduction. This assumption is, once again, supported by still growing empirical data about studied species. Since it depends on the given environmental conditions which phenotypes constitute (dis)advantages, it is only a question of time that populations evolve differently under different environmental conditions. Here again there are a lot of empirical data that speak in favour of the evolutionary approach (see for a detailed analysis e.g. Sober 2008b). This evolution contains both the extinction of existing species and the development of new species. Nonetheless, it seems questionable whether there exists only one general pattern of explanation for evolutionary change.

Going into this debate, let us distinguish between evolutionary theory in general and natural selection in particular (see Dawkins 1986, chapters 1–3, and Mayr 2002, chapters 6 and 10). Chance plays a crucial role for evolution. However, we understand chance, like probability, in an epistemic manner in this context, concerning our knowledge and not

The Theory of Evolution and Casual Structures in Biology   95

nature itself. Gene mutations are, from a biological perspective, a chancy process, whereby each case of a gene mutation may be subject to physical deterministic laws. The mechanism of natural selection, by contrast, is not a chance process from the biological perspective. Natural selection leads to evolution as soon as genetic differences are given, and these differences end up in differences in reproduction. One can thus maintain that the chancy single occurrences of gene mutations per se do not play any role in the *explanation* of, let's say, the direction of evolution, of what has become extinct or of why certain alleles have been fixed in a given population. By contrast, it is natural selection that constitutes the only mechanism bringing about adaptations (more on that later).

Fitness and environment are two essential notions in evolutionary theory. Natural selection occurs whenever there are effective fitness differences between individuals, and such differences depend on the given environment. What is the precise role that fitness plays in evolution (see Mayr 2002, chapter 6, and Stephens 2007)? Is it possible that there is evolution, like a change in allele or genotype frequencies, without natural selection? To what extent may evolution be characterized by a chronology of different adaptations in continuously changing environments? Because of such questions that focus on the explanatory status of evolutionary biology, we shall now consider in more detail the concept of fitness and the controversial position of adaptationism (see also M. Abrams 2007, Burian 1992, Godfrey-Smith and Wilkins 2008, Matthen and Ariew 2002, Mayr 2002, chapter 7, Sober 1998, 1999, chapter 5, 2008b, chapter 3, and Stephens 2007).

Natural selection is linked to one or both of the following two properties of organisms—their lifecycle or capability to survive (probability to survive) and their reproduction rate or probability to reproduce (average of offspring, absolute or per time unit). Fitness generally encompasses both properties, since no organism of a species lives forever so that there has to be reproduction for the species to survive. Fitness thereby is commonly defined by the average of offspring, which, in turn, depends on the probability to survive (see Okasha 2008a and Sober 1999, chapter 3). In what follows, natural selection is taken to be effective whenever there are fitness differences between organisms and whenever these differences are the result of *inheritable* properties. In other terms, without differences in fitness, there is no natural selection. Note that we do not consider sexual selection in particular, since it is a special case of natural selection (Stephens 2007; see as well Cronin 1992 and Spencer and Masters 1992). We do not consider the debate about the units of selection either—whether genes, organisms or groups are the units of selection—, since our discussion here is not based on a specific position in that debate.

Still, the reductionist strategy that we shall outline in the following two chapters contains an implicit strategy to reduce conservatively any focus

96 Conservative Reductionism

on groups or organisms to that on genes. After all, there are cases that cannot be accounted for by any non-gene-centred view and thus necessitate a focus on genes in order to provide explanations, in particular in the search for so-called evolutionary stable strategies (see classically Maynard Smith and Price 1973 and Maynard Smith 1974 and 1978). Such cases, however, do not exclude that, under certain environmental conditions, a focus on the organism or on the group is explanatory as well and even more unifying than the gene-centred view. Here, however, we only assume *that* there is natural selection—a process that applies to certain entities (units of selection) under certain conditions (see for that debate Brandon 1982, Dawkins 1976, Goodnight and Stephens 1997, Hurst and Werren 2001, Kitcher et al. 1990, Okasha 2008b, Sober 1988, 1990 and 1999, chapter 4, Sober and D. S. Wilson 1998, Sterelny 1996, Sterelny and Kitcher 1988, Waters 1991, D. S. Wilson 1989 and 1992, D. S. Wilson and Sober 1989, 1994a and 1994b, and R. A. Wilson 2007).

We take for granted that fitness supervenes on physical properties. The fitness of a gene, an individual or a group supervenes on the physical properties of the gene, individual or group and the physical properties of the relevant environment (see Rosenberg 1978, Sober 1999, chapter 3.5, and Weber 1996). Let us consider three aspects of the supervenience relation in order to specify the connection between biological and physical characteristics (see also section 1.1): (1) The physical properties determine the corresponding fitness. Scientific investigations support this claim, for example in the case of two gene occurrences that are physically identical and that are also identical as concerns their biological functionality in the cell and thus their fitness or fitness contribution to the organism (provided that the relevant environment, the two respective cells, organisms and the habitat are sufficiently similar in the two cases). (2) If fitness differences are present (while the relevant environment is sufficiently similar), then there have to be physical differences as well. This assumption is empirically confirmed as well—for instance in any case in which biological differences are explained by physical differences. (3) Under certain environmental conditions it is possible that physical differences are present without these differences leading to a fitness difference.

What is explained by fitness similarities or fitness differences? Simplified, whenever an individual has in average more than one offspring, the size of the population will grow. If, however, the average of offspring is smaller than 1, then the population size decreases. These facts suggest explaining the change of population size in terms of fitness. If for example a population becomes larger, whereas the size of another population is reduced, then we can explain these variations in terms of the first population possessing a higher fitness. But how does evolutionary biology explain such differences in the fitness of populations? Supervenience is not explanatory in itself, and explaining fitness differences in terms of some underlying physical differences would constitute a reductive and thus *non*-biological explanation

The Theory of Evolution and Casual Structures in Biology 97

(more on that below and in sections 4.2 and 5.1). Here, however, we want to focus on the explanatory capacities of biology, and the crucial point is that any biological explanation of evolutionary change that is couched in terms of fitness becomes circular if the fitness of an entity at t_1 is explained by the evolutionary effects it brings about at t_2. It is hardly explanatory to say that populations increase faster, the higher their fitness is, *and* what their fitness is depends on how quickly they increase in size. Consequently, a substantial part of the theory of evolution would not be falsifiable so that the theory could be criticized altogether as being unscientific. Such a conclusion would, however, be hasty (see also Rosenberg 1978, Sober 1999, chapter 3, and Stephens 2007). Taking evolution as a fact, it seems that there has to be a non-tautological explanation of fitness possible.

As we shall discuss later in detail, everything that can be explained is in principle explainable by physics (section 5.1). Against this background we accept the theoretical possibility of a physical explanation of changes in alleles or anything else that may characterize biological evolution. Such a theoretical physical explanation could draw on the facts that certain molecules, macromolecules and still more complex physical structures increase in number in the course of the time, while others decrease. Since such explanations are based on physical laws only, we usually assume that there is a non-tautological explanation of biological evolution. The question now is whether and how biology can explain evolution in a comparable non-tautological way.

Without using the concept of fitness, biology can likewise explain which genes, which organisms or which populations stand in which relationships to the given relevant environment—even though such explanations often employ physical and chemical laws. These are simple causal explanations, so-called *proximal* explanations. They are non-tautological in the same way as physical explanations are, being about local causal processes. However, the core of evolutionary biology is its so-called *ultimate* explanations, which trade in the concepts of fitness and natural selection (see also Sober 1999, chapter 1). Ultimate explanations answer the question why certain types of characteristic traits became fixed or disappeared during evolution. The fact that an inheritable characteristic in a population became (rather) fixed is usually explained with reference to fitness differences and the corresponding natural selection. Adaptations are taken to be the result of natural selection and thus the result of given fitness differences. What however is so particular about the concept of fitness and the principle of natural selection that their use leads to tautological explanations? How can the abstractions from physical details and/or proximal explanations, which are both not tautological, result in tautological explanations?

The obvious circularity in evolutionary biology has a concrete epistemic reason, which we see, following Rosenberg (1978), in the failure to distinguish between the *operational* and the *conceptual* understanding of fitness. It is theoretically possible by drawing on physical and chemical laws

98 *Conservative Reductionism*

to predict how many descendants which organism will probably have and thus determine its individual fitness value. In practice, it is however often not possible to carry out such a prediction. To put it differently, such a procedure is not operational. The operationally simplest way to *determine* the fitness value is to do so in retrospective by counting the number of descendants. However, having once retrospectively determined the fitness value of a population, it is possible to use this value to explain further evolutionary change if the context remains sufficiently similar. Against this background we understand fitness values or differences as abstract but genuine explanations of population developments or differences. We take the latter however to be a pragmatic means to determine the fitness values. Fitness, purely conceptually, refers in an abstract way to the physical traits of a gene, an organism or a population due to which it possesses a certain likelihood to have a certain number of offspring.

Having in mind this solution to the tautology problem we can discuss now the position according to which ultimate explanations often seem to be nothing more than *story telling* or *descriptions* of the phenomenon that has to be explained (Mills and Beatty 1979). Operationally, purely practically understood, this claim seems to be correct. However, drawing on the precedent distinction of the two notions of fitness, it is in principle possible to turn the ultimate explanations (that are called descriptions) into genuine causal explanations by adding the theoretically available corresponding proximal explanations. Each case of circularity within the theory of evolution is based on epistemic reasons, on confounding the mentioned two notions of fitness. In what follows, we essentially understand the explanatory value of the concepts of fitness, the average value of fitness or fitness differences as abstract placeholders for a complex conjunction of many detailed proximal explanations.

Let us now turn to the importance of ultimate explanations. Due to fitness values we can summarize in mathematical models, almost deduce, how population sizes change over time. Evolutionary models, if formulated carefully, appear often not to be empirical models, but rather mathematical truths—so that this abstract and general part of evolutionary biology seems to be void of empirical content (see Sober 1999, chapter 3; see furthermore the discussion between Fodor 2008a and 2008b on the one hand and Dennett 2008, Godfrey-Smith 2008 and Sober 2008a on the other). However, this apparently purely analytical part of evolutionary biology can be tested by empirical data, leading to a modification of the mathematical models. This point highlights again the fact that the concept of fitness includes more than just the operational aspect and is not limited to providing an unfalsifiable description. Furthermore, as already mentioned, the premises for natural selection and other issues can be falsified —like among others the thesis that there are intermediate forms between two related species or the thesis that there are homologous characteristics (see furthermore the discussion by Maynard Smith 1978).

The Theory of Evolution and Casual Structures in Biology 99

The problem how to understand the concept of fitness reappears in another context. It is questionable whether fitness is linked to *actual* success in survival and reproduction. If the environmental conditions are identical, then two biologically identical organisms possess the same fitness. If, however, only one of them actually has offspring, does this mean that this one has a higher fitness than the other one? In order to avoid this conclusion—since one would in this case fail to distinguish between the operational and the conceptual notion of fitness—one generally defines fitness by means of propensities or dispositions to survive and to have offspring and not by the actual survival and reproduction (Mills und Beatty 1979). We thus understand fitness as a dispositional property of organisms in the sense of the causal-functional theory of properties outlined in the second chapter (see also Weber 1996, Ariew and Lewontin 2004, Krimbas 2004, as well as Ariew and Ernst 2009 for clarifications and critical comments on the propensity interpretation of fitness that, however, mainly show effective problems to get to an explanatory conceptual notion of fitness in practice).

The comparison with a stock example of a macroscopic, chemical disposition, namely the disposition of sugar to dissolve in water, may help to illustrate our claim. The disposition of sugar to be water-soluble is ontologically speaking the property to dissolve in water, ceteris paribus. In the same vein, we understand "fitness" as an abstract concept referring to the set of dispositional properties of an organism to survive and to have offspring. On this basis, it is possible to provide abstract and ultimate explanations of the changes of populations and biological evolution. By contrast, proximal explanations concern the manifestation of the given dispositional properties. Sugar dissolves in water, because the polar water molecules change the structure of the sugar molecules in such a manner that their crystalline bounding breaks down. In a similar way, the respective fitness of an organism or a population can be causally explained in the sense of proximal explanations by pointing out what dispositions were manifested under the given environmental conditions in the course of time (leading to the death of x_1 at t_1, the fight between x_2 and x_3 at t_2, the development of x_4 from t_1 to t_2, the birth of x_5 at t_3, and so on). In this sense, we suggest that the ultimate explanations that are at the heart of the evolutionary theory are abstractions from causal details that are outlined in the corresponding proximal causal explanations. We shall spell out this view further later on in the framework of our reductionist strategy (see section 5.3; in addition, see Rosenberg 2006, Sober 1984 and Weber 2008).

We agree with Elliot Sober that abstract biological generalizations are laws, as for example Fisher's law (Sober 1999, pp. 14–18; see against such a position for example Beatty 1995 (no laws in the theory of evolution) or Rosenberg 1994, chapter 6, and 2006, chapters 4–6 (the law of natural selection, which is a physical law, being the only law in biology)). We essentially follow Sober's criticism of Beatty and Rosenberg (Sober 1997, see also Weber 2008) and share his position according to which the multiple

100 *Conservative Reductionism*

realization of biological properties does not hinder that there are laws in evolutionary biology. Of course, it depends on the initial conditions whether and which laws apply, but given certain conditions it is not a pure coincidence that the laws describe correctly certain causal relations. If certain conditions that can be formalized are fulfilled (which is an empirical question)—for example that resources are limited, that there is a competition for resources, that the outcome of this competition depends on certain properties that are at least partly inheritable—then we can infer that the corresponding gene frequencies will change in accordance with the principle of natural selection and that evolution will thus take place (see Sober 1984, 1997 and 1999).

Against this background, let us consider in more detail what the principle of natural selection explains (see also Stephens 2007). To put it differently, each time on earth when the mentioned premises for applying the principle of natural selection are fulfilled, does natural selection entirely determine evolution? Or are there also other determining factors? Let us ask moreover how specific nature is (or can be) in its selection. To put the question in a less metaphorical way, to what extent does evolution reflect a relative fitness optimization? For our following consideration, let us distinguish between *selection for* and *selection of* (see also Sober 1999, chapter 3.6). *Selection for* concerns the causes of selection, while *selection of* brings out the effects of selection.

A classical example can illustrate this distinction as well as the concept of adaptation. It is well known that the forelegs of turtles have the following two functional characteristics: they are used for movement and for eggs burying (see also Lewontin 1978 and West-Eberhard 1992). Assume that after their "first" occurrence (at t_1), the forelegs were exclusively used for progressive movement. Generations later, at t_2, the forelegs were also used for eggs burying, because changed environmental conditions made this possible. To move with forelegs is an adaptation if from the "first" occurrence of the forelegs on (at t_1) the turtles did so and if doing so had a selective advantage; in accordance with natural selection, moving with forelegs may even become fixed in the population. In such a case, there was a *selection for* forelegs, but just because of the possibility to use them to move. However, it is not possible that forelegs were already selected at t_1 for using them *later* on (t_2) for eggs burying. In this sense, there was no *selection for* eggs burying at t_1, but only a *selection of* this capacity (that was employed later on at t_2). This is why the capacity to use the forelegs for eggs burying is no adaptation (in this example).

Let us now consider in an abstract way all the biological properties that have a genetic basis. Any of them can be functionally defined—in terms of certain causal dispositions as we shall argue later on in detail (section 3.4). Adaptationism could be understood as claiming that the actual characteristic effects of a property are the reason why this property was selected in the first place—and thus any property represents an adaptation (that was

The Theory of Evolution and Casual Structures in Biology 101

selected *for*). Such a strong understanding of adaptationism is of course misleading since it excludes any change of function due to environmental change for instance. One would thereby contradict the spirit of evolutionary theory. For a more appropriate understanding of adaptationism, let us distinguish between being adaptive and being an adaptation (see also Stephens 2007). A property is adaptive if it amounts to a selective advantage under the *given* environmental conditions. Being adaptive, however, does not imply that the given selective advantage or something similar was already present at the "first" occurrence of the property in question.

Against this background, we propose to understand adaptationism in the following more modest form (see as well Matthen and Ariew 2002, Sober 1998 and 1999, chapter 5): natural selection is the primary reason why certain biological properties become or tend to be fixed after their "first" occurrence while others disappear. The characteristic effects of properties and thus their effective functionality may however change during evolution. According to this understanding, adaptationism claims that all or most properties that are widespread at a given time are or were adaptations because of certain of their effects. These effects, however, do not have to continue to be adaptive, and what most characterizes the property in question may change depending on the environmental context. To sum up, the primary question in the adaptationism debate is whether or not evolution was mainly influenced by the development and fixation of adaptations (whose characteristic effects may change over time).

There are, of course, other factors that influence evolution and that, metaphorically speaking, let nature select somehow less specific, that is, are not orientated towards a relative improvement of fitness. The concept of genetic drift sums up such factors (see M. Abrams 2007). An illustrative example is a volcanic eruption that kills individuals living in its environment independently of their different properties and supervening fitness values (see Beatty 1992). It is thus possible that, by "chance," only those individuals survive that are less fit than those that die. It is however a difficult empirical question to assess to what extent such events have influenced evolution and thus constitute an argument against adaptationism that takes such events as negligible accidents. It seems more important to evaluate the importance of environmental conditions that are occurring more frequently. Without going into detail here, let us consider some issues that show some explanatory limits of any exclusive focus on natural selection. Genetic constraints like heterozygote superiority imply that natural selection may not always lead to a fixation of a certain genotype. Furthermore, selection generally results in available compromises since genes may have both negative and positive effects that may be suppressed or amplified by other genes. The effect of natural selection on single alleles may thus be reduced since its fixation (or extinction) in the gene pool of a population may presuppose further evolutionary steps that may face similar obstacles. Notice further that the importance of any positive or negative effect of genes depends on

102 *Conservative Reductionism*

the environmental conditions that may include the size of the given population and the given genotype frequency. And, particularly in small populations, changes of allele and genotype frequencies are significantly influenced by non-selected forces (see classically Gould and Lewontin 1978 against adaptationism and for the recent discussion Beatty and Desjardins 2009, Forber 2009a and 2009b, Houston 2009, Lewens 2009, Potochnik 2009, Van Valen 2009 and Wilkins and Godfrey-Smith 2009).

To sum up the crucial issues, adaptationism constitutes an explanatory abstraction from certain details and the adequacy of such an approach is linked to conditions that are satisfied, partially satisfied or not at all satisfied. How can we now evaluate the given similarities and differences between individuals of one or different species? The fact that any human being possesses eyes suggests that this fixation is the result of a selective advantage—such that the adaptationist position seems to be the adequate position as concerns the development of eyes. The general point of this example is that the more common a given property is (was) in the population or species in question, the more *probable* it is (was) that the given property is important for the fitness of the organism in question. To put it differently, adaptationism seems to be quite adequate as concerns common or fixed properties. The argument behind this generalization is that the common distribution up to a fixation of a property is by far more probable if the given property makes an important contribution to the fitness value to the organism in question. In that sense, we take adaptationism to be the (more) appropriate position in what follows, since we consider especially abstract biological concepts that bring out central *functional similarities*. Still, in the next section, we shall develop our position, among others, in the context of neutralism.

3.2 THE RELEVANCE OF THE ENVIRONMENT

In this section, we consider the concept of a resource and the concept of a niche, since both these related concepts contribute to a better understanding of our previous discussion of the concept of fitness and the importance of natural selection. The guiding question is what conditions are relevant for the fitness contribution of a property and under what conditions the selective pressure for property differences change such that other mechanisms may constitute more important determinants than natural selection.

Whatever the unit of selection is, it defines what is a resource in its environment (Lewontin 1982). For simplicity reasons, let us take the perspective of an individual —even though our considerations can be generalized for any other possible unit of selection. A resource for an organism is what potentially increases its probability of survival and reproduction, that is, its fitness (P. Abrams 1992). We consider an organism to be an entity with certain causal-dispositional properties whose manifestation depends directly

The Theory of Evolution and Casual Structures in Biology   103

or indirectly on the given resources. We thereby lay stress on the relational aspect of resources: not only organisms define what a resource is in their environment, but also the given resource, understood as a causal-dispositional property as well, can be in quite different ways a resource for quite different individuals (of even different species). Thus, resources are what leads potentially to the display of properties of organisms whose manifestation generally improves the fitness of the organism.

Since resources are often limited, competition for the resources is widespread. Such competition does not necessarily imply physical battles (see Fox Keller 1992, pp. 68–73, Mayr 1963, pp. 42–43, and McIntosh 1992). The aspect of a quantitative usage or consumption of resources, if limited, comes along with an impact on the consumers. Illustrative models like the Lotka-Volterra equation describe such mutual impacts between predator and prey populations (Lotka 1998 [1934 and 1939]). In a similar way, other correlations within ecosystems can be formalized (see for instance P. Abrams 2000, Colyvan 2008 and Gintis 2000, chapter 8.5).

Against this background, let us consider the more comprehensive concept of the environment. The environment includes generally all external factors that play a role for the survival and the reproduction of the organism in question. These external factors may reach beyond resources that can be quantitatively reduced by consumption. Due to different external physical conditions at different places in the world, a different evolution of flora and fauna has taken place. A different evolution in turn leads to different external physical conditions, that, again lead to . . . and so on.

As in the case of resources, not any environmental factor is relevant in the same way for the manifestation of the causal-dispositional properties in question. In what follows, only those environmental factors come under the concept of the *relevant environment* that are pertinent to the manifestation of causal-dispositional properties that have an impact on the fitness of the organism in question. The environmental conditions change continuously, sometimes slowly, sometimes abruptly. In this context, a catastrophe means generally an extreme and abrupt change of the relevant environment. Apart from this particular issue, it is generally only a question of time that different causal-dispositional properties of organisms are manifested or manifested in a different way such that the fitness contribution changes accordingly.

Let us define the concept of the niche in order to conclude our discussion of the relevant environment. A niche can be conceived as the set of conditions that are sufficient for the survival of the given population (see M. Abrams 2009 and Colwell 1992). A niche, thus understood, is the essential relevant environment of the organism or population in question. It depends on the given environmental conditions whether an organism with its biological properties respectively its niche can survive and reproduce, that is, whether its causal-dispositional properties can be sufficiently manifested in such a way that the individual can survive

104   *Conservative Reductionism*

and reproduce. Since not all environmental factors are salient in the same way, the relevant environment are those factors that are pertinent in the context of selection. To put it differently, environmental factors (or changes of them) that have no impact on the probability to survive or reproduce do not fall under the concept of the relevant environment (see as well Brandon 1992 and his analysis of the "selective environment"; see furthermore M. Abrams 2009). In what follows, the concept of standard conditions is closely linked to that of the relevant environment: under standard conditions it is possible, as we shall outline later on in more detail, that certain physical differences of biological properties do not imply a functional difference. Depending on the change of environmental conditions, however, the physical differences in question may lead to fitness differences. This then is a change of the *relevant* environment.

Against this background, let us consider how natural selection provides for an explanation of adaptation. Let us distinguish between two factors—changing environmental conditions and the development of new properties. Starting with the first one, let us consider a population of individuals who are similar as regards certain properties and different as regards other properties. Under the given environmental conditions, we can assume that these differences do not lead to significant fitness differences. There thus is no high selective pressure on these differences. However, when the environmental conditions change, there then are different possibilities, ranging from the given environmental change still having no significant impact on the fitness of the individuals to its being that great a change of the relevant environment that the population becomes extinct (catastrophe). Between these extreme cases we can find the general cases that lead to evolution—even though extinction is part of evolution and evolution does not necessarily presuppose environmental changes. Most interestingly here are cases where the given differences between individuals that did not lead beforehand to fitness differences now do so.

Let us take up certain issues of the so-called neutralism debate in this context. Before Motoo Kimura (1924–1994) introduced the theory of neutralism in 1968, the common opinion was in the 1950s and 1960s that natural selection is generally the determining factor of evolution (see as regards Kimura also Crow 2007). What Kimura set out to show is that on the molecular level, most changes of the DNA are selectively *neutral* (Kimura 1968, see furthermore Kimura 1992 and Plutynski 2007). That is to say, without denying that form and function of customary phenotypic properties as for instance human eyes are the product of natural selection, Kimura claims that rather than natural selection, the mutation rate and genetic drift are the important factors for the evolution at the molecular scale. Neutralism, however, does not claim that mutation rates and genetic drift can exclusively explain any evolutionary change —as already said, the evolutionary history of the human eyes is

The Theory of Evolution and Casual Structures in Biology   105

well explained by natural selection. Neutralism is moreover an objection against a so-called panselectivism, since, according to Kimura, most molecular changes in the gene pool from one generation to the next one do not have any significant impact on the corresponding fitness (see also King and Jukes 1969 who argue for neutralism as well, even though in another way than Kimura; see for a comparison of both approaches and further details of the debate Nei 2005).

It is uncontroversial in this debate *that* there are genotypic and phenotypic properties and that changes of them can occur without any impact on the fitness of the organism in question. Already before Kimura's publication, there was a discussion on the proportion of such selectively neutral or almost neutral properties and differences and their pertinence for evolution (see Nei 2005 and Plutynski 2007). To put it differently, the question is what role certain environmental conditions and molecular mechanisms can play for an evolution that is not linked to an improvement of relative fitness. Against this background, Kimura claims that, on the molecular level, there are changes of amino acids or nucleotides for instance that accumulate in the course of generations and that are randomly fixed—or at least not fixed for selective reasons. Hence, at the molecular level, adaptationism is not or hardly the adequate position to describe and explain evolution.

The argument for Kimura's claim is based on the results of his experiments, from which he draws the general conclusion that the change rate is simply too high in the genome of an organism for natural selection to influence these changes in a pertinent way. In this sense the molecular changes are effectively seen as selectively neutral. Let us note, however, that there is an ongoing debate on the interpretation of these quantitative tests as well (see Nei 2005 and Kreitman 2000). One can however already say that the question is not *whether* neutralism *or* selectionism is right, but that the point is rather a *more-or-less* issue (Plutynski 2007).

Against this background, let us nonetheless take a stance on this debate since neutralism obviously challenges our position as outlined at the end of the previous section. As can be shown empirically, amino acid substitutions in proteins (resulting out of genmutations of the corresponding DNA sequence) are less often observed in those proteins that are quite important for the organism and that occur in functionally important parts of the protein in question (see Nei 2005). Without any doubt, there are genetic changes and these genetic changes, essentially due to mutation rates, lead to genetic differences within and across species. If such regularly occurring genetic differences have no effect on the fitness, natural selection cannot work on them. It is thereby possible that there are fixations of certain DNA sequences without these being guided by natural selection. In this sense, we agree to weaken the so-called Neodarwinism and concede that panselectivism is obviously not the correct position, since there are many examples to which it apparently does not

106 *Conservative Reductionism*

apply. In other terms, there are functional similarities possible that are somehow not the exclusive result of natural selection—to the extent that the precise DNA sequence was not selected for in favour of some molecularly different (but functionally similar) DNA sequence. We thus agree with the claim that there are genetic differences possible that do not imply functional differences under the given environmental conditions. However, as soon as genetic differences imply functional differences, natural selection has an impact on them.

Let us come back to our example of the finches at the Galápagos Islands. We assumed that the given differences between the finches on island *a* did not imply any fitness difference there. However, according to our example, there was a differential selection according to the relevant environments on islands *b* and *c*. On island *a* there was no differential selection and thus no selective pressure on the given differences like different size and shape of the beaks. Due to a changing environment for those finches that migrated to either island *b* or *c*, there in fact is a selective pressure for deep and large beaks on *b* and for flat and small beaks on *c*. Selection pressure can thereby be understood as the different probable results of the corresponding interaction between the causal-dispositional properties of the organisms in question and the causal-dispositional properties of the relevant environment. On island *b*, the result of the interaction between the causal disposition of deep and large beaks and the environment was, in terms of fitness contribution for the finches, more advantageous than the interaction between the causal disposition of flat and small beaks and the given environment. Thus, the selective pressure, that means the result of the interaction between genotype and relevant environment, was such that deep and large beaks became fixed while flat and small beaks disappeared on that island.

If no new properties develop in a population due to genetic mutation or recombination, selective pressure generally (generally here means in changing or temporally non-changing environments) ends up in decreasing the given genetic differences among the individuals, leading to the fixation of certain properties. More important than possible exceptions to fixations (because of e.g. heterozygote superiority) is the point that selective pressure per se never leads to an increase of genetic differences *within* populations. If, however, new properties develop, the given selective pressure plays an important role in determining which changes in the population are more probable and which ones are less probable. If for instance the emerging new property leads to a significantly higher fitness, the probability is accordingly high that this mutant will be fixed and replace the wild type. The selective pressure thereby increases with the changes in the relevant environment. For short, a changing environment, as Darwin already assumed, leads to new directions of evolution that were—before that change —less probable or not at all possible.

3.3 THE CRITERION FOR CAUSAL BIOLOGICAL STRUCTURES

What life is seems to be, on the one hand, quite familiar to us since we experience it every day in many ways. On the other hand, it is still not a trivial issue to define life precisely. One of the main difficulties is to find necessary and sufficient conditions that distinguish living beings from non-living ones. This section neither pretends to do so nor to consider in extension the current debate (see among others Griesemer 2008, Mayr 2002, chapter 3, Maynard Smith and Szathmáry 1999 and Szathmáry 2006). Still, we seek to provide an abstract reflection on the difference between complex causal structures that are commonly understood as non-living and complex causal structures that are commonly understood as living. Thereby, our aim is to indicate a naturalist account of the transition from physical to biological structures. This then enables us to highlight the basis of abstract explanations about evolutionary changes.

One of the reasons why the definition of living beings is a still open debate consists in the fact that the explanation of the development of living beings out of non-living constituents still is an open issue. One may wonder whether this issue will be solved one day, since there are promising approaches to close the gap (see classically Miller 1953; see as well Lazcano and Bada 2003). Beyond this more empirical challenge, there is also a conceptual debate how to define life in a non-circular way. It is generally taken for granted that life develops out of non-living structures without violating physical laws. Consequently, there is in principle a naturalistic explanation of life possible (even if not in general, then at least in each particular case). Without speculating about currently discussed empirical approaches, we shall elaborate on the probably essential and non-essential traits that enter into a naturalistic and non-circular explanation of life.

Let us take the quasi universality of the genetic code as starting point, which suggests the common descent of all living beings on earth. This fact does, however, not mean that there was only one precise common descent of life possible. Life seems to be possible without that very genetic code that, in addition, is in fact generally seen as a product of evolution, albeit an early one. This assumption is based on the complexity and specificity of the genetic code that, hence, requires several evolutionary steps until having obtained its actual fine-tuned shape (see Maynard Smith and Szathmáry 1999, chapters 1–5). Furthermore, the quasi universality of the genetic code seems hardly to constitute a necessary ingredient of life but rather constitutes a "frozen accident" that, once established, remains conserved (see Crick 1968). In addition, a particular molecular form of realization of genes cannot be a necessary condition for life either. Genes may not only be realized by DNA, but also by RNA, and RNA probably is the precedent of DNA in evolution (see Rosenberg 1994, chapter 6). To sum up, if there is a common feature of all living beings, neither a certain universality of the

108 *Conservative Reductionism*

genetic code nor a certain physical realization of genes are suitable candidates for constituting such a common feature.

Let us therefore take a step back from concrete details. Consider the hypothesis that life is essentially constituted by replication, variation and heredity. The general motivation for this hypothesis is this one: against the background of our previous discussion, we seek to obtain on the one hand a level of abstraction that includes other possible genetic codes and other possible realizations of genes than our ones. On the other hand, we look for a non-arbitrary criterion that, in the best case, reflects our intuitive distinction between living and non-living beings on earth and that fits within the explanatory scheme of evolutionary changes. To put it differently, we propose an abstract evolutionary perspective on living beings in order to spell out, at best, essential differences between living and non-living entities.

The proposed hypothesis includes a clear link with natural selection. If (a) replication is given, (b) there is some variation (for some reason or other, for instance in genes for molecular or physical reasons) and (c) these variations are transmitted from one generation to the next one, then the essential premises for natural selection to occur are satisfied (apart from possible situations as discussed in the context of adaptationism and neutralism).

This hypothesis thus directly invokes the question whether there can be life without natural selection. In order to answer this question, let us consider adaptation to environmental change. It seems clear that any living being has to possess in some way or other the capacity to adapt to environmental change, since environmental change is a fact. There is the theoretical possibility that life can exist without the capacity to adapt only if either there is a possible world in which no environmental change takes place or if the environmental change never puts into peril the existence of the living beings in question. If there is replication, variation and heredity, and thus natural selection, there consequently is the possibility for adaptation to environmental change. The subsequent question then is whether there can be continuous adaptation without replication, variation and heredity.

Once again theoretically speaking, it is possible that there are living beings that can adapt to environmental changes even in the long run without replication, variation and heredity. However, that possibility is practically excluded (or at least hardly likely) for the following reason: if living beings develop out of non-living beings, how can a living being possess the capacity to adapt to environmental change without replication, variation and heredity? It is an empirical question whether this is possible and if so, to what extent probable under which conditions. To continue our reasoning, it suffices to say that variation is, for emerged living beings, most likely to be realized by the capacity to replicate and inherit variation that occurs somewhere during the lifecycle or during the inheritance mechanisms. In any case all living beings, both the more and the less complex ones, evolve in that manner.

The Theory of Evolution and Casual Structures in Biology 109

Thus, if life is not probable without the capacity to adapt to environmental change and if the capacity to adapt to environmental change is not probable without replication, variation and heredity, it is plausible that natural selection is somehow constitutive of life or, to put it the other way round, natural selection is a hardly avoidable result of the existence of living beings. According to this line of reasoning, one may examine the development of life by establishing conditions that lead to natural selection, or, to use Dawkins' terminology, establishing conditions that lead to replicators (Dawkins 1986, chapter 5; see also Hull and J. S. Wilkins 2008 and Wilson 2007). To put it differently, life may start, independently of the physical realization, if replication, variation and heredity are given —and thus, when there is natural selection.

Natural selection is, in a very broad sense nothing else than the corresponding causally efficacious environment of the entity in question. That environment has no qualitatively different effects on living and non-living beings. That means that there are no new or different physical laws at stake when life develops. However, what is changing with the development of life is that certain properties become more pertinent than others. Therefore, natural selection can be understood more narrowly, namely as the reason for there being evolution that is somehow inevitably oriented towards a relative increase of fitness. Compare, for instance, the property of entities to be stable under certain environmental conditions and the property of entities to reproduce. Stability is, metaphorically speaking, fine, if there is no environmental change such that the former stability breaks down and the entity as such disappears. It is, however, just a question of time until an environmental change or influence occurs that destroys the entity in question. Replication thus is, still metaphorically speaking, better since the entity can survive in form of its replications as soon as the frequency of replication is higher than the frequency to break down. Let us illustrate this consideration by means of an abstract story.

Let the world be a distribution of microphysical objects in space-time that are linked in some way or other such that there are local physical structures (see section 2.4). One can ask what kind of local structures are likely to exist more often than others. We thereby make a shift from individuals to populations or types. One essential factor for the existence of a structure of a certain type is its probability to emerge —that its components meet somehow in space-time such that the structure is established. The other essential factor for the existence of such a structure is its stability —to persist in time. Both factors, of course, depend on the environmental conditions. In the former case, the availability of the corresponding components of the structure and the probability that these components form the structure in question are crucial. In the latter case, depending on the environmental conditions, the formed structure may persist for a more or less long period of time.

110   *Conservative Reductionism*

Without going into physical or chemical details, one may then ask how a structure may occur numerically more often than structures of another type. The existence of the structures of both types depends on the probability to develop out of the components and the stability to persist in time. Since both these factors depend on the given and changing environment, any direct or indirect positive influence of a given structure on the probability that structures of the same type develop and persist in time leads to an exponential increase in the number of structures of that type that exist. Furthermore, there may be a negative influence on the probability to develop or to persist in time for structures of the other type (especially if both types of structure have certain components in common and thus are based on the same resources so to speak).

Up to this point, one may hardly speak of life, since what has been pointed out is nothing more than a steady state for each type of structure, and such a steady state applies to almost everything in the world. To put it differently, there is hitherto no distinction between two classes of entities, such as the distinction between living and non-living entities. The interesting point is that with the integration of the emergence of variation and the transmission of that variation, one effectively obtains that very distinction. Let us explain.

The emergence of variation can be easily integrated into the outlined picture. The components of a given structure are linked to each other by means of different kinds of bindings and thus forces. The force of each binding can vary depending on the environmental conditions. It is thus easily imaginable that the binding of one component to the structure becomes so weak under certain environmental conditions that it breaks out of the structure and is replaced by another, physically different component. One may think of more temporary or more constant replacements that do or do not change the entire structure under certain given environmental conditions.

More important than any such possibility is the heredity of variations. All that is needed for some kind of heredity of variation is that the given variation has, as maybe the old structure as well, a direct or indirect influence on the emergence of structures that contain that very variation. If for instance the structure A-B-C changes such that there is the structure A-G-C and this variation has a direct or indirect influence on the emergence of further A-G-C-structures, then the variation form C to G is transmitted.

Depending on many factors like to what extent structures can vary as regards some of their components without losing their stability and probability to have some kind of influence on the emergence of structures of the same type, there now is a new kind of adaptation possible: new types of structures can emerge because of variations and their inheritance that are such that stability and replication are retained even when the environmental context changes. Some kind of optimization in the physical realization of our genes and the genetic code seems to be an earlier or later product of such a process (as well as any more comprehensive reproduction in contrast to pure replication).

The Theory of Evolution and Casual Structures in Biology   111

What is the upshot of this abstract story? Keep in mind that the idea is to identify a *non*-arbitrary criterion that may distinguish living from non-living beings. By means of doing so, one avoids having to take a stance on the question of what list of more or less concrete characteristic traits any or most living beings have to satisfy. If the mentioned reasoning is correct, any form of life is probably the *result* of a process such as the outlined one. Of course, due to hybridization or other processes, living entities like mules or worker bees may emerge that may no longer pass on their genes to the next generation. This fact, however, does not constitute an objection to the outlined analysis. First of all, the apparent problem disappears from a gene-centred perspective. Second, from the perspective of the organism or the group, hybridization and other processes like horizontal gene transfer seem to constitute evolutionary stable strategies only if they imply some kind of reproductive advantage *somewhere*. Worker bees, for instance, increase the fitness of others that contain the same genes (or so they "hope"). If there were no increase of fitness at all, there would be, depending on the given and changing environment, a correspondingly high selective pressure against the emergence of such life forms. Thus, at least in the long run, living beings remain units of natural selection ("natural selection" understood here in the narrow sense). Keep in mind that the proposed correlation between being a living entity and being a unit of selection does not rely on the very idea of a common descent. Possible forms of life that constitute units of selection do not have to go back to a common descent (see Sober and Orzack 2003).

Against this background, let us come back to our mentioned doubt towards any life-defining list that is based on criteria beyond replication, variation and heredity. Taking into account more complex properties such as the metabolism, specific replication or reproduction mechanisms, perception, and possible distinction between self-replication and self-reproduction does, of course, provide a better understanding of the living being in question. These details, however, constitute only proximal explanations that provide the basis for more abstract explanations of micro- and macro-evolutionary changes. They do not seem to be necessary for any distinction between non-living entities and living beings that evolve. In other terms, they can be left aside since their consideration does not alter the substantial pattern of evolutionary explanation in terms of continuous adaptations to environmental change. One does not have to draw on any concrete physical realization in order to be in the position to distinguish entities that are capable of being a unit of natural selection.

3.4 BIOLOGICAL FUNCTIONS AND FUNCTIONAL EXPLANATIONS

In the last section of this chapter, we shall consider the concept of biological functions and functional explanations. We thereby put the concept of causal biological structures into the general frame of the first two

112 *Conservative Reductionism*

chapters. The notion of biological function has changed from a concept with teleological connotations to one that can be defined naturalistically, broadly either in terms of selected effects or in terms of causal dispositions to contribute to certain capacities or the fitness of biological systems. This conceptual change reflects the development of modern science, due among other factors to evolutionary biology, and aims at a naturalisation of biological functions (see also Lewens 2007). Let us consider the two main positions discussed in the current literature (see Wouters 2003 and 2005 for an overview).

The etiological approach defines biological functions in a historical manner, by means of referring to the evolutionary past of the biological property in question (see classically L. Wright 1973; see also Godfrey-Smith 1993 and 1994, Griffiths 1993 and 2009, Millikan 1989 and 2002, Mitchel 1993, Neander 1991 and Schwartz 1999). For instance, the heart of an organism is defined functionally by means of the selective advantages of the preceding organisms with a heart. In order to spell out the argument for this approach, consider the criteria one may use to characterize something as functional. According to the causal theory of properties, a property generally consists in the power to produce certain effects (section 2.1). By contrast to physics, biology focuses only on certain, *characteristic* effects and not on any possible physical effect of a given property.

What is the criterion to distinguish characteristic effects—such that, in the best case, one obtains a non-arbitrary difference between physical and biological descriptions? A heart produces many effects. To pump blood seems to be more characteristic than other effects like making noise, appearing red, and contributing mass to the organism. How is it possible to spell out why the effect to pump blood is objectively more characteristic of a heart than the other effects?

The idea of the etiological approach is to look at the evolutionary past: in the past, organisms with a heart have survived especially because of the heart's effect to pump blood —and not because of the other effects of the heart. Hence, it is the effect to pump blood that is the (more) characteristic effect. The function of the heart thus is what constituted the selective advantage in the past, the selected effect. One thereby answers also the question why there are still organisms with hearts. One furthermore brings out the difference with physical descriptions that are not concerned with selective advantages in particular (but with any possible effect).

The disadvantage of the etiological approach becomes obvious when one considers the first occurrence of a biological functional property, since in that case, there is no evolutionary past. The first heart, so to speak, was no functional property, since there was no evolutionary past to base its function on. Similarly, changes of functions constitute a problem for the etiological approach. If the environment changes such that the function of a property changes accordingly, it is not possible to consider this functional change by a reference to the past (where the environment was different).

The Theory of Evolution and Casual Structures in Biology   113

We can generalize these objections such that any approach to define biological functions becomes problematic the more it is static. To have a clear and objective normative criterion at one's disposal, as the etiological approach provides, is on the one hand a clear advantage. On the other hand, defining biological functions in such a way that they cannot change does not cohere with the spirit of evolutionary biology. Fitness—and thus biological functions—seem to depend on the present environment and not on the past one even though the reference to the evolutionary past explains why certain properties still exist while others have been disappeared. To put it differently, since the relevant environment changes, it is not plausible to assume that a property remains functionally identical in time. It is therefore appropriate to take the environmental change explicitly into account in order to be in the position to consider functional changes and define biological properties accordingly.

The causal-dispositional approach defines biological functions as causal dispositions to have effects in the given environment. Here, the normative criterion to identify the characteristic causal dispositions is based either on an analysis of the contribution to capacities of the biological system (systemic approach) or by a focus on fitness contributions (see classically Cummins 1975; see also Amundson and Lauder 1994, Bigelow and Pargetter 1987, Manning 1997, Mossio et al. 2009 and Weber 2005, chapter 2.4; see furthermore Arp 2008, Walsh 1996 and Kitcher 1993 for a compatibility of such approaches with the etiological one). In what follows, we do not explicitly distinguish between contributions to certain capacities or the fitness of biological systems since we take the latter one as some kind of ultimate capacity of biological systems that is salient in the context of evolution. Consider another example that both serves to illustrate this approach and discuss possible objections against it. Imagine a flower with a gene for red blossoms. According to the causal-dispositional approach, the gene is in the case of the production of red blossoms the function or functional property to do so, contributing to certain capacities or to the fitness of the flower by producing red blossoms. This approach can consider new properties (like mutants) or changes of properties. If a mutant that hypothetically leads to pink blossoms makes a contribution to the fitness of the corresponding organism, it is functional. It is not necessary that there is any evolutionary past in which the mutant has already made a fitness contribution. In a similar way, changes of functions are taken into account.

The obvious advantage of this approach is to provide for a flexible and context-dependent concept of biological functions. But a certain price has to be paid to gain this advantage. It seems that there no longer is *the* function of all hearts, genes, and so on. Any function changes at some time, since the environment changes. To put the crucial point differently, there are for instance gene tokens of a certain type that do not always contribute the same fitness to the organism. What then have these tokens in common so that they come under the same type? For instance, what is the

114 *Conservative Reductionism*

function of a gene for the colour of the blossoms in a flower in Europe and in the Sahara, the environmental conditions being such that red blossoms are only produced in Europe but not in the Sahara. Or what is the function of that very gene in winter in Europe when there is no manifestation of the red blossoms either? In brief, it seems that the gene tokens do not exist as tokens of biological functional types when no effect that contributes to the fitness of the organism is manifested.

Obviously, the gene token makes a contribution to the fitness of the organism only when red blossoms are produced. However, we have to keep in mind that a permanent production of red blossoms, independently of the given environmental conditions, would decrease the fitness of the organism in a serious way. A hypothetical production of red blossoms in winter in Europe or in the Sahara would cost a lot of energy without having a positive effect for reproduction since no insects are around at that time. Hence, a manifestation of red blossoms only under environmental conditions where a fitness contribution is given or very likely makes the gene a better fitness contributor than if it would lead to the manifestation of red blossoms under any environmental conditions. The absence of the manifestation of red blossoms under cold or dry conditions can thus be taken into account in the functional definition of the gene. To put it differently, genes are dispositions to produce certain effects but whether theses effects are actually produced can be regulated. It is this disposition for regulation that makes our gene for red blossoms quite functional, even in winter.

Ontologically speaking, the causal-dispositional properties that fundamental physics considers always bring about some effects (see sections 2.1 and 2.5). This is not so for biological functional dispositions. They are ontologically speaking always there, since they are identical with certain configurations of physical properties that always produce some physical effects. But, biologically speaking, they are not always manifested —since not any manifestation of effects is a biologically pertinent manifestation. To be more precise, the fitness contribution of physical configurations is context dependent, and this context dependency is a clear advantage for fitness, since the environmental context constantly changes.

To sum up, it is no objection against the causal-dispositional theory of properties that the manifestation of red blossoms in spring is more characteristic for the gene in question than the non-manifestation of red blossoms in winter or in the Sahara. Biological functional properties are constituted by such context-dependent variation. One generally speaks of reaction norms or fitness functions, these being functions about fitness values for the different environmental contexts. In other words, gene tokens come under the same type if they manifest the same effects under the same environmental conditions (thus having the same reaction norm). It is therefore only an epistemic problem how to bring gene tokens under one type if the environmental conditions are different. This problem concerns any approach, the causal-dispositional as well as the etiological one. That notwithstanding,

The Theory of Evolution and Casual Structures in Biology   115

ontologically speaking, the gene function (spelled out by a complex reaction norm) is always there.

Against this background, let us compare this approach to the etiological one and put our discussion into the context of this chapter and the general frame of the book. While the etiological approach refers to past occurrences and thus mainly to manifested and pertinent dispositions and therefore is somehow similar to ultimate explanations based on phylogeny, the systemic and causal-dispositional approach sticks more to local causal capacities of systems or dispositions to contribute to the fitness of organisms (or other units of selection) and thus can be connected with ontogenetic mechanistic explanations (see also Craver 2001). By adopting a reductionist perspective that we shall outline in the following two chapters, it is possible to understand the etiological approach as a more abstract approach or concept of biological functions than the other one but nonetheless reducible to it. If this line of reasoning is conclusive, one may explain away the main difficulties and make more explicit the advantages of both approaches, similar to our discussion of the adequacy of adaptationism. In any case, it depends on the given and changing environmental conditions whether the application of more abstract concepts is justified. To put it differently, it is the environment that constitutes the normative aspect for any kind of functional ascription. If, for instance, minor physical differences have an impact on the function under the given environmental conditions, there is an argument to account for this fact, and this is, in the most extreme case, done by a local and non-historic focus in terms of causal dispositions. By contrast, many physical differences have no functional impact under certain environmental conditions such that more abstract approaches, even with a historical dimension, are admitted or even preferred to provide more unifying explanations.

4 Case Study
Classical and Molecular Genetics

4.0 INTRODUCTION TO CHAPTER 4

Does evolution presuppose genetic mechanisms? What is the impact of genetics to better understand evolutionary theory and the importance of natural selection? There are of course several answers possible to such general questions. As we have seen in the previous chapter, life and its evolution are closely linked to continuous adaptation to environmental change by natural selection. There is selection because certain advantageous or disadvantageous properties are transmitted from generation to generation. This transmission of heritable traits is the domain of genetics. Let us start with a little historical anecdote to illustrate the relation between evolutionary theory and genetics and then introduce this chapter and link it to the general frame of this book:

> Just two weeks before he died, Charles Darwin wrote a short paper about a tiny clam found clamped to the leg of a water beetle in a pond in the English Midlands. It was his last publication. The man who sent him the beetle was a young shoemaker and amateur naturalist named Walter Drawbridge Crick. The shoemaker eventually married and had a son named Harry, who himself had a son named Francis. In 1953, Francis Crick, together with a young American named James Watson, would make a discovery that has led inexorably to the triumphant vindication of almost everything Darwin deduced about evolution. (Ridley 2009)

The discovery of the molecular structure of the DNA and the then starting research leading up to establishing molecular genetics provides an enormous support for the theory of evolution. Coming back to the example of the finches on the Galápagos Islands, DNA analyses have confirmed Darwin's assumption that all the species of finches on theses islands have a common ancestry (Sato et al. 2001). Nonetheless, genetic research had already progressed and supported evolutionary theory before 1953 and furthermore spread into and thus connected other biological disciplines. In between Darwin's last publication and the discovery of the molecular structure of the DNA, there is the so-called great synthesis of genetics and evolutionary theory.

The aim of this chapter is to discuss essential issues of this great synthesis and the relation between classical and molecular genetics. In considering the relationship between classical and molecular genetics, we intend to introduce a general reflection on the scientific quality of abstract biological theories like evolutionary theory and the principle of natural selection. We finally seek to make intelligible how abstract approaches that apply to physically and biologically quite different properties or species provide nonetheless causal explanations. In the first section (section 4.1), we start with classical genetics that constitutes, subsequently to the rediscovery of Mendel's experiences at the beginning of the 20th century, a new research discipline within biology. In this context, we make a clear link to the previous chapter and thus implicitly consider the great synthesis by means of going into certain essential issues of this theoretical integration. Then, we shall focus on molecular genetics and its detailed causal mechanistic explanations (section 4.2). Against the background of the discussion of both genetic theories, we elaborate on the relation between both theories whereby several discussions of the previous chapters are taken up (section 4.3). In doing so, we shall argue for ontological reduction and lay the foundation for a new and general epistemological reductionist approach that will be set out in the next chapter. To put it differently, we intend to employ the case study—classical vs. molecular genetics—for a general philosophical discussion of abstract explanatory theories that can be reduced in a conservative way to molecular and finally physical theories.

4.1 FUNCTIONALIZATION OF CLASSICAL GENETICS

Genetics starts with Gregor Mendel (1822–1884) (Mendel 1865). The results of his breeding experiments on peas (*Pisum sativum*) were rediscovered and confirmed at the beginning of the 20th century, resulting in genetics becoming quickly a research discipline of its own within biology. In the course of time, the method, the technical terms and the so-called Mendelian laws were modified. It is common knowledge that the Mendelian laws are not universal genetic laws but depend on certain conditions that are either fulfilled or not. For instance, Mendel's law of independent assortment states that alleles of different genes assort independently of one another during gamete formation. This is actually not true for genes that are linked. Nonetheless, there is a core of classical genetics that is correct and that has an explanatory value. In this section, we will spell out to what extent a somehow reconstructed classical genetics still has a scientific quality and compare this theory in the following sections with molecular genetics. Figure 4.1 may help to get a general overview of this chapter.

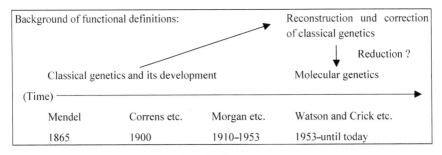

Figure 4.1 Classical genetics and its developments.

We implicitly reconstruct and correct classical genetics by focussing first of all on functional definition of genes—that genes are simplified, causal-dispositional properties that can be transmitted hereditarily and that are mainly defined by their phenotypic effects, which are manifested under certain environmental conditions (see Sterelny and Griffiths 1999, pp. 87–93, Waters 1994 and 2007 and furthermore Weber 2005, chapter 7). It will become clear at the end of this chapter how to integrate the well-known Mendelian laws into our consideration of functional definitions of gene types. We will extend these considerations to any abstract biological law at the end of chapter 5. There we shall show how Mendelian laws or the principle of natural selection can be interpreted as abstractions from functional definitions of gene types or other biological property types.

Despite the increasing use of various chemical and physical methods in genetics, the introduction and modification of technical terms and the different goals of classical genetics (like gene mapping), Mendel's implicit distinction between genotype and phenotype always held firm. The genotype of an organism is its genetic information or genes that are causally disposed (a) to be transmitted to the next generation and (b) to produce certain phenotypic effects. The phenotype thus is, simplified, what one can observe—the manifestation of causal-dispositional properties of the genotype. The concept of the phenotype, however, is nowadays used for more than what we can easily observe like the colour of eyes or blossoms. A phenotype is generally what a gene can cause (given certain conditions), like the regulated production of proteins, which then directly or indirectly results in effects that are observable with the naked eye (Kitcher 1984). In the course of genetic research, it became clear that genes can have a causal influence on more than one single phenotypic effect and also that a phenotypic effect can depend on more than a single gene. The fact that the relation between genes and phenotypic effects may be quite complex and depend on the environment does, however, not touch the core of the conceptual distinction between genotype and phenotype. Genes can still be construed as certain causal-dispositional properties of organisms—dispositions to be transmitted hereditarily and dispositions to have phenotypic effects depending on the environmental conditions (see along these lines the conception of genes as "difference makers" by Waters 1994 and 2007).

There obviously is a continuous transition from classical to molecular genetics and any clear distinction between both theories appears to be somehow artificial. However, even if there are for instance technical terms that are used in both theories, there is the following contrast between classical and molecular genetics: molecular genetics can explain in causal-mechanical details heredity processes and the impact of the genotype on the phenotype, while classical genetics cannot do so, or at least not in a detailed manner. Classical genetics moreover stipulates *that* there are genes that can be transmitted to the next generation and *that* these genes have phenotypic effects under certain environmental conditions. It furthermore constructs law-like generalizations about these causal relations, couched in terms of independent assortment or dominance and recessiveness. However, it is beyond its scope to specify the required, so-called standard environmental conditions for heredity or the manifestation of genetic dispositions like dominance. In order to do so, one has to draw on molecular biology, chemistry and physics. What the underlying mechanisms are, for instance as concerns the protein production that leads to yellow blossoms, comes, if at all, only indirectly into the focus of classical genetics.

Such an indirect link, however, was shown before molecular genetics was established. The chromosome theory of inheritance of H. T. Boveri (1862–1915) und W. S. Sutton (1877–1916) suggests that genes lie on chromosomes like peals on a chain. Since those days, one of the main aims of genetic research is to establish gene maps (see as well Weber 1998). However, it was only due to observable phenotypic properties and statistical correlations that one concluded that genes stand in this or that relation to each other, being located, or linked so to speak, on this or that chromosome. The molecular basis of genes and the molecular mechanisms are in the domain of molecular genetics, which did not get started before the discovery of the molecular structure of the DNA in 1953.

It is common ground in today's philosophy of biology that all gene tokens are identical with something physical. More precisely, any gene token, a so-called allele, is identical with a concrete molecular structure or configuration. Classical genetics focuses on the fact *that* there are genes, *that* they are transmitted in this or that way, and on *what* these genes cause (Waters 2007). To put it differently, independently of the facts that there is a physical basis for any gene token and what this basis is like in each case, classical genetics can formulate concepts of genes in a functional manner. These concepts are

120　*Conservative Reductionism*

defined mainly in terms of the characteristic effects of their referents and in the last resort in terms of dispositions for fitness contributions.

There are thus functionally defined genes like for the colour of the eyes and for the size and shape of the beaks. If there are different phenotypic effects of genes—like different shapes of the beaks in the case of certain finches on a particular Galápagos Island—then there are different alleles of the genes. More precisely, alleles of the same type bring about the same phenotypic effects under the same environmental conditions that include, from the perspective of the allele in question, also the given alleles in the cell. However, it is not the case that *any* observable difference or similarity between individuals is linked to a corresponding genetic difference or similarity. Under different environmental conditions both genetically different individuals may develop similar phenotypic effects, and genetically similar individuals may develop different phenotypic effects. We are hence not committed to genetic determinism (see Rosenberg 2006, chapter 8, for a discussion of genetic determinism).

Classical genetics provides functional explanations that are causal explanations focussing on biological functional properties and relations, against the background of evolutionary theory. In this context, we understand a gene token, like any biological property token, as a causal disposition whose manifestation depends on the relevant environmental conditions. The functional definition of genes, formulated in terms of classical genetics and considering the concept of biological functions in the evolutionary context, thereby brings out what fitness contribution the according manifestation (of the causal disposition of the gene token in question) implies for the organism in question. To put it differently, the characteristic effects of gene tokens that come under the concept F of classical genetics are, in the relevant environment W, the phenotypic effects F_E. In that sense, any gene concept of classical genetics is implicitly or explicitly defined by its fitness contribution.

When the (sometimes more detailed and sometimes more abstract) functional explanations of classical genetics and evolutionary theory are based on generalized definitions, that is, nomological functional definitions, then they contain a scientific quality in the following sense: they reveal the essential causal relations between genotype and phenotype depending on the relevant environment in the context of fitness and natural selection. (See figure 4.2.)

Functional definitions of a gene type of classical genetics that express the cause-effect relation in the context of evolutionary theory:

(Gene-type) $F \rightarrow F_E$ (Phenotypic effect of the gene / fitness contribution)

Figure 4.2　Functional definition of a gene type.

Let us sum up three main interconnected issues.

(1) Functional explanations of classical genetics are causal explanations that are generally not detailed ones in the sense that they do not reveal the causal mechanisms in question and cannot specify sufficiently the standard conditions in their own terms. In the vocabulary of classical genetics, the manifestation of phenotypic effects may be functionally explained by reference to the corresponding gene that is or was selectively advantageous. Such an explanation, however, does not lay out the mechanism how a gene brings about its effects and what environmental conditions are required for its manifestation. Molecular genetics provides a more complete account.

(2) The abstraction from causal mechanical details and the required standard conditions has the consequence that the functional definitions of classical genetics are more abstract than definitions in terms of molecular genetics. As we shall discuss later in more detail, molecularly different gene tokens may come under one and the same functional definition of classical genetics. There then is multiple realization or reference. The detailed consideration of the multiple realization of the gene types of classical genetics can be seen as representative of any other form of multiple realization of biological property types.

(3) Linked to abstract functional definitions of genes, there are certain generalizations of classical genetics that have a restricted domain of application, that have only predictive but no explanatory power, or that are even wrong (see for instance Sarkar 1998, chapter 5). As we have already mentioned, certain even more abstract generalizations like the Mendelian laws were modified in the course of time until the 1930s when a coherent genetic theory with more clearly formulated conditions for exceptions was achieved. Furthermore, the conditions in which the generalizations of classical genetics hold are often not well understood without the knowledge of the underlying molecular mechanisms and constraints.

While the last point suggests a reductive approach to classical genetics, the second one seems to block reduction. We shall come back to this issue in the last section of this chapter (section 4.3), when we compare both genetic theories after having considered molecular genetics.

4.2 CAUSAL MECHANISMS IN MOLECULAR GENETICS

What molecular genetics precisely is and is about constitutes an even more difficult question than in the case of classical genetics. It is helpful to take up a distinction between a broad and narrow definition of molecular *biology* (see Olby 1990). In a narrow sense, molecular biology is molecular

122 Conservative Reductionism

genetics, being mainly about the transmission of genetic information and the closely connected molecular mechanisms. Molecular biology in this sense is concerned with the molecular mechanisms that are pertinent for heredity and that play a role in the manifestation of causal-dispositional properties that bring about the phenotypic effects. Molecular biology, in the broad sense, is generally about the causal dispositions of biological macromolecules, organelles, membranes, proteins, nucleic acids, and so on and their components. One may thereby take molecular genetics as one of many special disciplines of biology (since it focuses on certain biological properties in particular), while molecular biology is an experimental and theoretical paradigm that concerns biology in its entirety (since it can be applied, with ongoing explanatory success, to any biological property).

In 1953, James D. Watson (*1928) and Francis H. C. Crick (1916–2004) discovered the molecular structure of DNA (Watson and Crick 1953a, 1953b and 1954). This is somehow the beginning of molecular genetics, which is nowadays also known for other subsequent discoveries like the operon model (Jacob and Monod 1961), the allosteric model of protein interaction (Changeux 1964), the genetic code (see Nirenberg and Matthaei 1961 and Nirenberg and Leder 1964), to mention but a few of the famous early discoveries of molecular genetics.

In this book, we focus on the DNA and the genetic code. We consider the main philosophical problem for the possibility of theory reduction of biological theories as being situated in the context of DNA and the genetic code— and thus linked to the debate about the relationship between classical and molecular genetics (for a reductionist approach towards developmental biology see Rosenberg 2006). The reason for this assessment is based on our later discussion of multiple realization (section 4.3) that witnesses its most extreme cases—and thus the most challenging cases for a theory reduction—in the context of the DNA and the redundancy of the genetic code.

Let us consider in a simplified manner the central causal dispositions of the DNA. In order to do so, let us turn in the first place to the process of transcription, which is essentially a synthesis of RNA according to the DNA sequence that figures as a template. RNA is a ribonucleic acid that is, though no double helix like the DNA, structurally speaking quite similar to it (and thus dispositionally speaking as well, which can be easily seen in cases where RNA constitutes genes on its own in certain species). Both mainly differ in the sugar base. While DNA is composed of guanine, cytosine, thymine and adenine as bases, RNA contains uracil instead of thymine. The molecular mechanism of transcription is mainly carried out by a special protein called RNA polymerase that synthesizes the RNA molecule in the form of a negative copy of the DNA sequences (see figure 4.3). Similarly, we may secondly mention that the transcribed RNA either constitutes in itself a functional property for the cell or is translated so to speak into a functional property. There is a process called translation from the transcribed and so-called messenger RNA (mRNA) sequence to a chain of amino acids that, after diverse possible modifications,

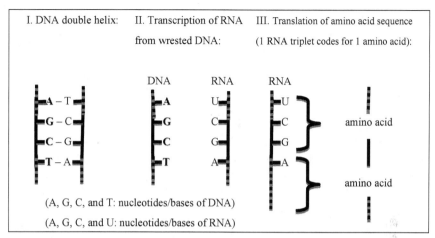

Figure 4.3 Translation and transcription.

constitute proteins. Since most of the transcribed RNA is translated into a chain of amino acids, the following scheme focuses on the relation from DNA to the primary structure (chain of amino acids) of proteins.

Let us consider proteins, since they are often the characteristic effects of DNA sequences that thus explain why certain DNA sequences were selected for in the course of evolution. Any type of protein is functionally defined by means of its effects on the state of the cell and the entire organism with its observable properties. These observable properties are, simplified, those phenotypic effects that define functionally the gene types in terms of classical genetics. Most functionally defined gene types of classical genetics can be described as DNA sequences in terms of molecular genetics (apart from genes that are in fact RNA sequences; in that case, however, a similar approach can be spelled out). By the molecular approach to genes we mean the functional definition of certain DNA sequences—that is to say their causal dispositions, their manifestation under certain molecular conditions and also the effects of these manifestations for the organisms and their fitness in the relevant environment. The molecular context depends on the causal disposition under consideration. For the duplication of DNA, among others, DNA polymerases and the necessary DNA bases have to be given. One part of the complex process of cell division is that spindle fibres separate the chromosomes, which are organized buildings of DNA and proteins, into daughter cells. As concerns certain effects of DNA sequences within cells—like the production of certain proteins—among others, special proteins, ATP and RNA molecules and amino acids are necessary.

It thus seems that the functionally defined gene types of classical genetics refer to entities that are (in most cases) described as certain DNA sequences

124 Conservative Reductionism

in terms of molecular genetics (plus the molecular context). At this point, let us just stipulate ontological reductionism in the sense of token identity, being a position that is widely accepted in the debate; we shall argue for this position later (see for instance Brigandt and Love 2008, Kitcher 1984 and 1999, or Rosenberg 1994, chapter 3). The entities that classical genetics functionally define in its proper terms and in the context of evolutionary theory are identical with certain molecular configurations, even though it may sometimes still be an open empirical question what exactly these molecular configurations are, how they are regulated, how they are influenced by the environment, and so on. Despite still open questions, molecular genetics can provide more detailed causal explanations of the functionally defined properties of classical genetics.

While the functional definitions and law-like generalizations of classical genetics presuppose standard conditions that cannot be completely specified in its terms, molecular genetics is in a better position to do so. This is why exceptions of law-like generalizations of classical genetics are often explained in terms of molecular genetics. The causal dispositions of DNA, RNA, proteins, and the like (and thus genes and phenotypic effects considered by classical genetics) depend on more or less local conditions, and molecular genetics, sometimes by referring to chemical or physical details, can completely explain the required environmental conditions. There are, to put it differently, functional definitions of classical genetics that refer to mechanisms at the molecular level that can be explained in a relatively complete manner in terms of molecular genetics.

There is a relative completeness of molecular genetics in comparison to classical genetics. The success of molecular genetics provides evidence for its causal, nomological and explanatory completeness with respect to classical genetics. In order to avoid misunderstandings, let us clarify two issues here. (1) Molecular genetics often draws on concepts and explanations from chemistry and physics. In comparison to these theories, molecular genetics is not complete. That is why the completeness claim of molecular genetics is only a relative one—in comparison to classical genetics. (2) This relative completeness is given even though, for epistemic reasons, molecular genetics often makes use of concepts and explanations of classical genetics in practice—such that, as already mentioned, the terms of both theories are in fact not strictly separated.

The completeness claim in question can be spelled out more precisely as follows. For any property token p_2 of molecular genetics, insofar as p_2 has a cause, it has a complete molecular cause, say p_1. This completeness is a relative one since it is possible that p_2 has a purely chemical or physical cause that cannot be considered in the terms of molecular genetics. In such a case, however, the cause of p_2 cannot be expressed in the terms of classical genetics either. In an analogous manner, there is a relative nomological and explanatory completeness of molecular genetics: insofar as p_2 has an explanation and comes under laws, it has a complete molecular explanation and comes under molecular laws (see Figure 4.4).

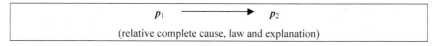

Figure 4.4 Relative completeness.

Against the background of this clarification, let us outline the argument in favour of token identity (see as well Kitcher 1984, Rosenberg 1978 and Sachse 2007, chapter 4.4). As shown in section 2.6, any causally efficacious property token described in terms of a theory of the special sciences is identical with a local physical structure. Since the concepts of classical genetics are functionally defined in order to provide causal-functional explanations—like those of the relationship between genotype and phenotype for instance—its functional definitions refer to certain physical configurations. The expression "gene for deep and large beaks" can stand for a simplified example of a functional definition in terms of classical genetics that refers to gene tokens of certain finches on the Galápagos Islands. Against the background of the relative completeness of molecular genetics, any of the gene tokens referred to are local molecular structures that can be, in a more complete manner, described and explained in terms of molecular genetics. It is not possible that classical genetics describes or explains causal relations that cannot, in a more complete manner, be described and explained in terms of molecular genetics. While these structures are, from the perspective of classical genetics, functionally defined, molecular genetics refers to them in the first place in terms of their composition. DNA sequences, for instance, are generally defined in terms of the base sequences. This kind of description is, however, a causal one as well, though an implicit one. It outlines what effects the components of structures have by being arranged in the way they are.

Since thus (1) classical genetics provides causal explanations in terms of biological functions and (2) the properties of classical genetics supervene on physical properties (see Rosenberg 1978, Weber 1996) and (3) molecular genetics is causally, nomologically and explanatorily complete with respect to classical genetics (cf. Papineau 2002, appendix), molecular genetics hence is in the position to explain the causal interactions between for instance genotypes, phenotypes and the environment and can on that basis explain evolutionary changes of the genotypes among other things. There is no non-molecular or at least no non-physical causal force involved here. These premises taken together suggest the token identity of any property of classical genetics with a molecular property token.

4.3 COMPARISON BETWEEN BOTH THEORIES

In this section, we shall elaborate in more detail on the relationship between classical and molecular genetics and consider whether it is possible to

126 *Conservative Reductionism*

obtain nomologically coextensive concepts of both theories. If this turns out to be in principle possible, then the necessary and sufficient conditions for a reduction of classical to molecular genetics are satisfied. We shall outline in detail our account of theory reduction in the next chapter. Here, the primary questions are how abstract the concepts of molecular genetics and how precise the concepts of classical genetics can be. Based on a causal argument, we set out to show that, in principle, a nomological coextension between certain concepts of classical genetics (so-called sub-types) and certain concepts of molecular genetics can be established.

Coextension of concepts is necessary and sufficient to deduce the laws of classical genetics from laws of molecular genetics (see Sachse 2007, chapter 7). Let F be as usual a functional definition of a gene type whose tokens are identical with some molecular configuration or other. These gene tokens are dispositions to have certain effects that are functionally defined as well (F_E). Think about *Escherichia coli*, a bacterium that is often used in genetic research: it contains genes or regions in the genome that are responsible for its cell-wall biosynthesis. To simplify, let us focus on genes that code for membrane proteins. In what follows, we refer to such properties by means of the general term "membrane component," which is more precise than just talking in terms of phenotypic effects. Since the synthesis of these proteins or membrane components is required for the growth of the cell before cell division, it is accordingly possible to functionally define the genetic bases: the rate of protein synthesis means a contribution to the possible growth rate, which can be, under optimal growth conditions, equated with fitness. To put it differently, functional definitions of genes are generally embedded in evolutionary theory: in the last resort, the fitness contribution is the characteristic effect. In the context of our example, the gene tokens cause the production of a certain component of the membrane that is for its part relevant for the fitness of the bacterium under certain (if not most) environmental conditions.

Against this background, law-like generalization of the type "If F, then F_E" express a causal relation between gene tokens (coming under F) and phenotypic effects (coming under F_E). Any such generalization is a ceteris paribus law presupposing standard conditions that cannot be completely spelled out in terms of classical genetics. It is beyond the scope of classical genetics to specify what the conditions are (within the cell and the environment) that are necessary and sufficient for the gene token to bring about the production of the membrane component in question.

Any true description of causal relations between property tokens by means of a law of classical genetics implies that there are also laws of molecular genetics that sufficiently (and even more completely) describe that very causal relation. Otherwise, there would be a contradiction with ontological reductionism and the relative completeness of molecular genetics. We thus take for granted that for any causal relation, brought out by a law-like generalization of the type "If F, then F_E" (classical genetics), there is a corresponding (maybe complex) law-like description in terms of molecular

Case Study 127

genetics available as well. There thus is a underlying molecular mechanism from for instance certain gene tokens to the production of membrane components—simplified a causal relation from the DNA to the production of the corresponding membrane component.

Let us now consider possible molecular differences among gene tokens that come under one single functional definition of classical genetics. The paradigmatic examples of molecular differences among gene tokens of a single classical gene type are generally based on the redundancy of the genetic code (but can also be based on other issues to which the following considerations apply as well). There are *different* DNA sequences possible that lead, by means of transcription into mRNA and translation of the mRNA into a chain of amino acids, to the production of proteins of the *same* type. This fact can be highlighted by a simple combinatorial reasoning. All amino acids in proteins are coded by triplets of bases, so-called codons. Since there are, due to the four possible bases, 64 triplets possible (4^3), but only 20 different amino acids to code for, the same amino acids can be coded for by different triplets (codons). Thus, there are different DNA sequences possible that are transcribed accordingly into different mRNA sequences that, despite their differences, code for the same chain of amino acids.

Gene tokens that are described by one concept F of classical genetics thus often differ molecularly and hence come under different molecular concepts (P_1, P_2, P_3). This is multiple reference (realization). Consequently, the concept F (such as "gene for membrane component F_E") is not coextensive with a single molecular concept. In the same way, the concept F_E (the concept for the membrane component in our example) refers to property tokens that may come under different molecular concepts as well (P_{E1}, P_{E2}, P_{E3}). The stock example for molecular differences of phenotypic effects is molecularly different proteins that still fall, from the perspective of classical genetics, under the same functional classification (type). There may be differences in the primary structure of proteins—the proteins may differ with respect to the chain of amino acids at some place—or there may be other differences like different ways in which the amino acid chain is twined such that the protein differs three-dimensionally. The reason why classical genetics cannot take into account all such possible differences is once again the fact that there are a lot of molecular differences possible that do not prevent the produced proteins from being functionally similar. Their molecular differences notwithstanding, proteins may bring about similar effects for the organism. Taking the molecular differences into account, there are different laws in molecular genetics, like "If P_1, then P_{E1}," "If P_2, then P_{E2}" and "If P_2, then P_{E3}" that bring out causal relations between property tokens that come under one homogenous law of classical genetics of the type "If F, then F_E" (see also Kitcher 1984 and 1999).

If at least one of the concepts that figure in a law of the type "If F, then F_E" is not coextensive with a concept of molecular genetics, then the corresponding law of classical genetics cannot be deduced from molecular genetics (see Figure 4.5). There then are different molecular causal mechanisms

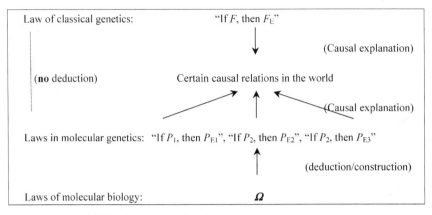

Figure 4.5 Multiple reference (realization).

that bring about an effect that is described homogeneously by "If F, then F_E." As we have seen in section 1.3, this asymmetry calls the scientific quality of that law in question. If it is not possible to build within molecular genetics concepts like "P" or "P_E" that are coextensive with "F" and "F_E," then the reference of the concepts of classical genetics is heterogeneous, since neither the property tokens that fall under F nor those that fall under F_E exhibit molecular similarities that make it possible to build molecular concepts, being apt to figure in molecular laws, that cover all and only those property tokens. It is then questionable how classical genetics can provide for homogeneous abstract causal explanations without coming in conflict with ontological reductionism and the relative completeness of molecular genetics. It seems that classical genetics brings out homogeneous causal powers that do not exist from the perspective of the more complete theory. Having coextensive concepts of both theories at one's disposal therefore is a necessary step to make intelligible how classical genetics can provide genuine causal explanations.

Coextension is also sufficient to obtain this result. To establish this point, let us for one moment ignore the possibility of multiple reference (realization). We thus assume that any concept figuring in the laws of classical genetics is coextensive with concepts of molecular genetics. F thus is coextensive with P, and F_E is coextensive with P_E. The causal explanation in form of the law "If F, then F_E" can therefore be deduced from "If P, then P_E" (see Figure 4.6).

In this case, there are homogeneous reductive molecular explanations available, making intelligible how classical genetics can provide for general causal explanations. Molecular genetics outlines in detail how the gene tokens bring about their characteristic effects. If there is no multiple realization, the causal explanations of both theories are coherent, since "If P, then P_E" is coextensive with "If F, then F_E."

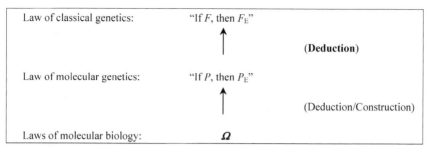

Figure 4.6 Deduction in the case of unique realization.

Let us now consider two complementary ways to obtain nomological coextension. Any functionally defined concept of classical genetics (F, for instance, "gene for membrane component") refers to property tokens in the world that are identical with a molecular causal structure each. Because of the relative completeness of molecular genetics, these property tokens with their causal dispositions are (relatively) completely describable in terms of molecular genetics. Consequently, for any single property token that falls under F, there is a reductive explanation in terms of molecular genetics available. Molecular genetics has the means to explain in a causal mechanical way under what conditions and in which manner the gene token in question brings about its characteristic effect, for instance the production of the membrane component.

In the case of multiple reference, it is not possible to build one molecular concept P that is coextensive with F, since there is no molecular similarity that picks out all and only those property tokens that fall under F and provides a coherent reductive explanation of them. There thus are molecular differences among the gene tokens. In order to establish a coherent reductive explanation of these gene tokens, corresponding to their molecular differences, different causal relations have to be taken into account and accordingly different laws *have to be considered*—like "If P_1, then P_{E1}," "If P_2, then P_{E2}," "If P_3, then P_{E3}", and so on.

Suppose that the law "If F, then F_E" refers to property tokens that are either referred to by "If P_1, then P_{E1}" or by "If P_2, then P_{E2}." There are for instance two different DNA sequences possible that come under F (see Figure 4.7). Hence, there are two different molecular mechanisms that lead to the production of proteins that end up in the phenotypic effects that come under F_E. We can think of two different ways in which DNA sequences, via transcription and translation, end up in the production of the membrane component in question.

There thus is multiple realization or reference if and only if there are molecular differences that *have* to be taken into account in order to provide reductive explanations in terms of molecular genetics. In the current philosophical debate it is often taken for granted that the different molecular mechanisms are limited to the molecular level. In the context of our

130   *Conservative Reductionism*

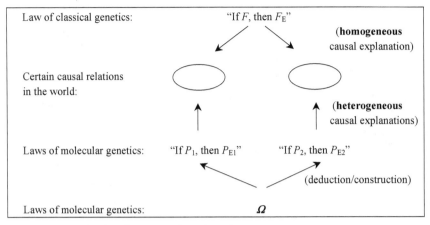

Figure 4.7 Multiple reference and explanation.

example, one generally assumes that the different ways in which the proteins are produced lead to sufficiently similar phenotypic effects so that these differences do not imply any functional differences for the organisms in question. The molecular differences between gene tokens that come under F and the molecular differences between the phenotypic effects that come under F_E are considered to be immaterial for the fitness of the organism in question. By contrast, we shall argue that such molecular differences have an impact on the fitness of the organism and that their impact is hence not limited to the molecular level.

If there are characteristic effects that are brought about in different molecular ways, then there are different molecular properties involved. If there are different molecular properties, there are different causal dispositions. As we have argued in section 2.1 in the context of the causal theory of properties, in being certain qualities, properties are powers to bring about certain effects (instead of being pure qualities). Therefore, if there are different properties, then they differ in the possible effects that they can bring about. Such differences in the effects may have an impact on the fitness of the organisms in question. Against this background, we have to consider three different cases. We shall consider here only the most important one and postpone the general discussion to section 5.2.

In addition to this argument from the metaphysics of properties that implies that molecular differences may have an impact on the level of classical genetics, let us now take into account some empirical case studies that establish that molecular differences among genes have an effect at the fitness level of the organism in question. Multiple realization is an object of empirical investigation in genetics. The situations are such that the characteristic effects coming under F_E are always produced but with difference in time. Gene tokens coming under F and P_1 produce the proteins, thus the effects coming under F_E, faster and with higher precision than those gene tokens that come under F and P_2. This difference in time and precision implies a possible fitness difference, since there are environments possible in which a faster and more precise production of proteins leads to an earlier and less resource-intensive reproduction. A population of bacteria that can produce the membrane components faster and more efficiently grows faster. The molecular differences then are clearly relevant to fitness.

Coming back to the genetic code, its standard version is that there are 61 so-called sense codons (triplets of bases that code for an amino acid) and three so-called stop codons that finish the translation of the mRNA. Research has shown that different species use or "prefer" different codons. There are even single genes that prefer certain codons more than other ones in order to code for the same amino acid. Scientists talk in terms of codon bias or preferences. In unicellular organisms, as in our example, there is a strong correlation between protein expression and the degree of codon preferences (see for instance Andersson and Kurland 1990 that sum up the previous research that started essentially at the end of the 1970s). In the case of *E. coli* and *Saccharomyces cerevisiae*, one can show that the redundancy of the genetic code is actually not entirely a redundancy, but is employed by the organisms in order to regulate the translation system and thus the protein synthesis.

The usage of certain codons and thus the codon preferences are linked to selective pressure. Thereby, it is possible that any codon that is a preferred one in some organisms or genes under certain conditions is not a preferred one under other conditions, in other organisms or other genes. Moreover, the given preferences can change (see Andersson und Kurland 1990). Simplified, there are more rare codons that are generally used to keep the gene expression low. If however a higher gene expression implies selective advantages (for instance due to changes in the environment), then the codon preference in question changes such that a corresponding mutation has a relatively high probability to become fixed or to increase by means of a relative high reproduction of the bacterium in question.

One may sum up these facts about codon preferences by saying that that they are the results of selective forces. However, other than selective forces may have an influence on the given codons as well. The occurrence of mutations is a generally chancy event (in the sense of an epistemological understanding of chance; see section 3.1). Therefore, and depending on the mutation frequency, there are of course regular changes of preferred codons into non-preferred ones; if the mutation frequency is sufficiently high, the given DNA sequence of a gene may hardly be something like the optimal or preferred one. In this context one may add that whatever preference there may be, if the gene is an important one, the selective pressure for the preferred composition is higher than for those genes that are not that important for the fitness of the organism in question. This relationship can be spelled out in terms of the selection-mutation theory (see Bulmer 1991).

132 Conservative Reductionism

The efficiency of the translation—in form of speed and precision—is generally relevant for fitness. Hence, the efficiency of the translation becomes more important for those genes that are often expressed. If the protein in question is not that important for the organism, the selection pressure and thus the codon bias for a particular DNA sequence is of course lower. However, for any such case, there are environmental conditions possible in which there is selection pressure.

There is growing research into codon preferences since the 1970s, leading to uncountable publications some of which we will cite at the end of this discussion. The research is mainly concerned with whether and which codon preferences are given in which organisms and under which conditions these codon preferences change. The empirical data show that there are codon preferences for any studied organism, even though the strength of the given codon preferences may differ (for reasons like those that we have already outlined). However, of course, it is not the case that *any* molecular difference *always* leads to functional differences. There are molecular differences possible among gene tokens (coming under *F*) that, under certain conditions, do not result in fitness differences. There are even codon preferences that result in a decreased fitness, since there are molecular mechanisms possible that have an influence on codon preferences without being linked to selective advantages. However, these facts do not imply that molecular differences *never* lead to functional differences or that codon preferences never change. The crucial point is that for any relevant molecular difference that amounts to a case of multiple realization, it is only a question of time and the environmental conditions that this difference leads to a functional difference (and also to such functional differences that are based on codon preferences resulting from selective pressure) (see furthermore Dennett 2008, Rosenberg 1994, p. 32, and Sachse 2007, chapter 7.3).

There is a whole debate in molecular genetics—the neutralism debate—that reflects the main issues mentioned here (see Crow 2007, Kimura 1968 and Nei 2005; see as well our introduction to this debate in section 3.2). It seems well grounded to assume that under certain environmental conditions there are molecular differences that are selectively neutral and that so-called selectively neutral mutations make a contribution to evolution that cannot be neglected—even though their relevance is still a matter of debate. It may help to consider Marshall Abrams' approach that takes both selection and genetic drift as factors on a probability distribution about future genotype frequencies and, by means of doing so, takes evolution into account. Selection is thereby the factor that is controlled by fitness differences. Genetic drift is the factor that is mainly controlled by the population size (M. Abrams 2007). The neutralism debate is about whether and under what conditions genetic drift is the more important factor for evolution. Genetic drift, as we have seen in section 3.2, plays a role in evolution, but its precise influence always depends on

Case Study   133

the conditions. As concerns these conditions, research has shown that changing the conditions may amount to selectively neutral gene differences becoming selectively relevant ones.

To be more precise, it is not possible that (1) there are selectively neutral processes and changes on the molecular level and (2) these processes and changes do generally not have an important influence on evolution, since (3) phenotypic differences supervene on molecular differences and (4) phenotypic differences are selected. It is possible that *under certain conditions* there are molecular differences that do not end up in phenotypic differences and thus are selectively neutral for a certain time. In short, for any molecular difference it is only a question of time and environment that it leads to a fitness difference and can thus be selected.

Our claims are mainly based on the research on so-called model organisms like *E. coli* and *Drosophila*, but also on viruses (see, chronologically ordered, some research results that support our argument according to which molecular differences of the DNA imply, under certain environmental conditions, functional differences: Hartl et al. 1994, Comeron and Kreitman 1998, Akashi 1999, Llopart and Aguadé 1999, Begun 2001, Morton 2001, Musto et al. 2001, Kern et al. 2002, Lynn et al. 2002, Piganeau and Eyre-Walker 2003, Plotkin and Dushoff 2003, Qin et al. 2004, dos Reis et al. 2004, Rispe et al. 2004, Bartolomé et al. 2005, Sharp et al. 2005, Burns et al. 2006, Cutter et al. 2006, Gilchrist 2007, Glémin 2007, Heger and Ponting 2007, Kimchi-Sarfaty et al. 2007, Morton and Wright 2007, Singh et al. 2007, Stoletzki and Eyre-Walker 2007, Haddrill et al. 2008, Mukhopadhyay et al. 2008, dos Reis and Wernisch 2009 and Gerland and Hwa 2009). Beyond this fruitful research on simple and well-studied model organisms, there are also similar studies and publications about mammals and human genomes (see for instance Louie et al. 2003, Comeron 2004 and 2006, Qu et al. 2006, Yang and Nielsen 2008, Moses and Durbin 2009). These studies support the claim that the proposed conclusion holds generally.

Note that we do not consider explicitly molecular differences in proteins, like a difference according to some amino acid in some protein (for instance due to so-called non-silent mutation). The reason for this neglect is that in such cases it is even more obvious and empirically easier to show to what extent the molecular difference in question leads under certain environmental conditions to a fitness difference (see for such implications in *Drosophila* for instance Loewe et al. 2006 and for analogous fitness differences in humans for instance Yampolsky et al. 2005). Let us sum up these results in figure 4.8.

Whenever there are fitness differences, it is possible to consider them in terms of classical genetics and thus distinguish the molecularly different gene tokens on the level of the descriptions of classical genetics as well. The differences in the molecular mechanisms can be taken into account. For instance, the time factor can be taken into account in the functional

134 *Conservative Reductionism*

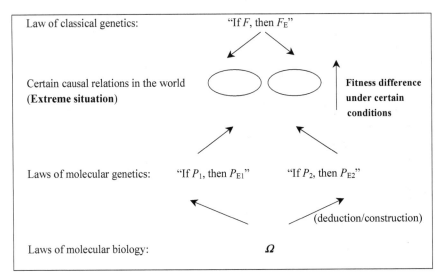

Figure 4.8 Fitness differences due to multiple realization.

definition of the gene tokens in question such that one can introduce subtypes of classical genetics that are coextensive with the respective types of molecular genetics. There are for instance genes that lead to a fast production of the membrane component, and the respective precise description in terms of molecular genetics, say F_1, is coextensive with the molecular description P_1. There are thus "genes for a fast production of F_E" ($= F_1$) and "genes for a slow production of F_E" ($= F_2$).

This possibility to introduce more fine-grained concepts in terms of classical genetics applies to all the other molecular differences as well that make a potential fitness contribution, like molecularly different proteins that come under a single concept of classical genetics. One can thus also introduce more fine-grained concepts F_{E1} and F_{E2} for the effects. In order not to complicate the issue, let us sketch out the construction of sub-types by means of figure 4.9.

It is thus only a matter of certain conditions for molecular differences to imply functional differences. The mentioned functional sub-types are therefore nomologically coextensive with the corresponding concepts of molecular genetics. Whenever the conditions in question obtain, the molecular differences lead to functional differences that can be taken into account in terms of classical genetics. The sub-types capture any possible functional differences implied by molecular differences manifested under certain environmental conditions. Introducing these sub-types does not amount to spelling out ceteris paribus conditions precisely in terms of classical genetics. It is sufficient for our argument that classical genetics can discern fitness differences statistically (like differences in time for protein

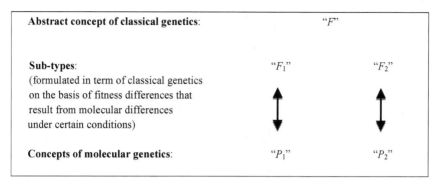

Figure 4.9 Sub-types.

production). Think about reaction norms of genes that are formulated more and more precisely in terms of classical genetics. One the basis of sub-types like F_1 and F_2, being nomologically coextensive with molecular types P_1 and P_2, classical genetics can formulate more detailed laws—sub-types laws—that can be deduced from molecular genetics.

Let us sum up the argument. By the construction of sub-types in the vocabulary of classical genetics, we mean functionally defined concepts of classical genetics that are nomologically coextensive with concepts of molecular genetics. The coextension is nomological, since for any actually given relevant molecular difference (multiple realization) and any possibly given relevant molecular difference (multiple realizability) there are situations possible in which the difference in question systematically implies a corresponding difference on the level of the functional descriptions of classical genetics. In other terms, relevant molecular differences are different ways in which certain causal relations described by classical genetics are brought about. Any such different way implies causal differences that are, under certain conditions, pertinent for the fitness of the organism so that classical genetics can take them into account.

Against the background of this nomological coextension, we can now discuss the question of the scientific quality of laws of classical genetics that are couched in terms of sub-types. Such theoretically constructed laws can be deduced from molecular genetics due to the nomological coextension of the concepts figuring in them. If F_1 is nomologically coextensive with P_1 and F_E with P_E, then the law "If F_1, then F_E" can be deduced from "If P_1, then P_E" (and "If F_2, then F_E" from "If P_2, then P_E"). For any of the sub-type laws, there are homogeneous reductive explanations possible in terms of molecular genetics. As outlined before, there thus is no conflict between the causal explanations in terms of the sub-type laws and the completeness claim of molecular genetics as well as ontological reductionism. However, we hesi-

136 Conservative Reductionism

tate to speak of a genuine scientific quality of the sub-type laws, since these extremely fine-grained sub-types will hardly enter into scientific practice.

Against this background, let us apply our strategy also to the well-known Mendelian laws. Mendel stipulated the existence of inheritable causally efficacious factors in order to explain his observed results. We understand these factors as functionally defined allele or gene types that can be conservatively reduced to molecular genetics. Furthermore, according to Mendel, the law of independent assortment, for instance, applies to any gene (allele). As we have already pointed out, this law does actually not apply to linked genes, like for instance those that are situated on the same chromosome. Without considering here crossing over or other possible cellular mechanisms, it is clear that the domain of application of the law is restricted. However, within that domain of application, the law of independent assortment applies to different genes and their heredity. Thus, the ways in which the independent assortment can be deduced from molecular laws and explanations about the formation of gametes differ from case to case. We thus face once again a case of multiple realization. The law of independent assortment is not coextensive to a single molecular equivalent law, even though, for instance meiosis is a general mechanism and quite similar in even very different organisms. The crucial point here is, however, that a detailed molecular reductive explanation of what is brought out homogenously by the law of independent assortment differs from allele to allele and organism to organism. Independent assortment "IA" cannot be deduced from one single constructed law of molecular genetics, but only from molecular laws ML_1 in certain cases, from MI_{t_2} in other cases, and so on.

Following the general procedure of our approach, one has to spell out more explicitly the functionalization step. How to do this is, however, not directly evident in the case of the law of independent assortment (and likewise for many other laws of classical genetics). Imagine for instance an allele a_1 (of type A) that is not linked to another allele b_1 (of type B) in an organism o (of type O) since both alleles are on different chromosomes. Still, it is possible that an allele a_2 (of the same type A) is actually linked to an allele b_2 (of the same type B) in an organism q (of type Q) since, there, both alleles are on the same chromosome. This possibility then suggests that independent assortment (IA) is not linked to specific gene types. It is thus not possible to take the law of independent assortment as a simple abstraction from certain aspects of gene types that are conservatively reducible, via their sub-types, to molecular genetics. Moreover, this law seems to be about the given relation of an allele to some parts of its genetic environment, in particular the relation to alleles that are on different chromosomes. And this particular relation becomes pertinent during the formation of gametes. Thus, as a first reaction, one may simply say that this law has nothing to do with the functional definition of particular property types but just constitutes an abstract consideration of certain results of meiosis and other mechanisms that are relevant in the heredity of alleles.

Case Study 137

However, even though such a point of view may represent the general way in which one can use classical genetics for *predictions*, there are several reasons to theoretically link the law of independent assortment (and thus any other law-like generalization) more explicitly to particular functional properties. Generally speaking, if there is no link to functional properties at all, then the *explanatory* power of the law in question is put into peril. It may only be used, at best, for predictions without improving any understanding of what is salient in the context of evolution. And actually, methods of classical genetics are not only employed to determine probabilities of certain genetic combinations, but also to put these probabilities into the larger context of possible dispositions for this or that phenotypic effect and thus selective advantages and disadvantages. The manifestation of genetic dispositions depends on the environmental context that includes the other given genes in the genotype. Hence, the law of independent assortment and the possible linkage of alleles are, given sufficient genetic knowledge, about probabilities that this or that genetic disposition may or may not be manifested in this or that organism. This law thus is about the impact of heredity mechanisms on the probabilities of the manifestation of genetic dispositions that are advantageous or not for the organism in question.

Against this background, the law of independent assortment (*IA*) turns out to be more explicitly linked to biological functions within its domain of application: independent assortment is about heredity processes and by means of that as well about probable changes of the relevant environment of alleles when it comes to heredity. Simplified, haploid gametes are formed out of diploid ones during meiosis and this constitutes a relevant environmental change for any allele. This change of the relevant environment goes on during fertilization by the fusion of two different gametes. There, the probabilities for the manifestation of genetic dispositions are once again changed, because of, among other factors, the new genetic combination. Most importantly for the application of the proposed sub-type strategy, the independent assortment of alleles during heredity contains functional side effects if there are molecular differences in the way in which the independent assortment is brought about.

In this functional framework, let us now illustrate the general idea behind the proposed sub-types strategy to the law in question. Because of possible molecular differences of alleles or their molecular context in the cell before, during and after meiosis and fertilization, there are different molecular ways to bring about the characteristic effects that are abstractly outlined by the law of independent assortment. However, as already outlined for the most extreme cases of multiple realization in the context of the redundancy of the genetic code, for any molecular difference, there are environmental conditions possible under which these differences become functionally relevant. Thus, in cases where the law of independent assortment applies to molecularly different alleles, different

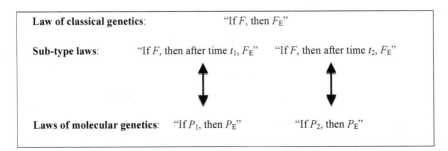

Figure 4.10 Sub-type laws.

processes like meiosis, different organisms, and the like, there are environmental conditions possible where these very differences have an impact on the functional level. To put it differently, as in our consideration of the possible impact of the multiple realization of gene types for the protein synthesis and the fitness for the organism, molecular differences of alleles have, under certain environmental conditions, an impact on the course of events during heredity.

Imagine two organisms o and q, each with two chromosomes. Assume furthermore that the law of independent assortment (IA) applies to some allele a_1 on the one chromosome of o in comparison to some other allele a_2 on the other chromosome. It also applies to some allele b_1 in q in comparison to some other allele b_2 on the other chromosome. Thus, although there are molecular differences between the four alleles, the two organisms, heredity processes, and so on, the law of independent assortment applies homogeneously to the possible heredity of these alleles. However, for any molecular difference (brought out by ML_1 and ML_2) between both organisms and the heredity of the alleles under consideration that amounts to multiple realization, there are environmental conditions possible where these differences imply a selective advantage for the one but not the other organism or allele in question. For instance, the independent assortment of alleles a_1 and a_2 will take more time or is less precise than that of b_1 and b_2 for one reason or another, for instance because their chromosomes differ in size. Such difference can be, in theory, taken into account in the application of the law of independent assortment if it is used for functional explanations. To put it differently, there are different ways in which alleles may assort independently, and these ways can be salient for selection. It thus seems plausible to take the law of independent assortment to be an abstraction from those functional details that may play a crucial role in heredity and that can be, in theory, brought out by sub-types of the law, say IA_1 and IA_2. These sub-type laws are nomologically coextensive to laws of molecular genetics (ML_1 and ML_2) and thus in no conflict with ontological reductionism and the relative completeness of molecular genetics.

Let us sum up and generalize our consideration of the law of independent assortment. Firstly, one has to specify the domain of application. Second, within the domain of application, one has to spell out the link to the functional framework. To put it differently, one has to make explicit the explanatory power of the law in question, showing how it is used for functional explanations. The third and fourth steps are to identify the entities from the perspective of the reducing theory and outline its reductive explanations. Given multiple realization, fifth, it is theoretically possible to determine functional side effects in any case of multiple realization (or multiple realizability) and construct functional sub-types (of the law in question). By means of the established nomological coextension with molecular laws, there is no conflict with ontological reductionism and the relative completeness of molecular genetics.

However, since the sub-types (or sub-type laws) are nomologically coextensive with types (or laws) of molecular genetics, this strong systematic link suggests rather the theoretical replacement of the sub-types with molecular types, molecular genetics offering more detailed causal explanations. It is therefore still an open question how to build a non-eliminativist reductionist strategy on the notion of functional sub-types. How one can in that manner vindicate the scientific quality of the well-known Mendelian laws for instance, or the principle of natural selection, is an open issue as yet. We shall consider this issue in the next chapter, setting out to make a new constructive contribution to the debate about the reducibility of classical to molecular genetics in particular and the reducibility of the special sciences in general (as regards the former debate see notably Goosens 1978, Hull 1972, 1974, 1979, Kimbrough 1979, Kitcher 1984 and 1999, Rosenberg 1978, 1985, 1994 and 2006, Ruse 1971 und 1974, Sarkar 1998, Schaffner 1967, 1969a, 1969b, 1974 and 1993, Sober 1999, Vance 1996, Waters 1990, 1994 and 2000 and Weber 1996 and 2005). The question thus is, against the background of this chapter, how one can argue for the scientific quality of abstract laws of the special sciences—such as the abstract laws of classical genetics—without getting into conflict with ontological reductionism and the completeness of molecular biology, or physics.

5 Conservative Functional Reduction

5.0 INTRODUCTION TO CHAPTER 5

Are we really nothing but a certain physical structure—in other words, a configuration of molecules? Yes, because we have ample reason to believe that the fundamental physical theories are complete with respect to the special sciences. There is not the slightest indication that there are non-physical forces in the world, such as an élan vital or an entelechie. Against the background of the completeness of physics, there is a strong causal argument leading to the conclusion that everything that is causally efficacious in the world is identical with something physical.

Setting out this argument often leads to some sort of disillusionment, which is more a consequence of the way in which the above mentioned question is asked than a well-grounded implication of the answer to this question. The way in which this question is often put suggests that something important gets lost if it turns out that we are identical with a certain physical structure. It seems as if admitting that the properties on which the special sciences focus are identical with physical properties has to be avoided at any cost, because it seems that there is no place in physical structures for the traits that are characteristic of life and the human personality.

However, what does really get lost of life and the human personality if biological and mental properties are identical with physical properties? The answer is nothing, because identity—and ontological reduction—is conservative. As already mentioned at the beginning of section 2.6, identity is a symmetric relation: if all biological and mental properties are identical with configurations of physical properties, then some configurations of physical properties simply are biological or mental properties. It is misguided to suppose that the identity of biological or mental properties with physical properties has an eliminativist flavour, that it implies that something gets lost. The properties on which the special sciences focus are identical with physical properties and therefore exist in the same way as physical properties do. The only consequence of this identity is that any property (in the sense of a property token) to which a description of a special science refers admits of a physical description as well. There are complex physical structures in the world to which not only physical concepts apply, but also concepts that are proper to the special sciences. Even if, following ontological reductionism, everything that there is in the world is something physical, this fact by no means hinders that there is life and the human personality. Ontological reductionism only implies that there also is a physical manner to access the properties on which the special sciences focus.

There are similar negative connotations of reductionism when it comes to the reduction of theories. Again, reduction is often taken to amount to elimination—as if the first and foremost aim of theory reduction were to replace the theories of the special sciences with physical theories. On the contrary, the primary objective of theory reduction is to achieve a better understanding of the relationship between the concepts, laws and explanations that the special sciences propose and physical concepts, laws and explanations, aiming at a coherent system of knowledge (see Dizadji-Bahmani et al. 2010 and 2011). Insofar as a theory of the special sciences that is to be reduced is not wrongheaded, its reduction leads only to minor corrections within that theory, but not to its elimination (see Kistler 2009, chapter 1). In this vein, it is the intention of this book to set out a conservative reductionism that vindicates the specific scientific quality of the special sciences.

From the perspective of the special sciences, we and the world appear as something fascinating. However, would that fascination remain if its price were to abandon the spirit of scientific enquiry? Certainly not. One cannot establish a satisfactory position by waiving argumentation. For this reason we pursue a reductionist strategy, since this strategy is the only way open to understand what is fascinating about us and the subject matter of the special sciences without coming into conflict with the completeness of physics. The perspective of the special sciences does not lose its fascination in conservative reductionism, since the particular manner in which it represents us and the world is retained and even grounded by our project. Everything that there is in the world is something physical. Everything that there is in the world admits of a complete physical description. We do not have to contradict these well-established statements in order to appreciate the fascination that goes with the description of the world that the special sciences propose.

This chapter focuses on the difference as well as the connection between explanations in physics and explanations in the special sciences. We first introduce the general model of functional and reductive explanations, which coheres well with the causal-functional theory of properties and which further pursues and generalizes the considerations of the two preceding chapters (section 5.1). We then work out in detail a strategy that shows a way out of the dilemma set out in the first chapter: by means of the introduction of functional sub-types, we get to functional concepts of the special sciences that are coextensive with physical concepts and that thereby enable a conservative reduction of the theories of the special sciences to physical theories (section 5.2). We have prepared this step at the

142   *Conservative Reductionism*

end of the preceding chapter in the context of biological research, using the relationship between classical and molecular genetics as case study. On that basis, we show how on the one hand the special sciences are reductively connected with physics and how on the other hand this framework enables them to make a contribution to the scientific description and explanation of the world that physics is not in the position to make (section 5.3). We thereby also solve the problem that has been left open at the end of the preceding chapter, namely how laws of classical genetics can be reduced to molecular genetics in a conservative manner.

5.1   FUNCTIONAL AND REDUCTIVE EXPLANATIONS

Theory reduction aims at explanation. Reductionism sets out to explain how all the phenomena we know enter into the world on a purely physical basis. As argued for in chapter 2, this volume, everything that there is in the domain of the special sciences is identical with local causal structures in the sense of modes (tropes). Consequently, property types—including types of configurations of properties—are concepts (see sections 1.2 and 2.5), which classify what there is in the world according to salient similarities. Such salient similarities constitute natural kinds. Generally speaking, the functional descriptions of the special sciences refer to certain causal relations among modes (more precisely, among objects or events in virtue of certain of their properties in the sense of modes, that is, ways in which they are). Thus, the concept of a gene focuses on the similarities among certain gene tokens, consisting in producing certain phenotypic effects, such as a cell wall component. Due to the similarity in producing certain specific effects, these gene tokens constitute a natural kind.

We can distinguish between perfect and imperfect similarities among property tokens in the sense of modes. This is an ontological distinction. Modes are perfectly similar if and only if they are exactly alike. All and only the fundamental physical modes are perfectly similar, as argued in section 2.5. For instance, all tokens of elementary negative charge in the world are qualitatively identical. Such a perfect similarity is sufficient to constitute a natural kind. Let us consider now configurations of fundamental physical modes that can also be described by concepts of the special sciences, such as, for instance, configurations that are a gene token. In this case, we can leave the possibility of a perfect physical similarity aside, since property tokens of the special sciences always exhibit some physical difference or other. Consequently, we deal here with less than perfect similarities, which may nevertheless be sufficient to constitute natural kinds.

Let us consider in the first place cases in which configurations of fundamental physical properties exhibit less than perfect similarities from the perspective of physics as well as from the perspective of the special sciences. According to the special sciences, some such configurations $(f_1, f_2, f_3,$

etc.) come under a certain concept F, if and only if F expresses what these configurations have in common and, hence, what distinguishes them from all the other configurations. There is a non-perfect similarity among these property tokens also from the point of view of physics if and only if physics can form a concept P that refers to all and only those tokens to which F refers and that is apt to figure in physical laws. Think for instance of gene tokens of a certain type of gene that are distinct only with respect to one fundamental physical property.

Let us now move on to cases in which modes exhibit significant similarities only from the point of view of a special science. Such modes hence come under a concept F of a special science, whereas there is no description of physical similarities by means of a physical concept P that applies to all and only these modes. Think for instance of gene tokens that on the one hand exhibit sufficient biological similarities in order to come under a gene type F, but that on the other hand are physically that distinct that physics is not in the position to express the less than perfect similarities among f_1, f_2, f_3, and so on, that F seizes in a homogeneous manner by forming a concept P that refers to all and only these tokens. In other words, we face here a case of multiple reference, having the consequence that there are no physical concepts that are coextensive with the concepts of the special sciences. Recall the example of the gene for the cell wall component. Since F expresses *causal* similarities among f_1, f_2, f_3, and so on, we can conclude against the background of ontological reductionism and the completeness of physics that the special sciences have the possibility to carry out certain *abstractions* and that physics lacks this possibility. There is no question of the special sciences referring to non-physical causal powers or the physical description and explanation of a given property token (such as f_1) being incomplete.

Let us take for granted that functionally defined concepts of the special sciences capture natural kinds, too. What then are the consequences for physics, given that physics is in a position to describe completely each member of such a kind, without disposing of the concept of the kind in question? What is the contribution that physics can make to the explanation of why there are natural kinds seized by the special sciences—such as genes, or trees, or mammals—in the world? Given token identity and the completeness of physics, there is no question that physics can consider the members of the natural kinds seized by the special sciences, because each token described by a special science admits of a complete description in a physical vocabulary. The history of science has shown that such physical descriptions can lead to important new insights. For instance, one gains a much better understanding of the genetic relationships on which classical genetics focuses by taking molecular biology and finally chemistry and physics into account. Let us now try to express the manner in which physics contributes to explaining the subject matter of the special sciences in a general scheme. Functional reduction is such a general scheme. It can be set out in terms of three consecutive steps.

144   *Conservative Reductionism*

Step 1: Functional Definition

Consider a natural kind that is the subject matter of a special science, its members coming under a concept F of a special science. The concept "gene for the cell wall component F_E" or the concept "gene for the colour of the skin and the hair," for instance, refer to tokens that constitute a certain natural kind of gene. Any such concept can be defined in a functional manner. That is to say, the concept indicates the characteristic effects that the modes coming under it (that is, the tokens of the natural kind in question) bring about, given normal conditions. The special sciences use concepts that are defined in such a functional manner, because they seek to make a contribution to explanations, and explanations of why there exist certain phenomena involve causal laws. In short, the rationale for recognizing the properties—and thus the natural kinds—in which the special sciences trade is that their tokens produce certain salient effects.

Accordingly, the causal model of explanations seems to prevail in the ongoing debate about explanations. The reason is that the deductive-nomological model of explanations (Hempel and Oppenheim 1948), the statistical relevance model of explanations (Salmon 1971) and the model of explanation through unification (Friedman 1974, Kitcher 1989) are considered as being insufficient in many cases (see Woodward 2003). The causal model of explanations is able to solve the problems of the other models by posing causal factors as determinants of the development of the world in time and thus as providing for an answer to the question why certain property tokens occur at certain positions in space and time (see, for instance, Cartwright 1983, chapter 1, and Salmon 1998, chapters 4 and 7). By contrast, one cannot answer this question by merely considering correlations or statistical relevance. We therefore have good reasons for assuming that a concept, integrated into a theory, contributes to explanations by expressing what the effects are that the tokens to which it refers can have.

Consequently, the concepts of the special sciences figure as functionally defined concepts in causal laws that can also be unificatory laws. We thereby take the model of explanation as unification within our causal conception into account, these models being compatible with one another. In other words, the description of a natural kind of the special sciences is a functional description that, being embedded in a theory with its law-like generalizations, yields causal explanations of tokens of the kind in question. These explanations can be abstract and in that sense unificatory. Thus, insofar as, for instance, a functional explanation in biology refers to causal relations in the world that are described and explained by different concepts of physics (multiple reference), such a biological explanation is a causal explanation that has a unificatory character.

This first step, consisting in the functional definition of concepts so that they can contribute to (unificatory) causal explanations, is not purely conceptual, since the causal explanations and predictions are subject to

Conservative Functional Reduction 145

empirical confirmation, and the success of many theories of the special sciences is an argument in favour of a realist conception of, for instance, genes, cells or organisms. Furthermore, this step is neutral with respect to philosophical theory in the following sense: independently of the metaphysical position that one endorses, one can take up from the practice of the special sciences that they define the properties in which they trade in a causal manner by indicating their salient effects under normal conditions.

Step 2: Ontological Reduction

Due to token identity, whenever a property token admits of a description in terms of a special science, there also is a physical description of that token. Each gene token that produces a certain phenotypic effect is identical with a complex, local physical structure and therefore admits a physical description. The descriptions of the special sciences are functional and thus causal in the sense that they aim at the effects that the complex, local physical structures in question have *as a whole* under normal conditions. By contrast, the physical description concentrates on the *composition* of these local structures. Thus, physics describes a gene that biology characterizes in functional terms by bringing out its molecular composition. The latter one also is a causal description in that the physical properties are causal properties as well. However, the physical description focalizes on the effects that the components of such a structure bring about by being related with each other in a certain manner, without having the effects in view that the structure or the configuration in question produces as a whole under certain environmental conditions.

Step 3: Reductive Explanation

Against the background of the first two steps, let us now consider the contribution to explanations that physics achieves and that cannot be matched by the special sciences, justifying the talk in terms of reduction. Given the principle of the completeness of physics, it is evident that a physical explanation of a given property token can be much more detailed than any explanation that a special science can provide. Let us make this point more precise by drawing on the concept of a causal reductive explanation, which brings out the difference between physics and the special sciences.

Property tokens in the sense of modes come under a functionally defined concept of the special sciences if and only if they have effects in common that are salient in a given environment so that concepts of a special science are formed in order to seize these effects. However, the special sciences do not explain these causal relations, at least not in detail. We have discussed this point already when we considered classical genetics: classical genetics is not in a position to explain the manner in which gene tokens produce phenotypic effects (section 4.3). Only physics is able to provide a complete

146 *Conservative Reductionism*

explanation of these causal relations, because it is capable of tracing the causal mechanisms in question in a detailed manner. In general, physics is able to explain how the objects that constitute a local structure produce taken together the effects that characterize a property type of a special science due to the way in which these objects are related with one another. For instance, in classical genetics, one takes for granted that genes have the power to produce certain phenotypic effects, such as components of cell walls or a certain colour of the hair or the skin, without classical genetics being able to explain that power. Molecular genetics and in the last resort physics, by contrast, is in the position to achieve such an explanation by considering the molecular composition of the structures in question.

In that vein, one can talk in terms of a reductive explanation when it comes to explaining characteristic effects on which a theory of the special sciences focuses in the vocabulary of a more fundamental theory. In this sense, the explanation of genetic relationships in the vocabulary of chemistry or statistical or classical mechanics is a reductive explanation. Since physics can explain everything that the special sciences seek to explain and can furthermore explain phenomena that are outside the scope of the special sciences, one can speak of reduction in the following sense: all causal relations in the world are physical causal relations, and physics can explain them in the most detailed manner.

In sum, we can characterize the explanations that the special sciences provide as abstract causal explanations, which enable general predictions that often abstract from the exact causal mechanisms producing the effects in question. These mechanisms are taken into account the more one focuses on physical details (see Machamer et al. 2000 as well as Craver 2001 and 2007). Thus, the abstract, functional explanations of the special sciences can be made more precise by detailed causal explanations of physics, which is the aim of reductive explanations. However, given multiple realization or multiple reference, functional reduction as it stands (see notably Kim 1998, chapter 4, and Kim 2005, chapter 4) is only able to explain each single token that comes under a concept (type) of a special science in a reductive manner, but not to reduce whole theories and laws of the special sciences to theories and laws of physics. We have discussed this point in connection with classical genetics: its laws and explanations cannot be deduced from molecular genetics; nonetheless, it is possible to explain each token of a causal relation between a gene token and a phenotypic effect in a molecular or physical vocabulary.

The special sciences, by contrast, are in the position to describe tokens that are physically *different* in a *homogeneous* manner, abstracting from the physical differences so that physics is not able to form concepts that apply to all and only the tokens that come under a given concept of a special science. This is a consequence of multiple reference: causal structures that are described in a homogeneous manner by a concept *F* of a special science can be composed in different physical manners. There thus are different physical mechanisms to bring about the effects that define the concept *F*. Consequently, there are different physical descriptions and hence different physical, reductive explanations.

Nonetheless, it is physics that describes and explains each single token that comes under *F* in the most detailed manner (reductive explanation). In contrast to physics, however, it is possible for the special sciences to abstract from physical details in order to point out salient causal similarities among local structures that are composed in different physical manners. Thus, classical genetics is in the position to bring out salient functional similarities among different DNA sequences and thereby provide for homogeneous, unificatory causal explanations. In that manner, one can explain many observable phenotypic properties of organisms by referring to causal powers of genes. As already mentioned, it is the causal power to bring about certain phenotypic effects that characterizes a gene—without going into the physical details of the mechanisms leading from the gene to its phenotypic effects. There consequently is a unificatory causal explanation provided by the special sciences, whereas physics does not achieve that homogeneity due to multiple reference.

Since the properties with which the special sciences deal are defined by their characteristic effects, the abstract, unificatory explanations of the special sciences are causal explanations as well. They are in accordance both with the model of causal explanations and with the model of explanation through unification, which is an important strength of the explanations in the special sciences. For instance, a certain phenotype of an organism, such as the one for a certain cell wall component or the one for the colour of the skin or the hair, is explained by the existence of one or several genes in the cells in question, which are the main cause of the cell wall component in question or the colour of the skin or the hair. By contrast, due to multiple reference, there is not such a unificatory physical causal explanation. However, the causal explanation of the special science in question does not provide a detailed account of the causal connection that leads from the gene to the phenotype. Only physics can achieve such an explanation for each single case.

Nonetheless, physics has also a unificatory character, consisting in universal theories that apply to everything in the world. Even if physics considers structures that are composed in different manners and that therefore come under different physical concepts, whereas there is a single concept of a special science that applies to many such different physical structures, physics explains all these structures by drawing on the same fundamental and universal laws. The special sciences cannot achieve such a degree of unification, because even their most abstract laws are not universal laws. In this sense, we can say that the causal explanations of the special sciences abstract from the underlying causal mechanisms. The advantage of such abstract causal explanations is that, whenever there is multiple reference, they point out salient causal similarities among physically different structures and employ these

148   *Conservative Reductionism*

similarities in unificatory causal explanations. By contrast, the unificatory character of physics does not consist in proposing abstract concepts, but in putting forward laws that have universal application.

We shall show in the next sections how the dilemma of epiphenomenalism and eliminativism, which is connected with multiple realization or multiple reference, can be avoided by means of the following conservative reductionist strategy: we shall introduce more precise functional concepts of the special sciences (sub-types) that are that fine-grained that they are coextensive with physical concepts describing the composition of the structures in question. We have already introduced this first step in section 4.3 when discussing the relationship between classical and molecular genetics and providing concrete examples from genetic research. Such a nomological coextension is a necessary and sufficient condition for theory reduction. Against this background, we can then establish the scientific quality of the abstract functional concepts and laws of the special sciences in the following manner: through the functional sub-types, these concepts and laws are linked with physical concepts and laws. However, they cannot be eliminated in favour of physical concepts and laws, for physics does not have the means at its disposal to bring out the salient causal similarities on which the abstract concepts of the special sciences focus in a homogeneous manner. In a nutshell, the physical descriptions and explanations remain complete and universal, but in certain cases, the special sciences are in the position to provide more focused unificatory descriptions and explanations in their vocabulary.

5.2   FUNCTIONAL SUB-TYPES AND THE LINK BETWEEN THE SPECIAL SCIENCES AND PHYSICS

In this section, we first point out that coextension between concepts of the special sciences and physical concepts is a necessary and sufficient condition for theory reduction. We then discuss the degrees of abstraction as well as degrees of precision that physical concepts and concepts of the special sciences admit. Against the background of the causal theory of properties, we show how one can reach a nomological coextension between fine-grained functional concepts of the special sciences (so-called sub-types) and physical concepts. On this basis, we achieve in the following section a systematic and reductive connection between the special sciences and physics, which is conservative instead of being eliminativist.

Only on the basis of the concepts of a theory T_1 being coextensive with concepts of a theory T_2 is it possible to deduce the laws of T_1 from the laws of T_2 (see notably Endicott 1998 and Fazekas 2009 as well as Dizadji-Bahmani et al. 2010). By contrast to the classical conception of theory reduction by Ernest Nagel (1961, chapter 11), the conception of functional reduction set out by Jaegwon Kim (1998, 2005) does not rely

Conservative Functional Reduction 149

explicitly on bridge principles. However, as has been pointed out in recent literature (see over and above Endicott 1998, section 8, and Fazekas 2009 also Hüttemann 2004, chapter 4.3, Kistler 2005, section 3, and Marras 2005, pp. 344–347), functional reduction also requires bridge principles in order to be in the position to link the physical vocabulary with the functional vocabulary of the special sciences. Any reductive explanation, even if it is limited to certain groups or applies only to certain individual cases, bases itself on one-way conditionals of the type "If a structure comes under the physical concept P, then it comes under the concept F of a special science as well." If there is multiple realization or multiple reference, the inverse conditional does not hold. Nonetheless, in order to get from a reductive explanation of individual cases or certain groups to a theory reduction, we have to be in the position to transform such one-way conditionals into biconditionals. The reason is that it is possible to derive the laws of a special science from physical laws if and only if each concept that is proper to the special science in question is coextensive with a physical concept.

We can consider statements about the characteristic causal powers of properties as simple, paradigmatic examples of laws of a special science. Let F stand for a functional definition of a property type of a special science whose tokens bring about certain specific effects, which are defined in a functional manner as well (F_E). The causal relation described by F, capturing the relationship between the tokens to which F refers and the tokens to which F_E refers, corresponds to a law, say simply the law "If F, then F_E." This is a ceteris paribus law, presupposing certain normal conditions, which cannot be completely accounted for in the vocabulary of the special sciences.

Let us suppose that for any token of a causal relation, coming under a law of the form "If F, then F_E" of a special science, there is an underlying complex physical causal relation. Let us suppose furthermore that the tokens to which F refers are physically different so that they come under different physical concepts (P_1, P_2, P_3). This is multiple reference. There is no physical concept that is coextensive with F. In the same manner, F_E refers to tokens that come under different physical concepts (P_{E1}, P_{E2}, P_{E3}). Thus, there are different physical laws of the form "If P_1, then P_{E1}," "If P_2, then P_{E2}" and "If P_3, then P_{E3}", capturing the causal relations between property tokens that the law "If F, then F_E" expresses in a homogeneous manner (see Putnam 1967/1975 and Fodor 1974).

Taking for granted that a functionally defined concept of a special science (F) refers to property tokens that there are in the world, ontological reductionism implies that these tokens are each identical with a certain local, causal physical structure. Due to the causal completeness of physics, the physical concepts are able to seize completely what these structures can do. We thus get to the conclusion that any property token that is described by a functional concept of a special science admits of a reductive

150 *Conservative Reductionism*

explanation. Since multiple reference teaches us that we cannot take coextension for granted, let us presuppose that there are different physical concepts describing the tokens coming under F.

Let us distinguish two cases. The first case is about minimal physical differences. Let us imagine tokens of a certain type of gene, described all by F, some of which have a few additional electrons. At first glance, one may think that this is a case of multiple reference, since the gene tokens are identical with different physical structures and thus also exhibit some causal differences or other. However, let us go into the reductive explanations of these gene tokens, including the causal law "If F, then F_E," in more detail and let us suppose that these slight physical differences are of no importance at all for the reductive explanation of the tokens coming under F. In other words, the physical descriptions of the gene tokens coming under F are not different, insofar as these physical descriptions are necessary and sufficient for a complete reductive explanation of the effects on which F focuses, or for a reduction of the law "If F, then F_E".

In such a case, there is no multiple reference, since it is possible to abstract from physical details within the physical theories in question in order to achieve coextension between the description provided by F and a homogeneous physical description. It is possible within the framework of the conceptual tools of the fundamental physical theories to achieve a homogeneous physical description P and a law of the form "If P, then P_E," which are sufficient in order to obtain a homogeneous reductive explanation of "If F, then F_E" (see Figure 5.1). When we talk about physical concepts in the following, we take such an abstraction for granted, which nonetheless considers all the relevant physical causal powers in order to achieve a homogeneous reductive explanation.

Let us now consider the case in which it is not possible to introduce such a homogeneous physical description P that is coextensive with F. There

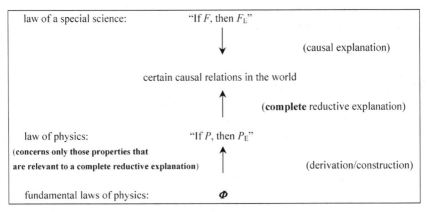

Figure 5.1 Deduction and reductive explanation.

Conservative Functional Reduction   151

thus are physical differences between the tokens coming under F or F_E, respectively, that are pertinent to the production of the effects on which the functional concepts of the special science in question focus. Consequently, the only homogeneous description that seizes all and only these tokens is the one expressed by F, or F_E, respectively. It is hence not possible to build within the physical vocabulary concepts P and P_E, figuring in a law of the form "If P, then P_E" from which one can derive a special science law of the form "If F, then F_E." In other words, there is no law of the form "If P, then P_E" that would provide for a homogeneous reductive explanation of the causal relation that the law "If F, then F_E" expresses. The law "If F, then F_E" refers to tokens of causal relations in the world to which the law "If P, then P_E" does not always apply, because the concepts "P" and "P_E" do not cover all the tokens to which "F" and "F_E" apply. Consequently, we have to employ *different* physical descriptions and laws of the form "If P_1, then P_{E1}," "If P_2, then P_{E2}" or "If P_3, then P_{E3}" in order to achieve reductive explanations.

The special science law "If F, then F_E" hence expresses a causal relation, and the effects to which F_E refers are both physically different and brought about in physically different manners. The causal explanation provided by "If F, then F_E" thus refers to physically different causal relations. Let us suppose for the sake of simplicity that the physical configurations to which F and F_E refer come under two different physical types, P_1 and P_{E1}, as well as P_2 and P_{E2}. Thus, the reductive explanations in question rely either on the law "If P_1, then P_{E1}" or on the law "If P_2, then P_{E2}" (see Figure 5.2). For instance, there may be two different physical (molecular) types of DNA sequences, corresponding to one and the same gene type F. Consequently, there are two different types of physical causal relations, leading to the production of physically different proteins, which however

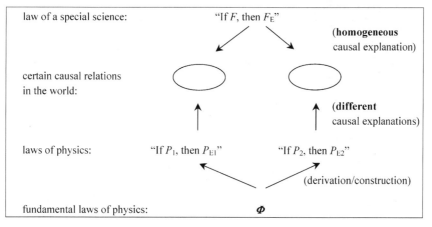

Figure 5.2   Multiple reference (realization).

coincide in producing the phenotypic effect F_E under normal conditions. One can exemplify these two different ways of producing a phenotypic effect of the same type in terms of two different types of causal relations between the DNA sequence in question and the protein synthesis in the cells in question, as illustrated in the preceding chapter. The causal relation described by "If P_1, then P_{E1}" is physically different from the one described by "If P_2, then P_{E2}."

In such a case, the law "If F, then F_E" expresses a type of causal relation in which different types of physical properties are involved. Let us represent those physical properties by P_1 and P_2, as well as P_{E1} and P_{E2}, respectively. Against the background of the causal theory of properties, there are two different types of physical properties if and only if the tokens coming under these types differ in the effects that they can bring about. In short, there is no qualitative difference between properties without a causal difference. Causal relations of different kinds thus obtain between the properties described by P_1 and P_2 and their physical environment. Against this background, we can distinguish three types of cases.

In the first place, there is the possibility that in certain situations—let us call them *extreme situations at the edge of normal conditions*—the probabilities for the causal relation in question to be hampered or interrupted are different due to the physical differences. There can thus be situations in which the probability is relatively high that the causal relation expressed by "If P_1, then P_{E1}" is hampered or interrupted. By contrast, given the same conditions, the probability that the causal relation expressed by "If P_2, then P_{E2}" is hampered or interrupted is relatively low (see Figure 5.3). Certain external physical influences may with a relatively high probability prevent that structures coming under P_1 lead to structures coming under P_{E1} so that the special science law "If F, then F_E" does not apply in this case. However, these external physical influences prevent only with a low probability that structures coming under P_2 lead to structures coming under P_{E2}. The law "If F, then F_E" hence applies nearly always in this case. In other

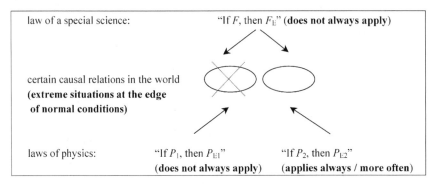

Figure 5.3 Extreme situations at the edge of normal conditions.

Conservative Functional Reduction 153

words, the physical differences between the structures coming under P_1 and the structures coming under P_2 become statistically relevant under certain physical circumstances. One can imagine circumstances in which the DNA sequences coming under P_1 are not stable enough to accomplish the protein synthesis in question, whereas the DNA sequences coming under P_2 are stable enough to accomplish the protein synthesis in question in these physical circumstances.

The second case is such that there are two different possible physical *ways* or mechanisms to implement the causal relation expressed by "If F, then F_E." One can conceive situations—let us call them *extreme situations within normal conditions*—in which the causal relation expressed by "If P_1, then P_{E1}" is that different from the causal relation expressed by "If P_2, then P_{E2}" that the difference in question is not limited to the exclusively physical domain. These situations are such that the effects described by P_{E1} or P_{E2} are always brought about, but that there is, for instance, a systematic difference in time in the production of the characteristic effects between the tokens described by "If P_1, then P_{E1}" and the tokens described by "If P_2, then P_{E2}." There is ample empirical evidence for such situations in genetics, as explained in the preceding chapter (see Figure 5.4). These situations are such that, simplifying a complicated matter, the DNA sequences coming under P_1 lead slower and with less precision to the protein synthesis in question than the DNA sequences coming under P_2. This example also shows that there is no sharp barrier between the first case and the second case discussed in this paragraph.

Before considering the third and last case, let us go into the phenotypic effects in the mentioned two cases. Our discussion of the first two cases is independent of whether or not the phenotypic effects in question are physically different. In *extreme situations at the edge of normal conditions* (case 1), there are different probabilities for the production of the phenotypic effects in question, even if these are physically the same phenotypic effects. Thus, due to the redundancy of the genetic code, it is possible that different

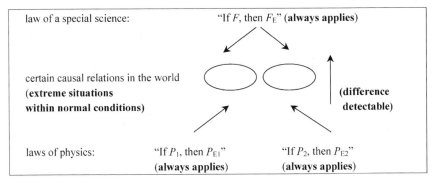

Figure 5.4 Extreme situations within normal conditions.

154 *Conservative Reductionism*

DNA sequences lead to the production of physically the same proteins, coming under one and the same physical concept P_E. In such a case, there are also different causal relations between the different DNA sequences and the production of the proteins. There can thus be situations in which the probability for the causal relation expressed by "If P_1, then P_E" to be hampered or interrupted is relatively high. By contrast, in the same conditions, the probability for the causal relation expressed by "If P_2, then P_E" to be hampered or interrupted is significantly lower. One can think of situations in which certain physical influences prevent with a certain probability structures coming under "P_1" from leading to structures coming under "P_E" (so that the special science law "If F, then F_E" does not apply in this case). However, the same physical influences prevent only with a significantly lower probability structures coming under "P_2" from leading to structures coming under "P_E" (so that the special science law "If F, then F_E" applies in this case).

If there are physical differences (P_{E1} and P_{E2}) also between the phenotypic effects (F_E), one can conceive with respect to these physical differences also *extreme situations at the edge of normal conditions*, along the lines of the first case. In these situations, the physical differences between the phenotypic effects indicate different probabilities for the production of the characteristic effects that those phenotypic effects can bring about in turn. Since the phenotypic effects coming under F_E are themselves defined in a functional manner, we can introduce a law of the form "If F_E, then F_{EE}." Supposing that the tokens coming under F_{EE} are themselves physically different, there thus are the corresponding physical laws "If P_{E1}, then P_{EE1}" and "If P_{E2}, then P_{EE2}." In this case, there can be situations in which the probability for the causal relation described by "If P_{E1}, then P_{EE1}" to be hampered or interrupted is relatively high. By contrast, in the same situations, the probability for the causal relation described by "If P_{E2}, then P_{EE2}" to be hampered or interrupted is significantly lower.

Thus, one can think of certain physical influences preventing with a certain probability structures coming under "P_{E1}" from leading to structures coming under "P_{EE1}" (so that the special science law "If F_E, then F_{EE}" does not apply in this case). On the contrary, the same physical influences prevent with a significantly lower probability structures coming under P_{E2} from leading to structures coming under P_{EE2} (so that the special science law "If F_E, then F_{EE}" applies in this case). The physical differences hence become statistically relevant under certain conditions. In other words, one can indicate physical influences due to which the proteins described by P_{E1} enter into different interactions so that the effects described by F_{EE} do not obtain. By contrast, these physical influences have no such consequences as far as the proteins described by P_{E2} are concerned. Physically different proteins may, for instance, have different three-dimensional structures so that there are different probabilities for passing cell membranes and, consequently, different probabilities for producing the characteristic

Conservative Functional Reduction   155

effects. Furthermore, physically different proteins exhibit different degrees of denaturation (a different resistance to acids, salts or organic solutions). There hence is empirical evidence for situations actually existing in which physically different proteins have the consequence of there being different probabilities to bring about the characteristic effects in question (see the discussion in section 4.3).

By the same token, physical differences in *extreme situations within normal conditions* (case 2) lead to different manners in bringing about the phenotypic effects in question, even if these effects are not different and come all under the one homogeneous physical concept P_E. The causal relation expressed by "If P_1, then P_{E1}" is that different from the causal relation expressed by "If P_2, then P_{E2}" that this difference is not limited to the physical level. These situations are such that effects coming under P_E are always produced, but that there are, for instance, differences in time between the cases coming under "If P_1, then P_{E1}" and the cases coming under "If P_2, then P_{E2}."

If the phenotypic effects (F_E) are physically different (P_{E1} and P_{E2}), then it is also possible to consider situations along the lines of *extreme situations within normal conditions* (case 2) as regards these differences. In these situations, the physical differences have the consequence that there are different ways of producing the phenotypic effects in question. The phenotypic effects coming under F_E are defined in a functional manner and figure in the law "If F_E, then F_{EE}." Supposing that the tokens coming under F_{EE} are physically different, we thus have to distinguish between the physical laws "If P_{E1}, then P_{EE1}" and "If P_{E2}, then P_{EE2}." In this case, there can be situations, *extreme situations within normal conditions*, in which the causal relation expressed by "If P_{E1}, then P_{EE1}" is that different from the causal relation expressed by "If P_{E2}, then P_{EE2}" that this difference is not limited to the physical level. These situations are such that structures coming under P_{EE1} and structures coming under P_{EE2} are always brought about, but with, for instance, the mentioned time differences. There is empirical evidence for such situations in genetic research, genetics being more and more in the position to point out functional differences between physically different proteins (see the discussion in section 4.3). For instance, the proteins coming under P_{E1} produce the characteristic effects in question slower and with less precision than the proteins coming under P_{E2}.

Against this background, we can now consider the *third and last case*: the physical differences between structures coming under P_1 and structures coming under P_2 do not lead to differences as far as the effects coming under F_E are concerned. Thus, there are no detectable differences as regards the causal relation expressed by "If F, then F_E," since normal conditions obtain (see Figure 5.5). These are physical conditions in the environment that have no influence on the causal relation expressed by "If F, then F_E," insofar as this relation is considered by a special science.

This third case is the well-known case of normal conditions, whereas such normal conditions do not obtain in the first two cases. That is why,

156 Conservative Reductionism

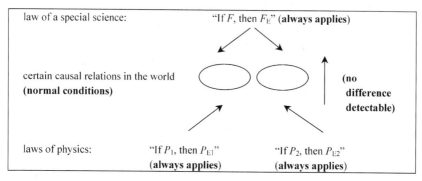

Figure 5.5 Normal conditions.

in the first two cases, it is possible to establish a distinction between the tokens coming under P_1 and the tokens coming under P_2 as regards the production of the effects coming under P_{E1} and P_{E2}, respectively. Even if it is true that the special sciences are never in the position to describe completely the normal conditions that they take for granted in the application of their laws, one may wonder whether, in the first two cases, it is possible to distinguish between structures coming under P_1 and structures coming under P_2 within the conceptual means of the special sciences.

Simplifying we can say that the law "If F, then F_E" tells us *that* there is a certain causal relation, without offering a detailed description of the mechanism of this causal relation. Nonetheless, in the first two cases, the special sciences are also in the position to distinguish between the physical structures coming under P_1 and the physical structures coming under P_2. In the first case, for instance, the special sciences are able to consider the differences in the probabilities with which structures coming under F bring about effects coming under F_E. In the second case, the special sciences are in the position to consider the different ways (mechanisms) in which the functional effects on which they focus are produced. Thus, for instance, the functional descriptions of the special sciences are able to take systematic differences in time in the production of these effects into account.

Paying heed to observable differences in probabilities or in the ways of producing the effects in question enables the special sciences to introduce functionally defined concepts in their own vocabulary that are coextensive with physical concepts. In other words, one can build concepts of the special sciences that are coextensive with P_1 and P_2 (as regards the possibility to introduce more precise functional concepts of the special sciences, see also Bechtel and Mundale 1999, pp. 201–204, who, however, tend to eliminate the more abstract functional concepts in favour of such precise functional concepts; see also Aizawa and Gillet 2011 as regards that option). These are what we propose to call sub-types, F_1 and F_2 (see Esfeld and Sachse 2007) (see Figure 5.6).

Conservative Functional Reduction 157

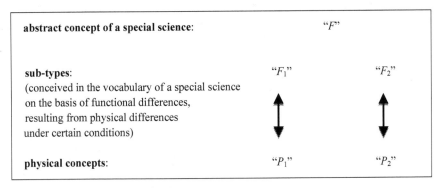

Figure 5.6 Construction of sub-types.

One can also apply this possibility to F_E, if there are physical differences in the effects, too. However, in order to simplify the discussion, we presuppose in the following that there is multiple reference only with respect to F, but not with respect to F_E. We thus have functional sub-types F_1 and F_2 in the vocabulary of the special sciences such that these sub-types are coextensive with the physical types P_1 and P_2. As regards the tokens coming under F_E, we presuppose in the following that there are no significant physical differences. Hence, the concept F_E is coextensive with P_E. Against this background, it is possible, as regards the first case, to conceive in the vocabulary of the special sciences more detailed laws, taking the form "If F_1, then, with probability c_1, F_E." or "If F_2, then, with probability c_2, F_E." By the same token, as regards the second case, there are the sub-types F_1 and F_2, taking for instance the time differences into account, as already set out in the preceding chapter (section 4.3). Consequently, we can formulate laws of the form "If F_1, then, taking time t_1, F_E" or "If F_2, then, taking time t_2, F_E".

By sub-types, we mean functionally defined concepts of the special sciences that are *nomologically* coextensive with physical concepts. Such a nomological coextension obtains in the first and the second case, because in these cases, there are for *any* relevant physical difference situations conceivable in which that difference is not limited to the exclusively physical domain. Any physically possible way in which a causal relation, described by a law of a special science, is brought about leads to causal differences that the special sciences can take into account in their own vocabulary. There is hence the principled possibility to conceive for any functional type of a special science functional sub-types in the vocabulary of the special science in question that are that fine-grained that they are nomologically coextensive with physical types.

The concept F has the same substantial "specification of the function" in all these sub-types since the sub-types are constructed out of it. Thereby, we take multiple realization or multiple reference to be an *intra-theoretic* issue, since the relation between F_1, F_2, and so on and F is

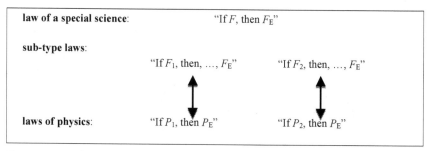

Figure 5.7 Sub-type laws.

a matter of variation of the degree of precision in the description of the causal roles proper to the different types of realizers of F. This contrasts with Lewis' and Kim's account, in which multiple realization or multiple reference remains an *inter-theoretic* issue, with respect to which, as argued in section 1.3, the introduction of group-specific concepts does not provide any help due to their hybrid—both physical and functional—individuation. This is why our proposal does not put the scientific quality of the concept F—its suitability to seize a natural kind—and the laws couched in terms of F in jeopardy.

Based on this nomological coextension we are in the position to vindicate a scientific quality for the sub-type laws of the special sciences. These laws can be derived from physics. If F_1 is coextensive with P_1, if F_2 is coextensive with P_2 and if F_E is coextensive with P_E, one can derive laws of the form "If F_1, then ... F_E" from "If P_1, then P_E", and so on. We thus get to homogeneous physical reductive explanations for those causal relations that the sub-type laws of the special sciences express. A scientific quality of the sub-type laws of the special sciences based on this possibility of a derivation from physics is coherent with token identity and the completeness of physics.

5.3 CONSERVATIVE THEORY REDUCTION AND THE SCIENTIFIC QUALITY OF THE SPECIAL SCIENCES

It is possible to deduce the sub-type laws of the special sciences from physical laws, given the coextension between the sub-types and physical types. Let us therefore now consider the relationship between the sub-types laws and the familiar, more abstract laws of the special sciences. The abstract law "If F, then F_E" seizes the causal relation between the tokens coming under F and the tokens coming under F_E. The same causal relation is expressed by "If F_1, then ... F_E" and by "If F_2, then ... F_E", with the difference that more details are taken into account—such as probabilities, or the different manners in which the effects coming under F_E can be brought about. The relationship between the sub-type laws and the more abstract laws therefore is one of abstraction within a given theory. The sub-type laws provide the most detailed causal explanations that can be reached within a theory of the special sciences, such as classical genetics, taking into account extreme situations within normal conditions or at the edge of normal conditions, as is done in genetic research. By contrast, the abstract laws implicitly take *normal* conditions for granted, as described in the third case considered in the preceding section (see Figure 5.8).

How can one argue against this background for a contribution of the abstract laws of the special sciences to the description and explanation of the world, a contribution that physics has not the conceptual means to make? As already mentioned, due to the nomological coextension with physical types, the sub-type laws can possess a scientific quality that does not come into conflict with physics. However, this nomological coextension also opens up the way to eliminate the sub-type laws: they do not reveal anything about the world that is not already contained in the corresponding physical concepts and laws. Since the latter ones are more precise and embedded in fundamental and universal theories, they are to be preferred. This is where the preceding chapter ended: the sub-types and sub-type laws of classical genetics do not tell us anything that is not already brought out by the coextensive concepts and laws of molecular genetics or physics.

Nonetheless, the functional sub-types of the special sciences are indispensable as bridge principles between the physical concepts and laws and the abstract concepts and laws of the special sciences. We get to these

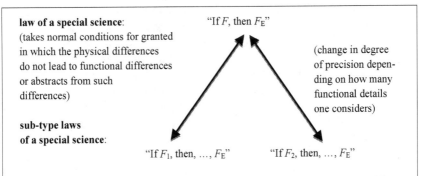

Figure 5.8 Difference between law and sub-type laws.

160   *Conservative Reductionism*

concepts and laws first by building functional sub-types and laws of the special sciences that are coextensive with physical concepts and laws and then by abstracting from functional details. Such an abstraction is legitimate in order to point out what these sub-types have in common. Being thus linked to physical concepts and laws, the abstract functional concepts and laws of the special sciences with which we are familiar do not come into conflict with the completeness of physics. Most importantly, by contrast to the sub-types and the sub-type laws, the abstract concepts and laws of the special sciences cannot be eliminated in favour of physical concepts and laws: they bring out salient causal similarities in the world that obtain under certain contingent environmental conditions in which physical differences do not imply functional differences. Physics does not have the conceptual means at its disposal to express these salient, contingent causal similarities. That is why the special sciences make a contribution to the scientific description and explanation of the world that physics is not able to make, without coming into conflict with the causal, nomological and explanatory completeness of physics. For instance, the law of independent assortment of classical genetics can be systematically linked to molecular genetics via its sub-types (section 4.3). However, since the law of independent assortment obtains under certain contingent environmental conditions in which molecular differences do not imply functional differences, it brings out salient similarities of its sub-types that cannot be brought out homogenously by molecular genetics. There, no coextensive equivalent exists that could provide such a unifying causal explanation. Within this framework, it is thus possible to vindicate the scientific quality of the abstract law of independent assortment without coming into conflict with the relative completeness of molecular genetics and, in the last resort, physics.

Let us now set out a synopsis of the steps taken and then come back to the issue of natural kinds of the special sciences. The starting-points are token identity and the completeness of physics. Multiple realization or multiple reference conceived as an anti-reductionist argument leads to a dilemma, because thus conceived multiple realization or multiple reference undermines the systematic connection between the special sciences and physics, and the special sciences are poised to lose if they enter into conflict with physics. Against this background, we have shown that the causal theory of properties enables us in any case of multiple reference to conceive more fine-grained functional concepts and laws of the special sciences—so-called sub-type laws—that are coextensive with those of physics that seize the complex, local physical structures that are identical with property tokens of a special science. Since coextension is sufficient for reduction, this step grounds on the one hand a possible scientific quality of the sub-type laws that does not come into conflict with the completeness of physics, but that on the other hand does not prevent these sub-types from being eliminated in favour of physical concepts and laws, since they do not add anything to the description and explanation of what there is in the world that is not already provided by physics. By abstracting from details as regards the ways in which the significant effects in question are brought about, it is possible to get within a theory of the special sciences from the sub-type laws to the corresponding abstract laws. These are thus linked with physics without being threatened with elimination, since physics is not in a position to build concepts that seize all and only those structures that have significant effects in common under certain environmental conditions, although they are composed in different manners.

Consequently, multiple reference no longer constitutes an anti-reductionist argument. It is possible to derive the laws of the special sciences by abstraction from the sub-type laws that are reductively linked with physical laws through nomological coextension. These abstract laws and the abstract concepts (such as F) reveal natural kinds, since they seize salient similarities in the effects that certain local physical structures have under normal conditions. These effects are described in a more detailed manner by the sub-type laws, taking further functional details into account. The natural kind expressed by F therefore figures in the same way in the sub-types F_1 and F_2 (see Figure 5.9).

Whereas the natural kind in question, which is the object of a special science, is still expressed by the sub-types such as F_1 and F_2, physics does not have the conceptual means at its disposal to express that kind in a homogeneous manner. But this is not a deep metaphysical or epistemological fact preventing reduction. It is simply a matter of the division of scientific labour. When talking about complex structures such as, for instance, genes, or whole organisms, the physical concepts focus on the composition of these objects. Due to selection there are salient causal similarities among effects that such complex objects produce as a whole under certain environmental conditions although they differ in composition. The concepts seizing these similarities are therefore not considered to be physical concepts, but classified as concepts of the special sciences.

We can dissolve the apparent tension between the conceptual capacities of the special sciences and those of physics by considering the contingent development of the evolution of species on earth. As already elaborated on in section 3.3, natural biological kinds have developed on earth that are significantly similar in the effects that they produce under certain environmental conditions, although they are composed in different manners. This fact then explains why there is multiple reference (see Papineau 1993, chapter 2). Whereas the mechanism of selection of simple systems concerns mainly their stability, the mechanism of selection profoundly changes as soon as replication properties come into existence, defining the domain of living beings. As far as the persistence of biological kinds is concerned, the frequency of replication rather

162   Conservative Reductionism

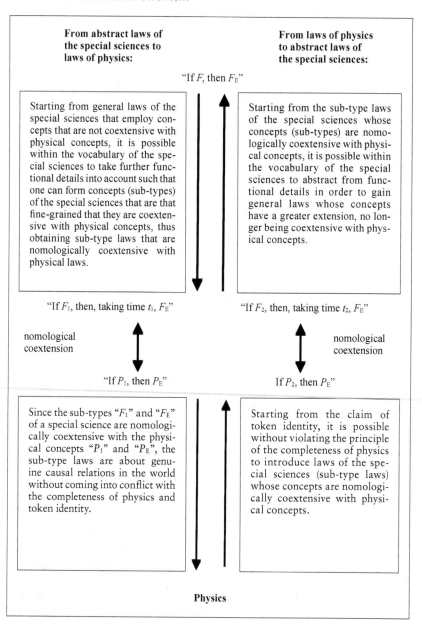

Figure 5.9 Conservative reduction.

than the stability of individual organisms is of primary importance. The issue of physically *identical* replications is under the following condition no longer important: if the replication of a physical structure leads to physical differences that do not have any negative consequences on the frequency of subsequent replications in the given environment, these

Conservative Functional Reduction 163

physical differences persist with a certain probability. Since it is a contingent matter of fact that on earth there often are environmental conditions in which such physical differences are not important for selection, the abstract concepts of biology express natural kinds. These are the normal conditions that the abstract concepts and laws of the special sciences implicitly presuppose. If such normal conditions do not obtain, the physical differences make a difference for selection as well. The subtypes express this link between physical differences and differences for selection that are revealed as soon as normal conditions do not obtain.

Against this background, we can claim that the special sciences have the conceptual capacity to bring out by means of their concepts and laws other natural kinds than physics. Taking for granted that there are physical natural kinds—such as, for instance, electrons—it is possible to argue for biological natural kinds within our conservative reductionist position. In order to vindicate this position, let us briefly consider four criteria that are at the centre of the contemporary debate about natural kinds (see LaPorte 2004).

In the first place, it is required that the members of a natural kind have natural properties in common. The members of a natural kind of physics have causal properties in common—all electrons, for instance, have a negative elementary charge and the same rest mass. Within biology, gene tokens in classical genetics, for instance, belong to the same kind if and only if they have significant phenotypic effects in common. This first criterion does not lead to a conflict between physics and the special sciences. There is no contradiction neither with ontological reductionism nor with the completeness of physics, since the causal similarities that the special sciences point out depend in such a way on environmental conditions that physical differences do not lead to functional differences.

Secondly, natural kinds should figure in laws. This is evident as regards natural kinds of physics. Any physical natural kind is described by concepts that figure in physical laws. In contrast to physics, it is debatable whether there are laws of the special sciences. Based on our discussion of evolutionary biology and classical genetics, we have in this chapter argued for the position that there are laws of the special sciences. These sciences describe tokens in the world in a functional manner and their functional definitions constitute law-like descriptions of causal relations in the world. The difference with physical laws consists in that statements of laws in fundamental physics express strict laws, whereas the laws of the special sciences are ceteris paribus laws. Nonetheless, there is no conflict between the special sciences and physics within our reductionist programme here. There is no violation of the nomological completeness of physics, since the laws of the special sciences can be connected with physical laws in a systematic and reductive manner via the mentioned sub-type laws.

The third criterion is that the members of a natural kind have to constitute a genuine, that is non-arbitrary, kind. They must not rest purely

164 *Conservative Reductionism*

on conventions. Let us take for granted that this criterion is satisfied in physics, even if physics will without doubt continue to change. However, the special sciences refer to property tokens in the world that are already described sufficiently in the vocabulary of physics. That is why one may think that the descriptions of the special sciences are purely conventional, relying only on pragmatic aspects. Without contradicting the pragmatic aspect of the special sciences, we have shown within our reductionist framework that the special sciences produce with good reason abstract descriptions of certain physical structures. The main reason is that certain physical differences do not have any functional relevance under certain environmental conditions. Consequently, there is an objective reason for the fact that biological descriptions point out functional similarities, abstracting from physical details and differences, that reason being based on the contingent way in which the evolution of biological species has developed on earth. Our conservative reductionism is hence compatible with recognizing several different descriptions of what there is in the world that are all non-arbitrary.

The fourth and last point is that natural kinds build a hierarchical system, if we take non-arbitrary classifications for granted. That is to say, natural kinds do not overlap. If they overlap, one of the kinds in question is a sub-class of the other one(s), or they are identical. As regards the relationship between the abstract concepts of a special science and the corresponding sub-types, there obviously is a hierarchy. However, the question is how to understand the relationship between biological concepts and natural kinds on the one hand and physical concepts and natural kinds on the other. Within the framework of our reductionist programme, any biological natural kind is connected with physics via its sub-types. Supposing that the biological sub-types (F_1, F_2, etc.) are a sub-class of the biological type in question (F) and that these sub-types are nomological coextensive with a physical type each (P_1, P_2, etc.), then these physical types are also a sub-class of the biological type in question (F). Of course, this is not to say that all physical natural kinds are sub-classes of biological natural kinds—physics is universal and hence also applies to properties in the world that do not fall within the domain of biology (or any other special science). Electrons or protons, for instance, are obviously not sub-classes of biological kinds. Only those complex physical structures whose physical descriptions are nomologically coextensive with biological sub-types are sub-classes of biological kinds. The fact that such complex physical structures are themselves composed of members of fundamental physical natural kinds does not hinder that there is a hierarchical system of natural kinds.

Let us now come back to the main thread of this book and build a bridge to the first and the second chapter in which we have pointed out a dilemma of the standard versions of functionalism and argued in favour of a causal theory of properties in the form of causal structures. We seek to lay stress on the following six points.

In the first place,

(1) the causal theory of properties is the presupposition in the sense of a necessary and sufficient condition for being able to introduce in any case of multiple reference functional sub-types that are that fine-grained that they are coextensive with physical types. If the physical properties were pure qualities instead of powers to produce certain effects in being certain qualities, multiple reference would always be trivially possible. There would then be no basis for the strategy to introduce functional sub-types since any functional description, however fine-grained, could always be satisfied by configurations of purely qualitative physical properties including structures of different types (see sections 1.3 and 2.3). By contrast, if properties are powers in being certain qualities, physical properties come under different physical concepts (types) if and only if there is a causal difference between them—that is to say, if and only they differ in the power to bring about certain effects.

By way of consequence, as we have pointed out in section 4.3 with respect to genetics and in a general manner in this chapter, it is in any case of multiple reference possible to introduce for each physical type a functional sub-type of the special science in question that is coextensive with the physical type in question. Precisely because the physical types (concepts) focus on the composition of the local structures in question, it is, against the background of the causal theory of properties, causal differences that establish the distinction between the different physical types that correspond in the case of multiple reference to one homogeneous type of a special science. For any such causal difference, there are environmental conditions conceivable and physically possible in which this causal difference is pertinent for selection and thus for fitness. It is therefore possible to take these causal differences in the vocabulary of the special science in question into account by means of introducing functional sub-types.

(2) The sub-types thus introduced are coextensive with physical types without being limited to certain groups (such as certain species). This is the main difference between our approach and the species-specific reduction proposed by Lewis and Kim as well as Bickle's "new wave reductionism" (see section 1.3). The sub-types are defined exclusively in the functional vocabulary of the special science in question. They are purely functional concepts of a special science, instead of being hybrid functional-cum-physical concepts (Lewis, Kim) or physical concepts that take the place of the functional concepts of the special science in question with respect to a certain group each (Bickle). On this basis, our approach is in the position to integrate the functional types of the special sciences instead of eliminating them. That is what distinguishes our approach as *conservative* reductionism.

(3) The sub-types introduced here are nomologically coextensive with physical types. When a physical type of a special science is that

166 *Conservative Reductionism*

abstract that the tokens falling under it come under different physical types, then there is, against the background of the causal theory of properties, a causal difference between these tokens in the manner in which they produce the effects that characterize the abstract type of the special science in question. Taking the causal theory of properties for granted, these causal differences are nomological differences: there are systematic differences in the manner in which the effects in question are brought about, having the consequence that the different physical types figure in different physical laws. Consequently, the physical types and the corresponding sub-types of a special science are nomologically correlated with each other, since both refer to the same systematic manners of producing certain significant effects. Nonetheless, it is not part of our programme to prescribe that the special sciences should systematically seek to construct such sub-types. We set out conservative reductionism as a position that accounts for the unity and the plurality of nature and the natural sciences, but it is not our aim to propose a methodological reductionism.

(4) The functional sub-types build a bridge between the special sciences and physics in the form of a nomological coextension and thereby satisfy the necessary and sufficient condition for theory reduction. However, precisely for this reason, the contribution of the special sciences to the description and explanation of the world does not consist in these sub-types. Since they are coextensive with physical types, they do not add anything to the description and explanation of the world that is not achieved by physical concepts alone. Comparing the sub-types and the corresponding physical concepts, the latter ones are to be preferred, since the laws in which they figure enable the most detailed causal explanations and are directly embedded into the universal laws of physics. Starting from the sub-types, we get through abstraction within one theory to the functional concepts and laws of the special sciences. These concepts and laws seize pertinent objective similarities that there are in the world and that physics cannot express within its conceptual means. It is a contingent matter of fact that such pertinent similarities have arisen during the evolution of biological species on earth, because it turned out that certain physical differences led under certain environmental conditions not to differences in selection and thus not to differences in fitness. That is why the special sciences make a contribution to the description of the world—describing pertinent similarities among physically different structures—as well as to the explanation of the world, providing for abstract causal laws and explanations that are about these pertinent similarities.

Nonetheless, what we have pointed out here is an ideal case. The reduction via sub-types usually goes together with a correction of the original concepts and laws of the special science in question in the light of the physical

Conservative Functional Reduction 167

knowledge. Thus, molecular genetics corrects classical genetics. Nonetheless, there remains a core of classical genetics that makes a contribution to the description and explanation of the world in the mentioned sense. In other words, the conservative reductionism that we propose vindicates in each case a scientific quality of a core of the special science theory in question.

(5) There is multiple realization or multiple reference in a substantial sense as soon as there is selection. When there is selection, there can be significantly similar functions that are brought about in different physical manners (see Papineau 1993, chapter 2). That is why multiple realization or reference then gives rise to anti-reductionist (or eliminativist) arguments. Against the background of the causal theory of properties, our sub-type strategy shows how reduction is nonetheless possible—a conservative reduction that takes the fact into account that physical causal differences do under certain environmental conditions not lead to functional differences in the sense of differences that are pertinent to selection.

Against the background of the theory of properties as modes, we are in the position to maintain that there are special sciences' properties out there in the world in the same way as physical properties: all there is in the world are property tokens in the sense of modes. All tokens of the same fundamental physical property type (fundamental physical kind) are perfectly similar (exactly the same, qualitatively identical). As soon as one goes beyond the domain of fundamental physics, there no longer is a question of perfect similarity. But there are pertinent similarities among the property tokens, amounting to there being natural kinds out there in nature independently of our descriptions. These pertinent similarities concern salient effects brought about under certain environmental conditions. Configurations of physical property tokens of different physical kinds can under certain environmental conditions all bring about salient biological effects of the same type (multiple reference) and therefore constitute a natural biological kind. To put it differently, according to our position, natural kinds in the special sciences are characterized by a causal role. They are thus not picked out by rigid designators, since they do not possess a common physical essence (see Lynch 2011 as regards the possibility to apply the multiple realization thesis to natural kinds). Nonetheless, our conservative reductionism vindicates natural kinds in the special sciences and shows how these kinds are related to physical kinds.

Going beyond natural kinds, the strategy built on sub-types is not limited to biological functional properties. It applies for instance also to machines. Any kind of machines is not defined by its physical composition, but by its function in the sense of certain salient effects that the machine produces as a whole and for which it is selected by its users. Nonetheless, differences in physical composition imply causal differences in the manner in which

168 *Conservative Reductionism*

these salient effects are produced, which can under certain circumstances become relevant to the users. For instance, the main computer programmes and Internet browsers are available for computers with Intel and with Mac processors, but with differences that are under certain circumstances relevant for the users. It is therefore not only in the case of biological natural kinds, but also in the case of technical or artificial kinds possible to introduce functional sub-types in the vocabulary of the special science in question that are that fine-grained that they are coextensive with types of physical structures.

This reasoning does not only apply to machines but in general to all domains for which the intentions of persons are essential and in which there are different physical manners or mechanisms to fulfil these intentions. In any such case it is in principle possible to seize these causal differences not only by means of physical types, but also by means of functional sub-types of the special science in question. That is why the sub-type strategy is the key not only for linking biology with physics through a conservative reduction but also for opening up the perspective to take psychology and the social and economic sciences into account.

(6) As pointed out at the end of section 2.6, ontological reductionism is a stable position only if it goes together with epistemological reductionism. If one seeks to establish the thesis of the property tokens of the special sciences being identical with local physical structures, one has to show how the concepts of the special sciences can be reductively linked up with physical concepts in the description of these structures. Otherwise, one is not in the position to establish the claim that physical concepts and concepts of the special sciences are descriptions of the same fine-grained entities in the sense of property tokens. The sub-type strategy hence establishes not only a conservative theory reduction, but thereby vindicates also ontological reductionism and its conservative character.

Conclusion

We have argued in this book for a position that may seem paradoxical at first glance: the scientific quality of the special sciences is established by showing how their theories are in principle reducible to in the last resort fundamental and universal theories of physics. The reduction to physics does not have the consequence that the special sciences can be dispensed with, but it is necessary to vindicate a place in the system of knowledge for them. The special sciences seize in their abstract, functional classifications and their laws pertinent similarities (natural kinds) that physics cannot express by means of its classifications. However, if one draws an anti-reductionist conclusion from this fact and conceives an opposition between the special sciences and physics, the special sciences will lose this competition. Ontological anti-reductionism has the consequence that it is not intelligible how the properties in which the special sciences trade can be causally efficacious; the rationale for recognizing these properties, however, just is that they are functional and thus causal properties. If one goes for epistemological anti-reductionism (no theory reduction), the principle of the causal, nomological and explanatory completeness of physics leads to the consequence to seek to construct in an exclusively physical vocabulary replacement theories for the theories of the special sciences that each apply to a physically homogeneous group (such as a species). It is then not possible to vindicate a scientific quality of the special sciences, because their supposed scientific quality is regarded as standing in opposition to the principle of the causal, nomological and explanatory completeness of physics.

Consequently, the special sciences can only gain from a systematic link with physics. We have shown in this book how such a link can be established by making the following two moves:

(1) In the first place, we have set out a theory of causal properties—more precisely causal structures—and based this theory on arguments that are independent of the debate about the relationship between physics and the special sciences.

(2) We have then employed this theory in order to show how it is possible to build by means of functional sub-types a biconditional link

170 *Conservative Reductionism*

between the special sciences and physics despite multiple realization or multiple reference and thus satisfy the necessary and sufficient condition for a reduction of the special sciences to physics.

In that manner, we are in the position to establish the scientific quality of the abstract, functional classifications of the special sciences, precisely because they are linked up with physical classifications via the mentioned functional sub-types.

Nonetheless, we do not maintain a methodological reductionism. We do not intend to prescribe to scientific practice to seek for reductions via functional sub-types. Our project is the one of a philosophical reflection on nature and the natural sciences, taking on the one hand the unity of nature and the natural sciences and on the other hand its plurality as starting point. The aim is to reach a reflexive equilibrium between these two poles and thus provide an answer to the question of what is the relationship between the various phenomena that there are in nature and the various theories treating these phenomena. Conservative reduction through functional sub-types against the background of the metaphysics of causal structures does justice to both these poles, the unity of nature and the natural sciences—expressed by the principle of the causal, nomological and explanatory completeness of physics—as well as its plurality—expressed by the scientific quality of the classifications and the laws of the special sciences, which support counterfactuals and yield abstract causal explanations, without these being classifications and laws that can be formulated in a physical vocabulary.

Constructing functional sub-types that build a bridge between the abstract functional classifications of the special sciences and physical classifications is an a posteriori business. In the first place, there are theories of physics and of the special sciences, which have developed more or less independently of each other. On this basis, one then seeks to build a link between both of them via functional sub-types. Against the background of the causal theory of properties in the form of causal structures, we have shown in this book that it is in principle possible to build such a link in each case, and we have presented a concrete case study, having considered the relationship between classical and molecular genetics.

Nonetheless, reductionism commits us to a stronger claim: if we had an ideally complete physical description of the world at our disposal, we could, under the counterfactual hypothesis of unlimited computational capacities, deduce from this description alone and thus a priori all the correct descriptions of phenomena in the world by the special sciences (cf. Jackson 2009). This is simply a logical consequence of the principle of the causal, nomological and explanatory completeness of physics and the principle of the global supervenience of everything that there is in the world on the distribution of the fundamental physical structures. If such a deduction were not possible, then there would be phenomena in the world for which there is

Conclusion 171

no complete physical explanation. Of course, given global supervenience, the distribution of the fundamental physical structures fixes all relations of similarity in the world. In other words, what there is in the fundamental physical domain fixes which macroscopic similarities are pertinent under which environmental conditions, such that these macroscopic similarities give rise to certain natural kinds and make true the corresponding classifications of the special sciences.

However, this reasoning establishes only the logical possibility of an a priori deduction of *ideal* special sciences from an *ideal* physics. We neither dispose of an ideal physics nor of ideal classifications of special sciences, and we will never do so. This logical consequence of reductionism hence does not impinge upon the fact that the reduction via functional sub-types that we can achieve always is an a posteriori and piecemeal affair—as shown in this book taking the relationship between classical and molecular genetics as a paradigmatic example.

Even if a super-intelligent being could carry out such an a priori deduction, this would not change anything as regards the fact that the classifications and theories of the special sciences are not physical classifications and theories and that they nonetheless possess a scientific quality, making a contribution to the description and explanation of what there is in the world that physics does not have the conceptual means to make. Such an intelligent being would be in the position to deduce from the complete physical description of the world (1) the physical concepts describing those local physical structures that produce as a whole certain significant effects in certain environments, (2) from these physical concepts the functional sub-types of the special sciences and finally (3) the abstract functional classifications of the special sciences and the corresponding laws. Nonetheless, the transition from (1) to (2) would still be the transition from physical concepts to concepts of the special sciences—the physical concepts focus on the composition of the local structures in question, the concepts of the special sciences on their pertinent effects as a whole in a given environment —only would this transition take the form of an a priori deduction.

We have based ourselves in this book on biology in order to show how conservative reductionism can be carried out in detail. On the one hand, biology is a paradigmatic example of a special science, trading in functional classifications that can be multiply realized; on the other hand, it is free of all those problems that turn the philosophy of psychology into a minefield. Nonetheless, the litmus test for the project of a conservative reductionism is the philosophy of mind. We are confident that the strategy of theory reduction via functional sub-types is applicable in philosophy of psychology as well (see Soom, Sachse and Esfeld 2010 for a first investigation), but, of course, a lot of more work needs to be done to establish this claim.

Summary of the Sub-chapters

(1.1) A satisfactory position as regards the relationship between the special sciences and physics has to achieve a reflective equilibrium between the following two poles: on the one hand, the unity of nature and the natural sciences, being based on the principles of global supervenience and the causal, nomological and explanatory completeness of physics; on the other hand, the variety of nature and the natural sciences, as expressed by the special sciences and their contribution to the description and explanation of the world. Functionalism is the only available position that offers the perspective of achieving such a reflective equilibrium. It conceives the properties with which the special sciences deal as functional and thus as causal properties. Certain configurations of physical properties realize these functional properties because they produce as a whole under normal conditions the effects that characterize a functional property of a certain type. Configurations of physical properties of different types can realize one and the same type of a functional property (multiple realization).

(1.2) Role functionalism (Putnam, Fodor) faces the problem of epiphenomenalism: insofar as functional role properties are not identical with physical properties, they cannot be causally efficacious (given the principles of supervenience and completeness of physics).

(1.3) Realizer functionalism (Lewis) admits only physical properties, and not functional properties of the special sciences. Recognizing only realizer properties, however, ends up in the consequence of an eliminativism with respect to the scientific quality of the special sciences. Physical theories are proposed that replace the theories of the special sciences for a particular group or species each.

(1.4) We suggest drawing two consequences from the dilemma of epiphenomenalism and eliminativism: it is wrong-headed to conceive an opposition between functional and physical properties (or functional and physical descriptions, respectively), and it is wrong-headed to build an anti-reductionist argument on multiple realization. The considerations set out in this

174 *Summary of the Sub-chapters*

book are built on the following two theses: all properties that there are in the world, including the physical ones, are functional properties in the sense of being causal properties. All true descriptions (laws, theories) that the special sciences propose can in principle be reduced to physical descriptions (laws, theories) by means of functional reduction, despite multiple realization.

(2.1) If one conceives properties as being categorical instead of causal – as pure qualities that are independent of the causal and nomological relationships in which they figure –, one is committed to quidditism: one has to recognize situations or worlds that are indiscernible as being qualitatively distinct nonetheless. Consequently, it is in principle not possible to gain an epistemic access to properties insofar as they are pure qualities (humility). Multiple realization of all causal relations by configurations of qualitative properties of different types then is always automatically possible. The central argument for the causal theory of properties is to avoid the consequences of quidditism and humility: in being certain qualities, properties are powers to produce certain specific effects.

(2.2) Today's fundamental physical theories – quantum theory and general relativity theory – shift the focus from intrinsic properties to structures. A physical structure is a network of concrete, qualitative relations among objects that do not possess an intrinsic identity.

(2.3) The objection of quidditism applies not only to intrinsic properties that are regarded as categorical properties and thus as pure qualities, but also to structures, if they are taken to be categorical. Conceiving the fundamental physical structures in a causal instead of a categorical manner provides moreover for a clear distinction between mathematical and physical structures.

(2.4) There are good arguments in the philosophy of physics to consider the quantum structures of entanglement and the metrical, gravitational structures of space-time as causal structures. By means of quantum state reductions, there is a transition from global structures of entanglement to local, classical physical structures. Some such local structures are the object of a special science, due to the effects that they have as a whole under normal conditions.

(2.5) There are good arguments from the metaphysics of properties to conceive properties including relations as modes, that is, as the ways in which the objects are.

(2.6) The premises of the causal theory of properties, of causal structures in physics and of properties including structures as modes enable us to

Summary of the Sub-chapters   175

set out a conservative identity theory: all the properties that the special sciences treat are identical with local, causal physical structures. Some of these structures are functional properties of the special sciences because they produce as a whole under certain environmental conditions the effects that characterize the latter properties. Against the background of the causal theory of properties, this identity theory vindicates the causal effectiveness of the properties that are the subject matter of the special sciences. This conservative ontological reductionism, however, is a stable position only if it can be combined with a conservative theory reduction.

(3.1) The theory of evolution is in the position to explain the coming into existence, the change and the extinction of natural biological kinds (living structures) by means of the principle of selection. Explanations that rely on the notion of fitness are not necessarily circular. The notion of fitness allows us to make predictions as well. There are good reasons for the position known as adaptationism, according to which evolution is essentially orientated towards a relative increase in fitness.

(3.2) Biological properties are causal-dispositional properties whose manifestation depends on normal conditions in the environment. The notion of a relevant environment can be made more precise by means of the concepts of resource, consumers and niche.

(3.3) Although we do not have a complete scientific explanation of the development of life on earth at our disposal as yet, we can define life in general by means of the concepts of reproduction, variation and inheritance and reconstruct in an abstract manner how purely physical structures can develop into living structures.

(3.4) There are good arguments for preferring the causal-dispositional theory of biological functional properties to the etiological theory. Moreover, this theory fits into the metaphysics of causal structures. Biological properties are, like all other properties, powers to produce certain specific effects. The biological function of a property consists in those effects that are relevant to the fitness of the organism (or the gene, or the population). Whereas the fundamental physical properties produce effects spontaneously, the biological properties are dispositions that depend on certain environmental conditions to bring about their characteristic effects. However, since these properties are identical with local physical structures, they exist (and produce some effects) also when these environmental conditions are not present.

(4.1) Classical genetics defines genes in a functional manner. But it does not offer any detailed causal explanations how genes produce their characteristic effects.

176   *Summary of the Sub-chapters*

(4.2) Molecular genetics reveals the molecular configurations with which genes are identical. Consequently, molecular genetics is in the position to provide relatively complete causal explanations of the manner in which genes produce their characteristic effects.

(4.3) On the basis of the causal theory of properties, it is possible to make the functional concepts (types) of classical genetics more precise such that one finally obtains functional sub-types of classical genetics that are that fine-grained that they are coextensive with molecular types. This strategy is not only a theoretical possibility, but there are concrete results of genetical research that support it.

(5.1) The programme of functional reduction developed so far in the literature makes it possible to explain in principle each token of a functional property of a special science in a reductive manner. However, this programme is not sufficient for theory reduction.

(5.2) Against the background of the causal theory of properties it is in general possible for each theory of a special science to define in its vocabulary functional concepts (sub-types) that are that precise that they are coextensive with physical concepts. These sub-types provide for the necessary and sufficient condition for theory reduction.

(5.3) By means of the strategy of constructing functional sub-types of the special sciences, and on the basis of the causal theory of properties, it is possible to develop the programme of functional reduction into a fully-fledged and conservative theory reduction. By contrast to the so called new wave reductionism, the sub-types are not limited to certain groups (such as certain species), and they are conceived exclusively in the vocabulary of the special science in question. This programme of a functional and conservative reduction within the framework of the metaphysics of causal structures vindicates the scientific quality of the special sciences: these are about natural kinds for which physical theories cannot form homogeneous concepts due to multiple reference. The special sciences provide for genuine, abstract causal explanations that are embedded into *ceteris paribus* laws. Their scientific quality does not come into conflict with the completeness of physics, because it is in principle possible to deduce the theories and laws of the special sciences from physics via the mentioned sub-types (*idealiter* in an *a priori* manner, but *de facto* in the sense of an *a posteriori* reductionism).

Bibliography

Abrams, Marshall (2007): "How do natural selection and random drift interact?" *Philosophy of Science* 74, pp. 666–679.

———. (2009): "What determines biological fitness? The problem of the reference environment." *Synthese* 166, pp. 21–40.

Abrams, Peter (1992): "Resource." In: E. Fox Keller and E. A. Lloyd (eds.): *Keywords in evolutionary biology*. Cambridge (Massachusetts): Harvard University Press. Pp. 282–285.

———. (2000): "The evolution of predator-prey interaction: theory and evidence." *Annual Review of Ecology and Systematics* 31, pp. 79–105.

Abzhanov, Arhat, Kuo, Winston, Hartmann, Christine, Grant, Rosemary, Grant, Peter and Tabin, Clifford (2006): "The calmodulin pathway and evolution of elongated beak morphology in Darwin's finches." *Nature* 442, pp. 563–567.

Abzhanov, Arhat, Protas, Meredith, Grant, Rosemary, Grant, Peter and Tabin, Clifford (2004): "Bmp4 and morphological variation of beaks in Darwin's finches." *Science* 305, pp. 1462–1465.

Ainsworth, Peter M. (2010): "What is ontic structural realism?" *Studies in History and Philosophy of Modern Physics* 41, pp. 50–57.

Aizawa, Ken and Gillett, Carl (2011): "The autonomy of psychology in the age of neuroscience." In: P. M. Illari, F. Russo and J. Williamson (eds.): *Causality in the Sciences*. Oxford: Oxford University Press.

Akashi, Hiroshi (1999): "Inferring the fitness effects of DNA mutations from polymorphism and divergence data: statistical power to detect directional selection under stationarity and free recombination." *Genetics* 151, pp. 221–238.

Albert, David Z. (2000): *Time and chance*. Cambridge (Massachusetts): Harvard University Press.

——— and Loewer, Barry (1996): "Tails of Schrödinger's cat." In: R. K. Clifton (ed.): *Perspectives on quantum reality*. Dordrecht: Kluwer. Pp. 81–91.

Allori, Valia, Goldstein, Sheldon, Tumulka, Roderich and Zanghì, Nino (2008): "On the common structure of Bohmian mechanics and the Ghirardi-Rimini-Weber theory." *British Journal for the Philosophy of Science* 59, pp. 353–389.

Amundson, Ron and Lauder, George V. (1994): "Function without purpose." *Biology and Philosophy* 9, pp. 443–469.

Andam, Chryl P., Williams, David and Gogarten, J. Peter (2010): "Natural taxonomy in light of horizontal gene transfer." *Biology and Philosophy* 25, pp. 589–602.

Andersson, Siv and Kurland, Charles (1990): "Codon preferences in free-living microorganisms." *Microbiological Reviews* 54, pp. 198–210.

Anjum, Rani Lill and Mumford, Stephen (2010): "Dispositional modality". In: C. F. Gethmann (ed.): *Lebenswelt und Wissenschaft. XXI. Deutscher Kongress für Philosophie. Kolloquien.* Hamburg: Meiner. Pp. 380–394.

178   *Bibliography*

Ariew, André and Lewontin, Richard, C. (2004): "Confusions of fitness." *British Journal for the Philosophy of Science* 55, pp. 347–363.

Ariew, André and Ernst, Zachary (2009): "What fitness can't be." *Erkenntnis* 71. pp. 289–301.

Armstrong, David M. (1968): *A materialist theory of the mind.* London: Routledge.

———. (1989): *Universals. An opinionated introduction.* Boulder: Westview Press.

———. (1999): "The causal theory of properties: properties according to Shoemaker, Ellis, and others." *Philosophical Topics* 26, pp. 25–37.

Arp, Robert (2007): "Evolution and two popular proposals for the definition of function." *Journal for General Philosophy of Science* 38, pp. 1–30.

Bain, Jonathan (2006): "Spacetime structuralism." In: D. Dieks (ed.): *The ontology of spacetime.* Amsterdam: Elsevier. Pp. 37–66.

Balashov, Yuri (2010): *Persistence and spacetime.* Oxford: Oxford University Press.

Bapteste, Eric and Burian, Richard M. (2010): "On the need for the integrative phylogenomics, and some steps toward its creation." *Biology and Philosophy* 25, pp. 711–736.

Bartels, Andreas (1996): "Modern essentialism and the problem of individuation of spacetime points." *Erkenntnis* 45, pp. 25–43.

———. (2010): "Dispositionen in Raumzeit-Theorien." In: C. F. Gethmann (ed.): *Lebenswelt und Wissenschaft. XXI. Deutscher Kongress für Philosophie. Kolloquien.* Hamburg: Meiner. Pp. 352–362.

Bartolomé, Carolina, Maside, Xulio, Yi, Soojin, Grant, Anna and Charlesworth, Brian (2005): "Patterns of selection on synonymous and nonsynonymous variants in *Drosophila miranda.*" *Genetics* 169, pp. 1495–1507.

Bassi, Angelo and Ghirardi, Gian Carlo (1999): "More about dynamical reduction and the enumeration principle". *British Journal for the Philosophy of Science* 50, pp. 719–734.

———. (2001): "Counting marbles: reply to Clifton and Monton." *British Journal for the Philosophy of Science* 52, pp. 125–130.

Beatty, John (1992): "Random drift." In: E. Fox Keller and E. A. Lloyd (eds.): *Keywords in evolutionary biology.* Cambridge (Massachusetts): Harvard University Press. Pp. 273–281.

———. (1995): "The evolutionary contingency thesis." In: G. Wolters and J. Lennox (eds.): *Concepts, theories, and rationality in the biological sciences: The second Pittsburgh-Konstanz Colloquium in the Philosophy of Science.* Pittsburgh: University of Pittsburgh Press. Pp. 45–81.

——— and Desjardins, Eric Cyr (2009): "Natural selection and history." *Biology and Philosophy* 24, pp. 231–246.

Bechtel, William and Mundale, Jennifer (1999): "Multiple realizability revisited: linking cognitive and neural states," *Philosophy of Science* 66, pp. 175–207.

Begun, David (2001): "The frequency distribution of nucleotide variation in *Drosophila simulans.*" *Molecular Biology and Evolution* 18, pp. 1343–1352.

Beiko, Robert G. (2010): "Gene sharing and genome evolution: networks in trees and trees in networks." *Biology and Philosophy* 25, pp. 659–673.

Bell, John S. (1964): "On the Einstein–Podolsky–Rosen-paradox." *Physics* 1, pp. 195–200.

———. (1987): "Are there quantum jumps?" In: C. W. Kilmister (ed.): *Schrödinger. Centenary celebration of a plymath.* Cambridge: Cambridge University Press. Pp. 41–52. Reprinted in J. S. Bell (1987): *Speakable and unspeakable in quantum mechanics.* Cambridge: Cambridge University Press. Pp. 201–212.

Bennett, Karen (2003): "Why the exclusion problem seems intractable, and how, just maybe, to tract it". *Noûs* 37, pp. 471–497.

Bickle, John (1998): *Psychoneural reduction: the new wave.* Cambridge (Massachusetts): MIT Press.

Bibliography 179

———. (2003): *Philosophy and neuroscience. A ruthlessly reductive account.* Dordrecht: Kluwer.

Bigelow, John and Pargetter, Robert (1987): "Functions." *Journal of Philosophy* 84, pp. 181–196.

Bird, Alexander (2007a): *Nature's metaphysics. Laws and properties.* Oxford: Oxford University Press.

———. (2007b): "The regress of pure powers?" *Philosophical Quarterly* 57, pp. 513–534.

———. (2009): "Structural properties revisited." In: T. Handfield (ed.): *Dispositions and causes.* Oxford: Oxford University Press. Pp. 215–241.

——— and Tomin, Emma (2008): "Natural kinds." In: E. N. Zalta (ed.): *The Stanford Encyclopedia of Philosophy.* http://plato.stanford.edu/entries/natural-kinds.

Black, Robert (2000): "Against quidditism." *Australasian Journal of Philosophy* 78, pp. 87–104.

Blackburn, Simon (1990): "Filling in space." *Analysis* 50, pp. 62–65. Reprinted in S. Blackburn (1993): *Essays in quasi-realism.* Oxford: Oxford University Press. Pp. 255–259.

Blackett, P. M. S. (1962): "Memories of Rutherford." In: J. B. Birks (ed.): *Rutherford at Manchester.* London: Heywood. Pp. 102–113.

Block, Ned (1990): "Can the mind change the world?" In: G. Boolos (ed.): *Meaning and method. Essays in honor of Hilary Putnam.* Cambridge: Cambridge University Press. Pp. 137–170.

Bohm, David (1951): *Quantum theory.* Englewood Cliffs: Prentice-Hall.

Boto, Luis (2010): "Horizontal gene transfer in evolution: facts and challenges." *Proceedings of the Royal Society B* 277, pp. 819–827.

Bouchard, Frédéric (2010): "Symbiois, lateral function transfer and the (many) saplings of life." *Biology and Philosophy* 25, pp. 623–641.

Brandon, Robert (1982): "The levels of selection." *Proceedings of the Philosophy of Science Association,* 1, pp. 315–323.

———. (1992): "Environment." In: E. Fox Keller and E. A. Lloyd (eds.): *Keywords in evolutionary biology.* Cambridge (Massachusetts): Harvard University Press. Pp. 81–86.

Brigandt, Ingo (2003): "Species pluralism does not imply species eliminativism." *Philosophy of Science* 70, pp. 1305–1316.

———. (2009): "Natural kinds in evolution and systematics: metaphysical and epistemological considerations". *Acta Biotheoretica* 57, pp. 77–97.

Brigandt, Ingo and Love, Alan C. (2008): "Reductionism in biology." In: E. N. Zalta (ed.): *The Stanford Encyclopedia of Philosophy.* http://plato.stanford.edu/entries/reduction-biology.

Bulmer, Michael (1991): "The selection-mutation-drift theory of synonymous codon usage." *Genetics* 129, pp. 897–907.

Burian, Richard M. (1992): "Adaptation: historical perspectives." In: E. Fox Keller and E. A. Lloyd (eds.): *Keywords in evolutionary biology.* Cambridge (Massachusetts): Harvard University Press. Pp. 7–12.

Burns, Cara Carthel, Shaw, Jing, Campagnoli, Ray, Jorba, Jaume, Vincent, Annelet, Quay, Jacqueline and Kew, Olen (2006): "Modulation of poliovirus replicative fitness in HeLa cells by deoptimization of synonymous codon usage in the capsid region." *Journal of Virology* 80, pp. 3259–3272.

Busse, Ralf (2008): "Fundamentale Eigenschaften und die Grundlagen des Ähnlichkeitsnominalismus." *Philosophia Naturalis* 45, pp. 167–210.

Cao, T. (2003): "Can we dissolve physical entities into mathematical structure?" *Synthese* 136, pp. 51–71.

Cartwright, Nancy (1983): *How the laws of physics lie.* Oxford: Oxford University Press.

180 Bibliography

———. (1989): *Nature's capacities and their measurement*. Oxford: Oxford University Press.

———. (2008a): "Reply to Mauricio Suárez." In: S. Hartmann, C. Hoefer and L. Bovens (eds.): *Nancy Cartwright's philosophy of science*. London: Routledge. Pp. 164–166.

———. (2008b): "Reply to Stathis Psillos." In: S. Hartmann, C. Hoefer and L. Bovens (eds.): *Nancy Cartwright's philosophy of science*. London: Routledge. Pp. 195–197.

Chakravartty, Anjan (2007): *A metaphysics for scientific realism: knowing the unobservable*. Cambridge: Cambridge University Press.

Changeux, Jean-Pierre (1964): "Allosteric interactions interpreted in terms of quaternary structure." *Brookhaven Symposia in Biology* 17, pp. 232–249.

Charlebois, Robert L. and Doolittle, W. Ford (2004): "Computing prokaryotic gene ubiquity: rescuing the core from extinction." *Genome Research* 14, pp. 2469–2477.

Clifton, Robert K. and Monton, Bradley (1999): "Losing your marbles in wave function collapse theories". *British Journal for the Philosophy of Science* 50, pp. 697–717.

Colwell, Robert (1992): "Niche: a bifurcation in the conceptual lineage of the term." In: E. Fox Keller and E. A. Lloyd (eds.): *Keywords in evolutionary biology*. Cambridge (Massachusetts): Harvard University Press. Pp. 241–248.

Colyvan, Mark (2008): "Population ecology." In: S. Sarkar and A. Plutynski (eds.): *A companion to the philosophy of biology*. Oxford: Blackwell. Pp. 301–320.

Comeron, Joseph (2004): "Selective and mutational patterns associated with gene expression in humans: influences on synonymous composition and intron presence." *Genetics* 167, pp. 1293–1304.

———. (2006): "Weak selection and recent mutational changes influence polymorphic synonymous mutations in humans." *Proceedings of the National Academy of Sciences of the United States of America* 103, pp. 6940–6945.

——— and Kreitman, Martin (1998): "The correlation between synonymous and nonsynonymous substitutions in Drosophila: Mutation, selection or relaxed constraints?" *Genetics* 150, pp. 767–775.

Coyne, Jerry A. (1994): "Ernst Mayer and the origin of species" *Evolution*, 48, pp. 19–30.

Craver, Carl F. (2001): "Role functions, mechanisms, and hierarchy." *Philosophy of Science* 68, pp. 53–74. .

———. (2007): *Explaining the brain: mechanisms and the mosaic unity of neuroscience*. Oxford: Oxford University Press.

Crick, Francis (1968): "The origin of the genetic code." *Journal of Molecular Biology* 38, pp. 367–379.

Cronin, Helena (1992): "Sexual selection: historical perspectives." In: E. Fox Keller and E. A. Lloyd (eds.): *Keywords in evolutionary biology*. Cambridge (Massachusetts): Harvard University Press. Pp. 286–293.

Crow, James F. (1988): "Sewall Wright (1889–1988)." *Genetics* 119, pp. 1–4.

———. (2007): "Motoo Kimura." In: M. Matthen and C. Stephens (ed.): *Handbook of the philosophy of science. Philosophy of biology*. Amsterdam: Elsevier. Pp. 102–107.

Cummins, Robert (1975): "Functional analysis." *Journal of Philosophy* 72, pp. 741–764. Reprinted in E. Sober (ed.) (1994): *Conceptual issues in evolutionary biology*. Cambridge (Massachusetts): MIT Press. Pp. 49–69.

Cutter, Asher, Wasmuth, James and Blaxter, Mark (2006): "The evolution of biased codon and amino acid usage in nematode genomes." *Molecular Biology and Evolution* 23, pp. 2303–2315.

Bibliography 181

Cuvier, George (1812): *Recherches sur les ossemens fossils de quadrupedes, ou l'on rétablit les caractères de plusiers espèces d'animaux que les révolutions du globe paroissent avoir détruits*. Paris: Deterville.

Damuth, John (1992): "Extinction." In: E. Fox Keller and E. A. Lloyd (eds.): *Keywords in evolutionary biology*. Cambridge (Massachusetts): Harvard University Press. Pp. 106–111.

Darwin, Charles (1859): *The origin of species by means of natural selection*. London: Murray.

Davidson, Donald (1970): "Mental events." In: L. Foster and J. W. Swanson (eds.): *Experience and theory*. Amherst: University of Massachusetts Press. Pp. 79–101. Reprinted in D. Davidson (1980): *Essays on actions and events*. Oxford: Oxford University Press. Essay 11, pp. 207–225.

Dawkins, Richard (1976): *The selfish same*. Oxford: Oxford University Press.

———. (1986): *The blind watchmaker. Why the evidence of evolution reveals a universe without design*. New York: Norton.

———. (1992): "Progress." In: E. Fox Keller and E. A. Lloyd (eds.): *Keywords in evolutionary biology*. Cambridge (Massachusetts): Harvard University Press. Pp. 263–272.

Dennett, Daniel C. (2008): "Fun and games in fantasyland." *Mind & Language* 23, pp. 25–31.

Dieks, Dennis and Versteegh, Marijn A. M. (2008): "Identical quantum particles and weak discernability." *Foundations of Physics* 38, pp. 923–934.

Dizadji-Bahmani, Foad, Frigg, Roman and Hartmann, Stephan (2010): "Who's afraid of Nagelian reduction?" in *Erkenntnis, 73*, pp. 393–412.

———. (2011): "Confirmation and reduction: a Bayesian account." Forthcoming in *Synthese* 179 (2).

Dobzhansky, Theodosius (1935): "A critique of the species concept in biology." *Philosophy of Science* 2, pp. 344–355.

———. (1937): *Genetics and the origin of species*. New York: Columbia University Press.

———. (1973): "Nothing in biology makes sense except in the light of evolution." *American Biology Teacher* 35, pp. 125–129.

Doolittle, W. Ford (2010): "The attempt on the life of the Tree of Life: science, philosophy and politics." *Biology and Philosophy* 25, pp. 455–473.

Dorato, Mauro (2005): *The software of the universe. An introduction to the history and philosophy of laws of nature*. Aldershot: Ashgate.

———. (2007): "Dispositions, relational properties, and the quantum world." In: M. Kistler and B. Gnassounou (eds.): *Dispositions and causal powers*. Aldershot: Ashgate. Pp. 249–270.

——— and Esfeld, Michael (2010): "GRW as an ontology of dispositions." *Studies in History and Philosophy of Modern Physics* 41, pp. 41–49.

dos Reis, Mario, Savva, Renos and Wernisch, Lorenz (2004): "Solving the riddle of codon usage preferences: a test for translational selection." *Nucleic Acids Research* 32, pp. 5036–5044.

dos Reis, Mario and Wernisch, Lorenz (2009): "Estimating translational selection in eukaryotic genomes." *Molecular Biology and Evolution* 26, pp. 451–461.

Dretske, Fred I. (1989): "Reasons and causes." In: J. E. Tomberlin (ed.): *Philosophical Perspectives 3: Philosophy of mind and action theory*. Oxford: Blackwell. Pp. 1–15.

Dupré, John (1981): "Natural kinds and biological taxa." *The Philosophical Review* 90, pp. 66–90.

———. (1992): "Species: theoretical contexts." In: E. Fox Keller and E. A. Lloyd (eds.): *Keywords in evolutionary biology*. Cambridge (Massachusetts): Harvard University Press. Pp. 312–317.

182 Bibliography

Earman, John and Norton, John (1987): "What price spacetime substantivalism? The hole story." *British Journal for the Philosophy of Science* 38, pp. 515–525.

Einstein, Albert (1948): "Quanten–Mechanik und Wirklichkeit." *Dialectica* 2, pp. 320–324.

———— and Podolsky, Boris and Rosen, Nathan (1935): "Can quantum-mechanical description of physical reality be considered complete?" *Physical Review* 47, pp. 777–780.

Endicott, Ronald P. (1998): "Collapse of the new wave." *Journal of Philosophy* 95, pp. 53–72.

Ereshefsky, Marc (2007): "Species, taxonomy, and systematics." In: M. Matthen and C. Stephens (eds.): *Handbook of the philosophy of science. Philosophy of biology*. Amsterdam: Elsevier. Pp. 406–427.

————. (2008): "Systematics and taxonomy." In: S. Sarkar and A. Plutynski (eds.): *A companion to the philosophy of biology*. Oxford: Blackwell. Pp. 99–118.

————. (2010): "Microbiology and the species problem." *Biology and Philosophy* 25, pp. 553–568.

Esfeld, Michael (1998): "Holism and analytic philosophy." *Mind* 107, pp. 365—380.

————. (2000): "Is quantum indeterminism relevant to free will?" *Philosophia Naturalis* 37, pp. 177–187.

————. (2001): *Holism in philosophy of mind and philosophy of physics*. Dordrecht: Kluwer.

————. (2004): "Quantum entanglement and a metaphysics of relations." *Studies in History and Philosophy of Modern Physics* 35, pp. 601–617.

————. (2006): "From being ontologically serious to serious ontology." In: M. Esfeld (ed.): *John Heil. Symposium on his ontological point of view*. Frankfurt (Main): Ontos. Pp. 191–206.

————. (2009): "The modal nature of structures in ontic structural realism." *International Studies in the Philosophy of Science* 23, pp. 179–194.

————. (2010): "Causal overdetermination for Humeans?" *Metaphysica* 11, pp. 99–104.

———— and Lam, Vincent (2008): "Moderate structural realism about space-time." *Synthese* 160, pp. 27–46.

———— and Lam, Vincent (2011): "Ontic structural realism as a metaphysics of objects." In: Alisa and Peter Bokulich (eds.): *Scientific structuralism*. Dordrecht: Springer. Pp. 143–159.

———— and Sachse, Christian (2007): "Theory reduction by means of functional sub-types." *International Studies in the Philosophy of Science* 21, pp. 1–17.

Everett, Hugh (1957): "'Relative state' formulation of quantum mechanics." *Reviews of Modern Physics* 29, pp. 454–462.

Fazekas, Peter (2009): "Reconsidering the role of bridge laws in inter-theoretical reductions." *Erkenntnis* 71, pp. 303–322.

Fisher, Ronald A. (1930): *The genetical theory of natural selection*. London: Dover.

Fodor, Jerry A. (1974): "Special sciences (or: The disunity of science as a working hypothesis)." *Synthese* 28, pp. 97–115. Reprinted in Ned Block (ed.) (1980): *Readings in the philosophy of psychology. Volume 1*. Cambridge (Massachusetts): Harvard University Press. Pp. 120–133.

————. (2008a): "Against Darwinism." *Mind & Language* 23, pp. 1–24.

————. (2008b): "Replies." *Mind & Language* 23, pp. 50–57.

Forber, Patrick (2009a): "Introduction: a primer on adaptationism." *Biology and Philosophy* 24, pp. 155–159.

————. (2009b): "*Spandrels* and a pervasive problem of evidence." *Biology and Philosophy* 24, pp. 247–266.

Bibliography 183

Fox Keller, Evelyne (1992): "Competition." In: E. Fox Keller and E. A. Lloyd (eds.): *Keywords in evolutionary biology*. Cambridge (Massachusetts): Harvard University Press. Pp. 68–73.

Franklin-Hall, L. R. (2010): "Trashing life's tree." *Biology and Philosophy* 25, pp. 689–709.

French, Steven (2006): "Structure as a weapon of the realist." *Proceedings of the Aristotelian Society* 106, pp. 167–185.

———. (2010): "The interdependence of structure, objects and dependence." *Synthese* 175, 89–109.

——— and Ladyman, James (2003): "Remodelling structural realism: quantum physics and the metaphysics of structure." *Synthese* 136, pp. 31–56.

——— and Ladyman, James (2010): "In defence of ontic structural realism." In: Alisa Bokulich and Peter Bokulich (eds.): *Scientific structuralism*. Dordrecht: Springer. Chapter 2.

Friedman, Michael (1974): "Explanation and scientific understanding." *Journal of Philosophy* 71, pp. 5–19.

Frigg, Roman and Hoefer, Carl (2007): "Probability in GRW theory." *Studies in History and Philosophy of Modern Physics* 38, pp. 371–389.

Frisch, Mathias (2009): "'The most sacred tenet?' Causal reasoning in physics." *British Journal for the Philosophy of Science* 60, pp. 459–474.

Gerland, Ulrich and Hwa, Terence (2009): "Evolutionary selection between alternative modes of gene regulation." *Proceedings of the National Academy of Sciences of the United States of America* 106, pp. 8841–8846.

Ghirardi, Gian Carlo, Rimini, Alberto and Weber, Tullio (1986): "Unified dynamics for microscopic and macroscopic systems." *Physical Review D* 34, pp. 470–491.

Gilchrist, Michael (2007): "Combining models of protein translation and population genetics to predict protein preduction rates from codon usage patterns." *Molecular Biology and Evolution* 24, pp. 2362–2372.

Gillet, Carl (2006): "Samuel Alexander's emergentism: or, higher causation for physicalists." *Synthese* 153, pp. 261–296.

———. (2007): "A mechanist manifesto for the philosophy of mind: a third way for functionalists." *Journal of Philosophical Research* 32, pp. 21–42.

——— and Rives, Bradley (2005): "The non-existence of determinables: or, a world of absolute determinates as default hypothesis." *Noûs* 39, pp. 483–504.

Gintis, Herbert (2000): *Game theory evolving. A problem-centered introduction to modeling strategic interaction*. Princeton: Princeton University Press.

Gisin, Nicolas (1984): "Quantum measurements and stochastic processes." *Physical Review Letters* 52, pp. 1657–1660.

———. (1991): "Propensities in a non-deterministic physics." *Synthese* 89, pp. 287–297.

Glémin, Sylvain (2007): "Mating systems and the efficacy of selection at the molecular level." *Genetics* 177, pp. 905–916.

Godfrey-Smith, Peter (1993): "Function: consensus without unity." *Pacific Philosophical Quarterly* 74, pp. 196–208.

———. (1994): "A modern history theory of functions." *Noûs* 28, pp. 344–362.

———. (2008): "Explanation in evolutionary biology: comments on Fodor." *Mind & Language* 23, pp. 32–41.

——— and Wilkins, Jon F. (2008): "Adapationism." In: S. Sarkar and A. Plutynski (eds.): *A companion to the philosophy of biology*. Oxford: Blackwell. Pp. 186–201.

Gogarten, Peter J. and Stevens, Lori (2005): "Horizontal gene transfer, genome innovation and evolution." *Nature Reviews Microbiology* 3, pp. 679–687.

Gogarten, Peter J. and Townsend, Jeffrey P. (2005): "Horizontal gene transfer, genome innovation and evolution," *Nature Reviews Microbiology* 3, pp. 679–687.

184 *Bibliography*

Goodnight, Charles J. and Stevens, Lori (1997): "Experimental studies of group selection: what do they tell us about group selection in nature?" *American Naturalist* 150, pp. S59–S79.

Goosens, William (1978): "Reduction by molecular genetics." *Philosophy of Science* 45, pp. 73–95.

Gould, Stephen J. and Lewontin, Richard C. (1978): "The spandrels of San Marco and the panglossian paradigm: a critique of the adaptionist programme." *Proceedings of the Royal Society of London B* 205, pp. 581–598. Reprinted in E. Sober (ed.) (1994): *Conceptual issues in evolutionary biology.* Cambridge (Massachusetts): MIT Press. Pp. 73–90.

Gould, Stephen Jay (1980): *The panda's thumb: more reflections in natural history.* New York: Norton.

Grant, Peter (1986): *Ecology and evolution of Darwin's finches.* Princeton: Princeton University Press.

Grant, Rosemary and Grant, Peter (1993): "Evolution of Darwin's finches caused by a rare climatic event." *Proceedings: Biological Sciences* 251 (1331), pp. 111–117.

———. (2002): "Unpredictable evolution in a 30-year study of Darwin's finches." *Science* 296, pp. 707–711.

———. (2006): "Evolution of character displacement in Darwin's finches." *Science* 313, pp. 224–226.

Graves, John C. (1971): *The conceptual foundations of contemporary relativity theory.* Cambridge (Massachusetts): MIT Press.

Griesemer, James (2008): "Origins of life studies." In: M. Ruse (ed.): *The Oxford handbook for philosophy of biology.* Oxford: Oxford University Press. Pp. 263–290.

Giffiths, Paul E. (1993): "Functional analysis and proper functions." *British Journal for the Philosophy of Science* 44, pp. 409–422.

———. (2009): "In what sense does 'Nothing make sense except in the light of evolution'?" *Acta Biotheoretica* 57, pp. 11–32.

Haag, Rudolf (1992): *Local quantum physics.* Berlin: Springer.

Hacking, Ian (1983): *Representing and intervening. Introductory topics in the philosophy of natural science.* Cambridge: Cambridge University Press.

———. (1989): "Extragalactic reality: the case of gravitational lensing." *Philosophy of Science* 56, pp. 555–581.

Haddrill, Penelope, Bachtrog, Doris and Andolfatto, Peter (2008): "Positive and negative selection on noncoding DNA in *Drosophila simulans.*" *Molecular Biology and Evolution* 25, pp. 1825–1834.

Haeckel, Ernst (1866): *Generelle Morphologie der Organismen.* Berlin: Georg Relmer.

Handfield, Toby (2008): "Humean dispositionalism." *Australasian Journal of Philosophy* 86, pp. 113–126.

Harbecke, Jens (2008): *Mental causation. Investigating the mind's powers in a natural world.* Frankfurt (Main): Ontos.

Harré, Rom and Madden, E. H. (1975): *Causal powers. A theory of natural necessity.* Oxford: Blackwell.

Hartl, Daniel, Moriyama, Etsuko and Sawyer, Stanley (1994): "Selection intensity for codon bias." *Genetics* 138, pp. 227–234.

Hawthorne, John (2001): "Causal structuralism." *Philosophical Perspectives* 15, pp. 361–378.

Heger, Andreas and Ponting, Chris (2007): "Variable strength of translational selection among 12 *Drosophila* species." *Genetics* 177, pp. 1337–1348.

Heil, John (2003): *From an ontological point of view.* Oxford: Oxford University Press.

———. (2006): "On being ontologically serious." In: M. Esfeld (ed.): *John Heil. Symposium on his ontological point of view.* Frankfurt (Main): Ontos. Pp. 15–27.

———. (2009): "Obituary. C. B. Martin." *Australasian Journal of Philosophy* 87, pp. 177–179.

——— and Mele, Alfred (eds.) (1993): *Mental causation*. Oxford: Oxford University Press.

Hempel, Carl Gustav and Oppenheim, Paul (1948): "Studies in the logic of explanation." *Philosophy of Science* 15, pp. 135–175.

Hoffmann, Vera (2010): *The metaphysics of extrinsic properties. An investigation of the intrinsic/extrinsic distinction and the role of extrinsic properties in the framework of physicalism*. Frankfurt (Main): Ontos.

Hooker, Clifford A. (1981): "Towards a general theory of reduction. Part I: Historical and scientific setting. Part II: Identity in reduction. Part III: Cross-categorial reduction." *Dialogue* 20, pp. 38–60, 201–236, 496–529.

Houston, Alasdair I. (2009): "San Marco and evolutionary biology." *Biology and Philosophy* 24, pp. 215–230.

Howard, Don (1985): "Einstein on locality and separability." *Studies in History and Philosophy of Science* 16, pp. 171–201.

Huber, Sarah K., De Léon, Luis Fernando, Hendry, Andrew P., Bermingham, Eldredge and Podos, Jeffrey (2007): "Reproductive isolation of sympatric morphs in a population of Darwin's finches." *Proceedings of the Royal Society B* 274, pp. 1709–1714.

Hüttemann, Andreas (1998): "Laws and dispositions". *Philosophy of Science* 65, pp. 121–135.

———. (2004): *What's wrong with microphysicalism?* London: Routledge.

Hull, David L. (1972): "Reduction in genetics—biology or philosophy?" *Philosophy of Science* 39, pp. 491–499.

———. (1974): *Philosophy of biological science*. Englewood Cliffs: Prentice-Hall.

———. (1979): "Reduction in genetics." *Philosophy of Science* 46, pp. 316–320.

——— and Wilkins, John S. (2008): "Replication." In: E. N. Zalta (ed.): *The Stanford Encyclopedia of Philosophy*. http://plato.stanford.edu/entries/replication/.

Hurst, Gregory D. D. and Werren, John H. (2001): "The role of selfish genetic elements in eukaryotic evolution." *Nature Review Genetics* 2, pp. 597–606.

Jackson, Frank (1998): *From metaphysics to ethics. A defence of conceptual analysis*. Oxford: Oxford University Press.

Jackson, Frank (2009): "A priori biconditionals and metaphysics." In: D. Braddon-Mitchell and R. Nola (eds.): *Conceptual analysis and philosophical naturalism*. Cambridge (Massachusetts): MIT Press. Pp. 99–112.

——— and Pettit, Philip (1990): "Program explanation: a general perspective." *Analysis* 50, pp. 107–117. Reprinted in F. Jackson, P. Pettit and M. Smith (eds.) (2004): *Mind, morality, and explanation. Selected collaborations*. Oxford: Oxford University Press. Pp. 119–130.

Jacob, François and Monod, Jacques (1961): "Genetic regulatory mechanisms in the synthesis of proteins." *Journal of Molecular Biology* 3, pp. 316–356.

Kern, Andrew, Jones, Corbin and Begun, David (2002): "Genomic effects of nucleotide substitutions in *Drosophila simulans*." *Genetics* 162, pp. 1753–1761.

Kiefer, Claus (2004): *Quantum gravity*. Oxford: Oxford University Press.

Kim, Jaegwon (1998): *Mind in a physical world. An essay on the mind-body problem and mental causation*. Cambridge (Massachusetts): MIT Press.

———. (1999): "Making sense of emergence." *Philosophical Studies* 95, pp. 3–36.

———. (2005): *Physicalism, or something near enough*. Princeton: Princeton University Press.

———. (2007): "Causation and mental causation." In: B. P. McLaughlin and J. Cohen (eds.): *Contemporary debates in philosophy of mind*. Oxford: Blackwell. Pp. 227–242.

186 *Bibliography*

———. (2008): "Reduction and reductive explanation: is one possible without the other?" In: J. Hohwy and J. Kallestrup (eds.): *Being reduced*. Oxford: Oxford University Press. Pp. 93–114.

———. (2009): "Mental causation." In: B. McLaughlin, A. Beckermann and S. Walter (eds.): *The Oxford handbook of philosophy of mind*. Oxford: Oxford University Press. Pp. 29–52.

Kimbrough, Steven Orla (1979): "On the reduction of genetics to molecular biology." *Philosophy of Science* 46, pp. 389–406.

Kimchi-Sarfaty, Oh, Jung Mi, Kim, In-Wha, Sauna, Zuben E., Calcagno, Anna Maria, Ambudkar, Suresh V. and Gottesman, Michael M. (2007): "A 'silent' polymorphism in the MDR1 gene changes substrate specificity." *Science* 315, pp. 525–528.

Kimura, Motoo (1968): "Evolutionary rate at the molecular level." *Nature* 217, pp. 624–626.

———. (1992): "Neutralism." In: E. Fox Keller and E. A. Lloyd (eds.): *Keywords in evolutionary biology*. Cambridge (Massachusetts): Harvard University Press. Pp. 225–230.

King, J. H. and Jukes, T. H. (1969): "Non-Darwinian evolution." *Science* 164, pp. 788–798.

Kistler, Max (2005): "Is functional reduction logical reduction?" *Croatian Journal of Philosophy* 14, pp. 219–234.

———. (2009): *La cognition entre réduction et émergence. Etude sur les niveaux de réalité*. Paris: Thèse d'habilitation.

Kitcher, Philip (1984): "1953 and all that. A tale of two sciences." *Philosophical Review* 93, pp. 335–373. Reprinted in P. Kitcher (2003): *In Mendel's mirror. Philosophical reflections on biology*. Oxford: Oxford University Press. Pp. 3–30.

———. (1985): "Darwin's achievement." In: N. Rescher (ed.): *Reason and rationality in natural science: a group of essays*. Washington (D.C.): University Press of America. Pp. 127–190.

———. (1989): "Explanatory unification and the causal structure of the world". In: P. Kitcher and W. C. Salmon (eds.): *Minnesota Studies in the philosophy of science. Volume XIII: Scientific explanation*. Minneapolis: University of Minnesota Press. Pp. 410–505.

———. (1993): "Function and design." In: P. A. French, T. E. Uehling and H. K. Wettstein (eds.): *Midwest Studies in Philosophy XVIII*. Minneapolis: University of Minnesota Press. Pp. 379–397.

———. (1999): "The hegemony of molecular biology." *Biology and Philosophy* 14, pp. 195–210. Reprinted in P. Kitcher (2003): *In Mendel's mirror. Philosophical reflections on biology*. Oxford: Oxford University Press. Pp. 31–44.

Kitcher, Philip, Sterelny, Kim and Waters, C. Kenneth (1990): "The illusory riches of Sober's monism." *Journal of Philosophy* 87, pp. 158–161.

Kreitman, Martin (2000): "Methods to detect selection in populations with applications to the human." *Annual Review of Genomics and Human Genetics* 1, pp. 539–569.

Krimbas, Costas B. (2004): "On fitness." *Biology and Philosophy* 19, pp. 185–203.

Kroedel, Thomas (2008): "Mental causation as multiple causation." *Philosophical Studies* 139, pp. 125–143.

Kuhlmann, Meinard: *The ultimate constituents of the material world. In search of an ontology for fundamental physics*. Frankfurt (Main): Ontos 2010.

Ladyman, James (1998): "What is structural realism?" *Studies in History and Philosophy of Modern Science* 29, pp. 409–424.

———. (2008): "Structural realism and the relationship between the special sciences and physics." *Philosophy of Science* 75, pp. 744–755.

Bibliography   187

———— and Bigaj, Tomasz F. (2010): "The principle of the identity of indiscernibles and quantum mechanics." *Philosophy of Science* 77, pp. 117–136.

———— and Ross, Don with Spurrett, David and Collier, John (2007): *Every thing must go. Metaphysics naturalised.* Oxford: Oxford University Press.

Lam, Vincent (2007): *Space-time within general relativity: a structural realist understanding.* University of Lausanne: PhD Thesis.

Langton, Rae (1998): *Kantian humility. Our ignorance of things in themselves.* Oxford: Oxford University Press.

———— and Lewis, David (1998): "Defining 'intrinsic'." *Philosophy and Phenomenological Research* 58, pp. 333–345. Reprinted in D. Lewis (1999): *Papers in metaphysics and epistemology.* Cambridge: Cambridge University Press. Pp. 116–132.

LaPorte, Joseph (2004): *Natural kinds and conceptual change.* Cambridge: Cambridge University Press.

Lazcano, Antonio and Bada, Jeffrey L. (2003): "The 1953 Stanley L. Miller experiment: fifty years of prebiotic organic chemistry." *Origins of Life and Evolution of the Biosphere* 33, pp. 235–242.

Lehmkuhl, Dennis (2010): "Mass-energy-momentum in general relativity. Only there because of spacetime?" Forthcoming in *British Journal for the Philosophy of Science.*

Lennox, James G. (2008): "Darwinism and Neo-Darwinism." In: S. Sarkar and A. Plutynski (eds.): *A companion to the philosophy of biology.* Oxford: Blackwell. Pp. 77–98.

Lewens, Tim (2007): "Functions." In: M. Matthen and C. Stephens (eds.): *Handbook of the philosophy of science. Philosophy of biology.* Amsterdam: Elsevier. Pp. 526–547.

————. (2009): "Seven types of adaptationism." *Biology and Philosophy* 24, pp. 161–182.

Lewis, David (1966): "An argument for the identity theory." *Journal of Philosophy* 63, pp. 17–25. Reprinted in D. Lewis (1983): *Philosophical papers. Volume 1.* Oxford: Oxford University Press. Pp. 99–107.

————. (1969): "Review of W. H. Capitan and D. D. Merrill (eds.) (1967): Art, mind and religion. Pittsburgh: University of Pittsburgh Press." *Journal of Philosophy* 66, pp. 23–35.

————. (1970): "How to define theoretical terms." *Journal of Philosophy* 67, pp. 427–446. Reprinted in D. Lewis (1983): *Philosophical papers. Volume 1.* Oxford: Oxford University Press. Pp. 78–95.

————. (1972): "Psychophysical and theoretical identifications." *Australasian Journal of Philosophy* 50, pp. 249–258. Reprinted in D. Lewis (1999): *Papers in metaphysics and epistemology.* Cambridge: Cambridge University Press. Pp. 248–261.

————. (1973): "Causation." *Journal of Philosophy* 70, pp. 556–567. Reprinted in D. Lewis (1986): *Philosophical papers. Volume 2.* Oxford: Oxford University Press. Pp. 159–172.

————. (1980): "Mad pain and Martian pain." In: N. Block (ed.): *Readings in the philosophy of psychology. Volume 1.* London: Methuen. Pp. 216–222. Reprinted in D. Lewis (1983): *Philosophical papers. Volume 1.* Oxford: Oxford University Press. Pp. 122–130.

————. (1986a): *Philosophical papers. Volume 2.* Oxford: Oxford University Press.

————. (1986b): *On the plurality of worlds.* Oxford: Blackwell.

————. (1994): "Humean supervenience debugged." *Mind* 103, pp. 473–490. Reprinted in D. Lewis (1999): *Papers in metaphysics and epistemology.* Cambridge: Cambridge University Press. Pp. 224–247.

————. (2009): "Ramseyan humility." In: D. Braddon-Mitchell and R. Nola (eds.): *Conceptual analysis and philosophical naturalism.* Cambridge (Massachusetts):

188 Bibliography

MIT Press. Pp. 203–222. Manuscript dated 7 June 2001. University of Melbourne Philosophy Department Preprint 1/01.

Lewis, Peter J. (1997): "Quantum mechanics, orthogonality, and counting." *British Journal for the Philosophy of Science* 48, pp. 313–328.

Lewontin, Richard C. (1978): "Adaptation." *Scientific American* 239, pp. 156–169.

———. (1980): "Theoretical population genetics in evolutionary synthesis." In: E. Mayr and W. Provine (eds.): *The evolutionary synthesis: perspectives on the unification of biology*. Cambridge (Massachusetts): Harvard University Press. Pp. 58–68.

———. (1982): "Organism and environment." In: E. H. C. Plotkin (ed.): *Learning, development and culture*. New York: Wiley. Pp. 151–170.

Livanios, Vassilios (2008): "Bird and the dispositional essentialist account of spatiotemporal relations." *Journal for General Philosophy of Science* 39, pp. 383–394.

Llopart, Ana and Aguadé, Monserrat (1999): "Synonymous rates at the *RpII215* gene of *Drosophila*: variation among species and across the coding region." *Genetics* 152, pp. 269–280.

Locke, Dustin (2009): "A partial defense of Ramseyan humility." In: D. Braddon-Mitchell and R. Nola (eds.): *Conceptual analysis and philosophical naturalism*. Cambridge (Massachusetts): MIT Press. Pp. 223–241.

Loewe, Laurence, Charlesworth, Brian, Bartolomé, Carolina and Noël, Véronique (2006): "Estimating selection on nonsynonymous mutations." *Genetics* 172, pp. 1079–1092.

Loewer, Barry (1996): "Freedom from physics: quantum mechanics and free will." *Philosophical Topics* 24, pp. 92–113.

———. (2007): "Mental causation, or something near enough." In: B. P. McLaughlin and J. Cohen (eds.): *Contemporary debates in philosophy of mind*. Oxford: Blackwell. Pp. 243–264.

Lotka, Alfred J. (1998): *Analytical theory of biological populations*. New York: Springer. First edition *Théorie analytique des associations biologiques. Première partie: Principes* (1934). *Deuxième partie: Analyse démographique avec application particulière à l'espèce humaine* (1939).

Louie, Elizabeth, Ott, Jurg and Majewski, Jacek (2003): "Nucleotide frequency variation across human genes." *Genome Research* 13, pp. 2594–2601.

Lyell, Charles (1830): *Principles of geology, being an attempt to explain the former changes of the earth's surface by reference to causes now in operation. Volume I*. London: John Murray.

Lynch, Kevin (2011): "A multiple realization thesis for natural kinds." *European Journal of Philosophy* 18.

Lynn, David, Singer, Gregory and Hickey, Donal (2002): "Synonymous codon usage is subject to selection in thermophilic bacteria." *Nucleic Acids Research* 30, pp. 4272–4277.

MacDonald, Cynthia and MacDonald, Graham (1986): "Mental causes and explanation of action." *Philosophical Quarterly* 36, pp. 145–158.

Machamer, Peter, Darden, Lindley and Craver, Carl F. (2000): "Thinking about mechanisms." *Philosophy of Science* 67, pp. 1–25.

Mallet, James (2005): "Ernst Mayr, the tree of life, and philosophy of biology." *Trends in Ecology and Evolution* 20, pp. 229–237.

———. (2010): "Why was Darwin's view of species rejected by twentieth century biologists?" *Biology and Philosophy* 25, pp. 497–527.

Manning, Richard N. (1997): "Biological function, selection, and reduction." *British Journal for the Philosophy of Science* 48, pp. 69–82.

Marras, Ausonio (2005): "Consciousness and reduction." *British Journal for the Philosophy of Science* 56, pp. 335–361.

Bibliography 189

———. (2007): "Kim's supervenience argument and nonreductive physicalism." *Erkenntnis* 66, pp. 305–327.

Martin, C. B. (1997): "On the need for properties: the road to Pythagoreanism and back." *Synthese* 112, pp. 193–231.

Matthen, Mohan and Ariew, André (2002): "Two ways of thinking about fitness and natural selection." *Journal of Philosophy* 99, pp. 55–83.

Maudlin, Tim (2007): *The metaphysics within physics*. Oxford: Oxford University Press.

———. (2008): "Non-local correlations in quantum theory: some ways the trick might be done." In: Q. Smith and W. L. Craig (eds.): *Einstein, relativity, and absolute simultaneity*. London: Routledge. Pp. 186–209.

Maynard Smith, John and Price, George R. (1973): "The logic of animal conflict." *Nature* 264, pp. 15–18.

Maynard Smith, John (1974): "The theory of games and the evolution of animal conflicts." *Journal of Theoretical Biology* 47, pp. 209–221.

———. (1978): "Optimization theory in evolution." *Annual Review of Ecology and Systematics* 9, pp. 31–56. Reprinted in E. Sober (ed.) (1993): *Conceptual issues in evolutionary theory. Second edition*. Cambridge (Massachusetts): MIT Press, pp. 91–118.

——— and Szathmáry, Eörs (1999): *The origins of life*. Oxford: Oxford University Press.

Mayr, Ernst (1942): *Systematics and the origin of species from the viewpoint of a zoologist*. New York: Columbia University Press.

———. (1963): *Animal species and evolution*. Cambridge (Massachusetts): Harvard University Press.

———. (1969): *Principles of systematic biology*. New York: McGraw-Hill.

———. (1985): "Darwin's five theories of evolution." In: D. Krohn (ed.): *The Darwinian heritage*. Princeton: Princeton University Press. Pp. 755–772.

———. (2002): *What evolution is*. London: Phoenix.

McIntosh, Robert (1992): "Competition: historical perspectives". In: E. Fox Keller and E. A. Lloyd (eds.): *Keywords in evolutionary biology*. Cambridge (Massachusetts): Harvard University Press. Pp. 61–67.

McLaughlin, Brian P. (2007): "Mental causation and Shoemaker-realization." *Erkenntnis* 67, pp. 149–172.

McLaughlin, Peter (1993): "Descartes on mind–body interaction and the conservation of motion." *Philosophical Review* 102, pp. 155–182.

Melnyk, Andrew (2003): *A physicalist manifesto*. Cambridge: Cambridge University Press.

Mendel, Gregor (1865): "Versuche über Pflanzen-Hybriden". *Verhandlungen des naturforschenden Vereins in Brünn*. Band IV für das Jahr 1865, pp. 3–47.

Miller, Stanley L. (1953): "Production of amino acids under possible primitive earth conditions." *Science* 117, p. 528.

Millikan, Ruth G. (1989): "In defense of proper functions." *Philosophy of Science* 56, pp. 288–302.

———. (2002): "Biofunctions: two paradigms." In: R. Cummins, A. Ariew and M. Perlman (eds.): *Functions: New readings in the philosophy of Psychology and biology*. Oxford: Oxford University Press. Pp. 113–143.

Mills, Susan K. and Beatty, John H. (1979): "The propensity interpretation of fitness." *Philosophy of Science* 46, pp. 263–286.

Misner, Charles W., Thorne, Kip S. and Wheeler, John A. (1973): *Gravitation*. San Francisco: Freeman.

Mitchell, Sandra D. (1993): "Dispositions or etiologies? A comment on Bigelow and Pargetter." *Journal of Philosophy* 90, pp. 249–259.

190   Bibliography

Mojzsis, S. J., Arrhenius, G., McKeegan, K. D., Harrison, T. M., Nutman, A. P. and Friend, C. R. L. (1996): "Evidence for life on earth before 3'800 million years ago." *Nature* 384, pp. 55–59.

Morton, Brian (2001): "Selection at the amino acid level can influence synonymous codon usage: implications for the study of codon adaptation in plastid genes." *Genetics* 159, pp. 347–358.

——— and Wright, Stephen (2007): "Selective constraints on codon usage of nuclear genes from *Arabidopsis thaliana.*" *Molecular Biology and Evolution* 24, pp. 122–129.

Moses, Alan and Durbin, Richard (2009): "Inferring selection on amino acid preference in protein domains." *Molecular Biology and Evolution* 26, pp. 527–536.

Mossio, Matteo, Saborido, Cristian and Moreno, Alavaro (2009): "An organizational account of biological functions", *The British Journal of the Philosophy of Science* 60, 813–841.

Mukhopadhyay, Pamela, Basak, Surajit and Ghosh, Tapash Chandra (2008): "Differential selective constraints shaping codon usage pattern of housekeeping and tissue-specific homologous genes of rice and Arabidopsis." *DNA Research* 15, pp. 347–356.

Muller, F. A. and Saunders, Simon (2008): "Discerning fermions." *British Journal for the Philosophy of Science* 59, pp. 499–548.

Muller, F. A. and Seevinck, Michel (2009): "Discerning elementary particles." *Philosophy of Science* 76, pp. 179–200.

Mumford, Stephen (1998): *Dispositions.* Oxford: Oxford University Press.

Musto, Héctor, Cruveiller, Stéphane, D'Onofrio, Guiseppe, Romero, Héctor and Bernardi, Giorgio (2001): "Translational selection on codon usage in *Xenopus laevis.*" *Molecular Biology and Evolution* 18, pp. 1703–1707.

Nagel, Ernest (1961): *The structure of science. Problems in the logic of scientific explanation.* London: Routledge.

Neander, Karen (1991): "Function as selected effects: the conceptual analyst's defense." *Philosophy of Science* 58, pp. 168–184.

Nei, Masatoshi (2005): "Selectionism and neutralism in molecular evolution." *Molecular Biology and Evolution*, 22, pp. 2318–2342.

Ney, Alyssa (2007): "Physicalism and our knowledge of intrinsic properties." *Australasian Journal of Philosophy* 85, pp. 41–60.

Nirenberg, Marshall W. and Leder, Philip (1964): "RNA codewords and protein synthesis." *Science* 145, pp. 1399–1407.

Nirenberg, Marshall W. and Matthaei, Heinrich (1961): "The dependence of cell-free protein synthesis in *E. coli* upon naturally occurring or synthetic polyribonucleotides." *Proceedings of the National Academy of Sciences of the United States of America* 47, pp. 1588–1602.

Noonan, Harold W. (2010): "Bird against the Humeans." *Ratio* 23, pp. 73–86.

Noordhof, Paul (1998): "Do tropes resolve the problem of mental causation?" *Philosophical Quarterly* 48, pp. 221–226.

Norton, John (2007a): "Causation as folk science." In: H. Price and R. Corry (eds.): *Causation, physics, and the constitution of reality. Russell's republic revisited.* Oxford: Oxford University Press. Pp. 11–44.

———. (2007b): "Do the causal principles of modern physics contradict causal anti-fundamentalism?" In: P. Machamer and G. Wolters (eds.): *Thinking about causes: from Greek philosophy to modern physics.* Pittsburgh: University of Pittsburgh Press. Pp. 222–234.

Okasha, Samir (2008a): "Fisher's fundamental theorem of natural selection—a philosophical analysis." *British Journal for the Philosophy of Science* 59, pp. 319–351.

Bibliography   191

————. (2008b): "The units and levels of selection." In: S. Sarkar and A. Plutynski (eds.): *A companion to the philosophy of biology*. Oxford: Blackwell. Pp. 138–156.

Olby, Robert (1990): "The molecular revolution in biology". In: R. Olby, G. Cantor, R. Christie and M. Hodge (eds.): *Companion to the history of modern science*. New York: Routledge. Pp. 503–520.

O'Malley, Maureen A. (2010): "Ernst Mayr, the tree of life, and philosophy of biology", *Biology and Philosophy* 25, pp. 529–552.

Papineau, David (1993): *Philosophical Naturalism*. Oxford: Blackwell.

————. (2002): *Thinking about consciousness*. Oxford: Oxford University Press.

Pearle, Philip (1976): "Reduction of statevector by a nonlinear Schrödinger equation." *Physical Review* D13, pp. 857–868.

Piganeau, Gwenaël and Eyre-Walker, Adam (2003): "Estimating the distribution of fitness effects from DNA sequence data: implication for the molecular clock." *Proceedings of the National Academy of Sciences of the United States of America* 100, pp. 10335–10340.

Pigliucci, Massimo and Kaplan, Jonathan (2006): *Making sense of evolution. The conceptual foundations of evolutionary biology*, Chicago: University of Chicago Press.

Plotkin, Joshua and Dushoff, Jonathan (2003): "Codon bias and frequency-dependent selection on the hemagglutinin epitopes of influenza A virus." *Proceedings of the National Academy of Sciences of the United States of America* 100, pp. 7152–7157.

Plutynski, Anya (2007): "Neutralism." In: M. Matthen and C. Stephens (eds.): *Handbook of the philosophy of science. Philosophy of biology*. Amsterdam: Elsevier. Pp. 129–140.

————. (2008): "Speciation and macroevolution." In: S. Sarkar and A. Plutynski (eds.): *A companion to the philosophy of biology*. Oxford: Blackwell. Pp. 169–185.

Popper, Karl R. (1959): "The propensity interpretation of probability." *British Journal for the Philosophy of Science* 10, pp. 25–43.

Potochnik, Angela (2009): "Optimality in a suboptimal world." *Biology and Philosophy* 24, pp. 183–197.

Psillos, Stathis (2006a): "The structure, the whole structure and nothing but the structure." *Philosophy of Science. Proceedings* 73, pp. 560–570.

————. (2006b): "What do powers do when they are not manifested?" *Philosophy and Phenomenological Research* 72, pp. 137–156.

————. (2008): "Cartwright's realist toil. From entities to capacities." In: S. Hartmann, C. Hoefer and L. Bovens (eds.): *Nancy Cartwright's philosophy of science*. London: Routledge. Pp. 167–194.

Provine, William B. (2004): "Ernst Mayr: genetics and speciation." *Genetics* 167, pp. 1041–1046.

Putnam, Hilary (1975): "The nature of mental states." In: H. Putnam (ed.): *Mind, language and reality. Philosophical papers. Volume 2*. Cambridge: Cambridge University Press. Pp. 429–440. First published as "Psychological predicates" in W. H. Capitan and D. D. Merrill (eds.) (1967): *Art, mind and religion*. Pittsburgh: University of Pittsburgh Press.

Qin, Hong, Wu, Wei Biao, Comeron, Joseph, Kreitman, Martin and Li, Wen-Hsiung (2004): "Intragenic spatial patterns of codon usage bias in prokaryotic and eukaryotic genomes." *Genetics* 168, pp. 2245–2260.

Qu, Hui-Qi, Lawrence, Steve, Guo, Fan, Majewski, Jacek and Polychronakos, Constantin (2006): "Strand bias in complementary single-nucleotide polymorphisms of transcribed human sequences: evidence for functional effects of synonymous polymorphisms." *BMC Genomics* 7, pp. 213.

192 *Bibliography*

Reydon, Thomas A. C. (2008): "Species in three and four dimensions." *Synthese* 164, pp. 161–184.

Richards, Richard A. (2008): "Species and taxonomy." In: M. Ruse (ed.): *The Oxford handbook of philosophy of biology.* Oxford: Oxford University Press. Pp. 161–188.

Richards, Robert J. (1992): "Evolution". In: E. Fox Keller and E. A. Lloyd (eds.): *Keywords in evolutionary biology.* Cambridge (Massachusetts): Harvard University Press. Pp. 95–105.

Ridley, Matt (2009): "Darwin's legacy." *National Geographic.* http://ngm.nationalgeographic.com/2009/02/darwin-legacy/ridley-text.

Rieppel, Olivier (2010): "The series, the network, and the tree: changing metaphors of order in nature." *Biology and Philosophy* 25, pp. 475–496.

Rispe, Claude, Delmotte, François and van Ham, Roeland (2004): "Mutational and selective pressures on codon and amino acid usage in *Buchnera*, endosymbiotic bacteria of aphids." *Genome Research* 14, pp. 44–53.

Robb, David (1997): "The properties of mental causation." *Philosophical Quarterly* 47, pp. 178–194.

———. (2001): "Reply to Noordhof on mental causation." *Philosophical Quarterly* 51, pp. 90–94.

Rosenberg, Alexander (1978): "The supervenience of biological concepts." *Philosophy of Science* 45, pp. 368–386.

———. (1985): *The structure of biological science.* Cambridge: Cambridge University Press.

———. (1994): *Instrumental biology or the disunity of science.* Chicago: University of Chicago Press.

———. (2006): *Darwinian reductionism. Or, how to stop worrying and love molecular biology.* Chicago: University of Chicago Press.

Rosing, Minik (1999): "^{13}C-depleted carbon microparticles in >3700-Ma sea-floor sedimentary rocks from West Greenland." *Science* 283, pp. 674–676.

Rovelli, Carlo (2007): "Quantum gravity." In: J. N. Butterfield and J. Earman (eds.): *Handbook of the philosophy of science. Philosophy of physics. Part B.* Amsterdam: Elsevier. Pp. 1287–1329.

Ruse, Michael (1971): "Reduction, replacement, and molecular biology." *Dialectica* 25, pp. 38–72.

———. (1974): "Reduction in genetics". In: K. F. Schaffner and R. S. Cohen (eds.): *PSA 1972. Proceedings of the 1972 biennial meeting of the Philosophy of Science Association.* Dordrecht: Reidel. Pp. 633–651.

———. (2007): "Charles Darwin". In: M. Matthen and C. Stephens (eds.): *Handbook of the philosophy of science. Philosophy of biology.* Amsterdam: Elsevier. Pp. 1–35.

Russell, Bertrand (1912): "On the notion of cause." *Proceedings of the Aristotelian Society* 13, pp. 1–26.

Sachse, Christian (2007): *Reductionism in the philosophy of science.* Frankfurt (Main): Ontos.

Salmon, Wesley C. (1971): "Statistical explanation." In: W. C. Salmon (ed.): *Statistical explanation and statistical relevance.* Pittsburgh: University of Pittsburgh Press. Pp. 29–87.

———. (1998): *Causality and explanation.* Oxford: Oxford University Press.

Sarkar, Sahotra (1998): *Genetics and reductionism.* Cambridge: Cambridge University Press.

———. (2007): "Haldane and the emergence of modern evolutionary theory." In: M. Matthen and C. Stephens (eds.): *Handbook of the philosophy of science. Philosophy of biology.* Amsterdam: Elsevier. Pp. 49–86.

Sato, Akie, Tichy, Herbert, O'H Uigin, Colm, Grant, Peter, Grant, Rosemary and Klein, Jan (2001): "On the origin of Darwin's finches." *Molecular Biology and Evolution* 18, pp. 299–311.

Bibliography 193

Saunders, Simon (2006): "Are quantum particles objects?" *Analysis* 66, pp. 52–63.

———, Barrett, Jonathan, Kent, Adrian and Wallace, David (eds.) (2010): *Many worlds? Everett, quantum theory, and reality.* Oxford: Oxford University Press.

Schaffner, Kenneth F. (1967): "Approaches to reduction." *Philosophy of Science* 34, pp. 137–147.

———. (1969a): "The Watson-Crick model and reductionism." *British Journal for the Philosophy of Science* 20, pp. 325–348.

———. (1969b): "Theories and explanation in biology." *Journal of the History of Biology* 2, pp. 19–33.

———. (1974): "Reduction in biology." In: K. F. Schaffner and R. S. Cohen (eds.): *PSA 1972. Proceedings of the 1972 biennial meeting of the Philosophy of Science Association.* Dordrecht: Reidel. Pp. 613–632.

———. (1993): *Discovery and explanation in biology and medicine.* Chicago: University of Chicago Press.

Schopf, William, Kudryavtsev, Anantoliy, Agresti, David, Wdowiak, Thomas and Czaja, Andrew (2002): "Laser-Raman imagery of earth's earliest fossils." *Nature* 416, pp. 73–76.

Schwartz, Peter H. (1999): "Proper function and recent selection." *Philosophy of Science* 66, pp. S210–S222.

Sepkoski, David (2008): "Macroevolution". In: M. Ruse (ed.): *The Oxford handbook for philosophy of biology.* Oxford: Oxford University Press, pp. 211–237.

Sharp, Paul, Bailes, Elizabeth, Grocock, Russel, Peden, John and Sockett, Elizabeth (2005): "Variation in the strength of selected usage bias among bacteria." *Nucleic Acids Research* 33, pp. 1141–1153.

Shoemaker, Sydney (1980): "Causality and properties." In: P. van Inwagen (ed.): *Time and cause.* Dordrecht: Reidel. Pp. 109–135. Reprinted in S. Shoemaker (1984): *Identity, cause, and mind. Philosophical essays.* Cambridge: Cambridge University Press. Pp. 206–233.

———. (2007): *Physical realization.* Oxford: Oxford University Press.

Singh, Nadia, DuMont, Vanessa L. Bauer, Hubisz, Melissa, Nielsen, Rasmus and Aguadro, Charles (2007): "Patterns of mutation and selection at synonymous sites in *Drosophila.*" *Molecular Biology and Evolution* 12, pp. 2687–2697.

Skipper, Robert A. (2007): "Sir Ronald Aylmer Fisher." In: M. Matthen and C. Stephens (eds.): *Handbook of the philosophy of science. Philosophy of biology.* Amsterdam: Elsevier. Pp. 37–48.

Smith, Peter (1992): "Modest reductions and the unity of science." In: D. Charles and K. Lennon (eds.): *Reduction, explanation and realism.* Oxford: Oxford University Press. Pp. 19–43.

Sober, Elliott (1984): *The nature of natural selection. Evolutionary theory in philosophical focus.* Cambridge (Massachusetts): MIT Press.

———. (1988): "What is evolutionary altruism?" *Canadian Journal of Philosophy*, Supplementary Volume 14, pp. 75–99. Reprinted in D. Hull and M. Ruse (eds.) (1998): *The philosophy of biology.* Oxford: Oxford University Press. Pp. 459–478.

———. (1990): "The poverty of pluralism: a reply to Sterelny and Kitcher." *Journal of Philosophy* 87, pp. 151–158.

———. (1997): "The outbreakness of lawlessness in recent philosophy of biology." *Philosophy of Science* 64, pp. S458–S467.

———. (1998): "Six sayings about adaptationism." In: D. Hull and M. Ruse (eds.): *The philosophy of biology.* Oxford: Oxford University Press. Pp. 72–86.

———. (1999): *Philosophy of biology. Second edition.* Boulder: Westview Press.

———. (2008a): "Fodor's *Bubbe Meise* against Darwinism." *Mind & Language* 23, pp. 42–49.

194   Bibliography

———. (2008b): *Evidence and evolution. The logic behind the science.* Cambridge: Cambridge University Press.

——— and Orzack, Steven Hecht (2003): "Common ancestry and natural selection". *British Journal for the Philosophy of Science* 54, pp. 423–437.

——— and Wilson, David Sloan (1998): *Unto others: the evolution and psychology of unselfish behaviour.* Cambridge: Harvard University Press.

Soom, Patrice, Sachse, Christian and Esfeld, Michael (2010): "Psycho-neural reduction through functional sub-types." *Journal of Consciousness Studies* 17, pp. 7–26.

Sparber, Georg (2009): *Unorthodox Humeanism.* Frankfurt (Main): Ontos.

Spencer, Hamish and Masters, Judith (1992): "Sexual selection: contemporary debates." In: E. Fox Keller and E. A. Lloyd (eds.): *Keywords in evolutionary biology.* Cambridge (Massachusetts): Harvard University Press. Pp. 294–301.

Stachel, John (2002): "'The relations between things' versus 'The things between relations': the deeper meaning of the hole argument." In: D. B. Malament (ed.): *Reading natural philosophy. Essays in the history and philosophy of science and mathematics.* Chicago: Open Court. Pp. 231–266.

Stephens, Christopher (2007): "Natural selection." In: M. Matthen and C. Stephens (eds.): *Handbook of the philosophy of science. Philosophy of biology.* Amsterdam: Elsevier. Pp. 111–127.

———. (2008): "Population genetics." In: S. Sarkar and A. Plutynski (eds.): *A companion to the philosophy of biology.* Oxford: Blackwell. Pp. 119–137.

Sterelny, Kim (1996): "Explanatory pluralism in evolutionary biology". *Biology and Philosophy* 11, pp. 193–214.

——— and Griffiths, Paul E. (1999): *Sex and death. An introduction to philosophy of biology.* Chicago: University of Chicago Press.

——— and Kitcher, Philip (1988): "The return of the gene." *Journal of Philosophy* 85, pp. 339–361.

Stevens, Peter (1992): "Species: historical perspectives." In: E. Fox Keller and E. A. Lloyd (eds.): *Keywords in evolutionary biology.* Cambridge (Massachusetts): Harvard University Press. Pp. 302–311.

Stoletzki, Nina and Eyre-Walker, Adam (2007): "Synonymous codon usage in *Escherichia coli*: selection for translational accuracy." *Molecular Biology and Evolution* 12, pp. 373–381.

Strawson, Galen (2008): "The identity of the categorical and the dispositional." *Analysis* 68, pp. 271–282.

Suárez, Mauricio (2004a): "On quantum propensities: two arguments revisited." *Erkenntnis* 61, pp. 1–16.

———. (2004b): "Quantum selections, propensities, and the problem of measurement." *British Journal for the Philosophy of Science* 55, pp. 219–255.

———. (2007): "Quantum propensities." *Studies in History and Philosophy of Modern Physics* 38, pp. 418–438.

———. (2008): "Experimental realism reconsidered. How inference to the most likely cause might be sound." In: S. Hartmann, C. Hoefer and L. Bovens (eds.): *Nancy Cartwright's philosophy of science.* London: Routledge. Pp. 137–163.

Szathmáry, Erös (2006): "The origin of replicators and reproducers." *Philosophical Transactions of the Royal Society Biological Sciences* 361, pp. 1761–1776.

Tumulka, Roderich (2006): "A relativistic version of the Ghirardi-Rimini-Weber model." *Journal of Statistical Physics* 125, pp. 821–840.

Van Valen, Leigh (2009): "How ubiquitous is adaptation? A critique of the epiphenomenist program." *Biology and Philosophy* 24, pp. 267–280.

Vance, Russell E. (1996): "Heroic antireductionism and genetics: a tale of one science." *Proceedings of the 1996 biennial meeting of the Philosophy of Science*

Association. Philosophy of Science 63 Supplement. East Lansing: Philosophy of Science Association. Pp. S36–S45.

Velasco, Joel D. and Sober, Elliott (2010): "Testing for treeness: lateral gene transfer, phylogenetic inference, and model selection." *Biology and Philosophy* 25, pp. 675–687.

Viljanen, Valtteri (2007): "Field metaphysic, power, and individuation in Spinoza." *Canadian Journal of Philosophy* 37, pp. 393–418.

Wallace, David (2008): "The interpretation of quantum mechanics." In: D. Rickles (ed.): *The Ashgate companion to the new philosophy of physics.* Aldershot: Ashgate. Pp. 16–98.

Walsh, D. M. (1996): "Fitness and function." *British Journal for the Philosophy of Science* 47, pp. 553–574.

Waters, C. Kenneth (1990): "Why the antireductionist consensus won't survive: the case of classical Mendelian genetics." In: A. Fine, M. Forbes and L. Wessels (eds.): *Proceedings of the 1990 Biennial Meeting of the Philosophy of Science Association.* East Lansing: Philosophy of Science Association. Pp. 125–139.

———. (1991): "Tempered realism about the force of selection", *Philosophy of Science* 58, pp. 553–573.

———. (1994): "Genes made molecular." *Philosophy of Science* 61, pp. 163–185.

———. (2000): "Molecules made molecular." *Revue internationale de Philosophie* 4, pp. 539–564.

———. (2007): "Causes that make a difference." *Journal of Philosophy* 104, pp. 551–579.

Watson, James D. and Crick, Francis H. C. (1953a): "A structure for deoxyribose nucleic acid." *Nature* 171, pp. 737–738.

———. (1953b): "Genetical implications of the structure of deoxyribonucleic acid." *Nature* 171, pp. 964–967.

———. (1954): "The complementary structure of deoxyribonucleic acid." *Proceedings of the Royal Society A* 223, pp. 80–96.

Weber, Marcel (1996): "Fitness made physical: the supervenience of biological concepts revisited." *Philosophy of Science* 63, pp. 411–431.

———. (1998): "Representing genes: classical mapping techniques and the growth of genetical knowledge." *Studies in History and Philosophy of Biology and Biomedical Sciences* 29, pp. 295–315.

———. (2001): "Determinism, realism, and probability in evolutionary theory." *Philosophy of Science* 68, pp. S213–S224.

———. (2005): *Philosophy of experimental biology.* Cambridge: Cambridge University Press.

———. (2008): "Review of Alexander Rosenberg, Darwinian reductionism. Or, how to stop worrying and love molecular biology. Chicago: University of Chicago Press 2006." *Biology and Philosophy* 23, pp. 143–152.

Weismann, August (1895): *Neue Gedanken zur Vererbungsfrage.* Jena: Fischer.

West-Eberhard, Mary Jane (1992): "Adaptation: current usage." In: E. Fox Keller and E. A. Lloyd (eds.): *Keywords in evolutionary biology.* Cambridge (Massachusetts): Harvard University Press. Pp. 13–18.

Wheeler, John A. (1962a): *Geometrodynamics.* New York: Academic Press.

———. (1962b): "Curved empty space as the building material of the physical world: an assessment." In: E. Nagel, P. Suppes and A. Tarski (eds.): *Logic, methodology and philosophy of science. Proceedings of the 1960 international congress.* Stanford: Stanford University Press. Pp. 361–374.

Whittle, Ann (2006): "On an argument for humility." *Philosophical Studies* 130, pp. 461–497.

———. (2007): "The co-instantiation thesis." *Australasian Journal of Philosophy* 85, pp. 61–79.

196 Bibliography

———. (2008): "A functionalist theory of properties." *Philosophy and Phenomenological Research* 77, pp. 59–82.

Wilkins, Jon F. and Godfrey-Smith, Peter (2009): "Adaptationism and the adaptive landscape." *Biology and Philosophy* 24, pp. 199–214.

Wilson, David Sloan (1989): "Levels of selection: an alternative to individualism in biology and the human science." *Social Networks* 11, pp. 257–272. Reprinted in E. Sober (ed.) (1993): *Conceptual issues in evolutionary biology. Second edition.* Cambridge (Massachusetts): MIT Press. Pp. 143–154.

———. (1992): "Group selection." In: E. Fox Keller and E. A. Loyd (eds.): *Keywords in evolutionary biology.* Cambridge (Massachusetts): Harvard University Press. Pp. 145–148.

———. (1994a): "A critical review of philosophical work on the units of selection problem". *Philosophy of Science* 61, pp. 534–555.

———. (1994b): "Reintroducing group selection to the human behavioural sciences." *Behavioral and Brain Sciences* 17, pp. 585–654.

Wilson, David Sloan and Sober, Elliott (1989): "Reviving the superorganism." *Journal of Theoretical Biology* 136, pp. 337–356.

Wilson, Robert A. (2007): "Levels of selection." In: M. Matthen and C. Stephens (eds.): *Handbook of the philosophy of science. Philosophy of biology.* Amsterdam: Elsevier. Pp. 141–162.

Woodward, James (2003): *Making things happen. A theory of causal explanation.* Oxford: Oxford University Press.

Wouters, Arno G. (2003): "Four notions of biological function." *Studies in History and Philosophy of Biological and Biomedical Sciences* 25, pp. 287–318.

———. (2005): "The function debate in philosophy." *Acta Biotheoretica* 53, pp. 123–151.

Wright, Larry (1973): "Functions." *Philosophical Review* 82, pp. 139–168. Reprinted in E. Sober (ed.) (1994): *Conceptual issues in evolutionary biology.* Cambridge (Massachusetts): MIT Press. Pp. 27–47.

Wright, Sewall (1931): "Evolution in Mendelian populations." *Genetics* 16, pp. 97–159.

Yablo, Stephen (1992): "Mental causation." *Philosophical Review* 101, pp. 245–280.

Yang, Ziheng and Nielsen, Rasmus (2008): "Mutation-selection models of codon substitution and their use to estimate selective strengths on codon usage." *Molecular Biology and Evolution* 25, pp. 568–579.

Yampolsky, Lev, Kondrashov, Fyodor and Kondrashov, Alexey (2005): "Distribution of the strength of selection against amino acid replacements in human proteins." *Human Molecular Genetics* 14, pp. 3191–3201.

Index of Names

A

Abrams, Marshall, 87, 95, 101, 103–104, 132
Abrams, Peter, 92, 102–103
Abzhanov, 90
Aguadé, 133
Aizawa, 156
Akashi, 133
Albert, 57, 60
Andersson, 131
Anjum, 39
Ariew, 95, 99, 101
Aristotle, 69–70
Armstrong, 22, 37, 69
Arp, 30, 113, 133, 153

B

Bain, 52
Bartels, 63
Bartolomé, 133
Beatty, 98–99, 101–102
Bechtel, 156
Begun, 133
Bell, 43, 66
Bennett, 17
Bickle, 27, 165
Bigelow, 113
Bird, 36–37, 63
Black, 33, 36
Blackburn, 32
Blackett, 1
Block, 17
Bohm, 43
Boveri, 119
Bradley, 80
Brandon, 96, 104
Brigandt, 93, 124
Bulmer, 132
Burian, 93, 95
Burns, 133

C

Cartwright, 40, 54, 144
Chakravartty, 36, 56
Changeux, 122
Colwell, 103
Comeron, 133
Coyne, 89
Craver, 115, 146
Crick, 107, 116, 122
Cronin, 95
Crow, 90, 104, 132
Cummins, 113
Cutter, 133
Cuvier, 86

D

Damuth, 86
Darwin, 85–94, 106, 116
Davidson, 82–83
Dawkins, 93–94, 96, 109
Dennett, 132
Descartes, 10, 47, 49
Desjardins, 102
Dieks, 44
Dizadji-Bahmani, 141, 148
Dobzhansky, 85, 89–90
Dorato, 40, 58–59
Dos Reis, 133
Dretske, 82
Dupré, 93
Durbin, 133
Dushoff, 133

E

Einstein, 43, 45, 64
Endicott, 148–149
Ereshefsky, 93
Ernst, 99
Esfeld, 18, 38, 43–45, 51, 58, 80, 156, 171

198 *Index of Names*

Everett, 61–62
Eyre-Walker, 133

F
Fazekas, 148–149
Fisher, 90, 99
Fodor, 15, 20, 80–81, 98, 149
Forber, 90, 102
Fox Keller, 92, 103
French, 44–45, 55–56, 69
Friedman, 144
Frigg, 59

G
Gerland, 133
Ghirardi, 57
Gilchrist, 133
Gillet, 32, 80–81, 156
Gintis, 103
Gisin, 57, 59
Glémin, 133
Godfrey-Smith, 95, 98, 102
Gogarten, 93
Goosens, 139
Gould, 86, 89, 102
Grant, Peter, 89–90
Grant, Rosemary, 89–90
Graves, 49

H
Haag, 52
Hacking, 53–54
Haddrill, 133
Haeckel, 93
Harbecke, 17
Harré, 36
Hartl, 133
Hawthorne, 36
Heger, 133
Heil, 36–37, 69, 79–80, 82
Hempel, 144
Hoefer, 59
Hoffmann, 23
Hooker, 27
Houston, 102
Hull, 109, 139
Hume, 23, 47
Hüttemann, 40, 149
Hutton, 86
Hwa, 112, 133

J
Jackson, 11, 16, 32–36, 49, 170
Jacob, 122

Jukes, 105

K
Kern, 133
Kiefer, 61
Kim, 17, 25, 79, 146, 148, 158, 165
Kimbrough, 139
Kimchi-Sarfaty, 133
Kimura, 104–105, 132
King, 105
Kistler, 82, 141, 149
Kitcher, 85, 96, 113, 118, 124–125,
    127, 139, 144
Kreitman, 105, 133
Kroedel, 17
Kurland, 131

L
Ladyman, 18, 44–45, 55–56, 69
Lam, 44–45, 52
Langton, 23, 33, 38
LaPorte, 93, 163
Leder, 122
Lehmkuhl, 41, 60
Leibniz, 10, 47, 52
Lewens, 102, 112
Lewis, David, 20, 22–23, 25, 34,
    38, 46, 48, 79, 81, 158,
    165
Lewis, Peter, 57
Lewontin, 90, 99–100, 102
Livanios, 63
Llopart, 133
Locke, 34
Loewe, 133
Loewer, 10, 17, 57
Lotka, 103
Louie, 133
Love, 124
Lyell, 86
Lynn, 133

M
MacDonald, Cynthia, 21
MacDonald, Graham, 21
Machamer, 146
Madden, 36
Malthus, 87
Marras, 17, 149
Martin, 36–37
Masters, 95
Matthaei, 122
Maudlin, 55, 61
Maynard Smith, John, 96, 98, 107

Index of Names 199

Mayr, 86–87, 89–90, 92–95, 103,107
McIntosh, 92, 103
McLaughlin, Brian P., 80
McLaughlin, Peter, 10
Mele, 82
Melnyk, 13
Mendel, 90, 117–118, 136
Mills, 98–99
Misner, 52
Mojzsis, 94
Monod, 122
Morton, 133
Moses, 133
Mossio, 113
Mukhopadhyay, 133
Muller, 44
Mumford, 36, 39
Mundale, 156
Musto, 133

N
Nagel, 148
Nei, 105, 132
Newton, 8, 12
Ney, 34
Nielsen, 133
Nirenberg, 122
Noordhof, 82–83
Norton, 45, 65

O
Okasha, 90, 95–96
Olby, 121
O'Malley, 89, 93
Oppenheim, 144
Orzack, 111

P
Papineau, 125, 161, 167
Pearle, 57
Pettit, 16
Piganeau, 133
Plato, 69
Plotkin, 133
Plutynski, 93, 104–105
Ponting, 133
Popper, 59
Potochnik, 102
Psillos, 33, 54, 56
Putnam, 15, 20, 80–81, 149

Q
Qin, 133
Qu, 133

R
Reydon, 67
Richards, 89, 92–93
Ridley, 89, 116
Rimini, 57
Rispe, 133
Rives, 80–81
Robb, 82–83
Rosenberg, 12, 32, 92, 96–97, 99, 107, 120, 122, 124–125, 132, 139
Rosing, 94
Rovelli, 63
Ruse, 85–86, 133, 139
Russell, 65

S
Sachse, 126, 156
Salmon, 144
Sarkar, 90, 121, 139
Sato, 90, 116
Saunders, 44, 62
Schopf, 94
Schrödinger, 57
Sharp, 30, 133, 153
Shoemaker, 36–37, 80–81
Singh, 133
Skipper, 90
Smith, Peter, 28
Sober, 92–101, 111, 139
Soom, 171
Sparber, 20, 47
Spencer, 95
Spinoza, 47, 69
Stephens, 87, 90, 95–97, 100–101
Sterelny, 93, 96, 118
Stevens, 93
Stoletzki, 133
Suárez, 54, 58–59
Sutton, 119
Szathmáry, 107

T
Thorne, 52
Townsend, 93
Tumulka, 61

V
Vance, 139
Versteegh, 44
Viljanen, 47

W
Wallace, 57, 62
Waters, 96, 118–119, 139

200 Index of Names

Watson, 116, 122
Weber, Marcel, 92, 96, 99, 113,
    118–119, 125, 139
Weber, Tullio 57
Weismann, 90
Wernisch, 133
West-Eberhard, 100
Wheeler, 49, 52
Whittle, 34, 75, 82
Wilkins, John S. 109
Wilkins, Jon F., 95, 102

Wilson, David Sloan 96
Wilson, Robert A. 96, 109
Woodward, 144
Wright, Larry, 112
Wright, Sewall, 90
Wright, Stephen, 133

Y

Yablo, 19, 80
Yampolsky, 133
Yang, 133

Index of Subjects

A

adaptive radiation, 93
adaptation, Adaptationism, 89, 92–102, 104, 105, 108, 110, 111
atomism, 47–48

B

Bell's theorem, 43
bridge principles, 149, 159

C

causation, 10–11, 18, 23, 56, 65, 79
charge, 22, 35–36, 38–44, 48, 59, 70–73, 76, 142, 163
coextension, 126–129, 135, 139, 148, 150, 157–161, 166
coherence, 53, 78
completeness
   of molecular genetics, 124–126, 128–129, 135, 138–139
   of physics, 8, 10, 12, 28–29, 76, 78, 80, 140–141, 143, 145, 149, 158, 160, 163, 169–170
configurations, 13–17, 19–25, 27, 32, 35, 67, 72–73, 75, 77, 81, 114, 119, 124–126, 140, 142–143, 145, 151, 165, 167
connections, necessary, 39–41, 47

D

decoherence, 62–63
determinism, 9, 30, 45
   genetic, 120
direction of time, 60, 63
dispositions, 22–24, 37–40, 58–60, 62–63, 72, 75, 80, 91, 99–100, 102–103, 106, 112–115, 118–120, 122–124, 126, 129, 137
dynamics, 5, 56–58, 60–62, 66–67

E

Einstein-Podolsky-Rosen correlations, 43
elimination, eliminativism, 1–2, 7, 26–29, 31, 49, 68, 75–81, 83, 139–141, 148, 156, 159–161, 165, 167
entanglement, quantum, 43–46, 49, 52, 56–68, 71–73, 75–76
entity realism, 53–54
environment, 14–15, 20–21, 27, 40, 45, 68, 72–74, 76–78, 83, 85–89, 91–97, 99–106, 108–115, 116–126, 131–134, 136–138, 145, 152, 155, 160–167, 171
   relevant environment, 96–97, 103–105
epiphenomena, epiphenomenalism, 2, 7, 11, 17–18, 21, 27–28, 31, 49, 68, 75–76, 79–80, 83
events, 38–39, 53, 64–68, 71–73, 82, 101, 131, 138, 142
explanations
   causal, 12, 16, 24, 50, 78, 83, 98–99, 117, 119–121, 124–125, 128, 135, 139, 144, 147–148, 151, 159–160, 166, 170
   functional, 27, 111, 120–121, 125, 138–139, 141, 144, 146
   homogeneous, 128, 150–151
   mechanistic, 115, 117, 119, 121, 124, 129, 146
   proximal, 97–99, 111
   reductive, 96, 128–129, 135–136, 139, 142, 145–147, 149–151, 158
   ultimate, 97–99, 115
   unificatory, 115, 144, 147–148

F

fitness, 92, 95–106, 109, 111–115, 120, 123, 126, 130–135, 138, 165–166
   operational concept, 98

202 *Index of Subjects*

supervenience of, 96
tautology, 97–98
fossils, 86, 94
function
    biological, 111
    causal-dispositional theory of, 100,
        111, 113–115
    etiological theory of, 111–113
    functional definition, 100, 114, 118–
        121, 123–127, 129, 134–136,
        143–145, 148–151, 154–157,
        160, 165
functionalism
    realizer, 7, 22–28
    reductionist, 79–80
    role, 7, 15–22, 28, 80

G

genetic drift, 101, 104, 132
genetic code, 14, 94, 107–108,
    110, 122, 127, 131, 137,
    153
    codon preferences, 131–132
    redundance, 122, 127, 131, 137,
        153
genetics
    classical, 23–24, 90, 116–139,
        142–143, 145–148, 159–160,
        163, 167, 170–171
    molecular, 116–119, 121–139, 142–
        143, 145–146, 148, 159–160,
        167, 170–171
genotype, 92–93, 95, 101–102, 106,
    118–120, 125, 132, 137
geometrodynamics, 49, 52
gradualism, 86, 91
gravitation, 8, 10, 38, 40–41, 46,
    49–50, 59, 61, 63–64, 72,
    75

H

haecceity, 20–21, 33–34
hole argument, 45–46
holism, 38, 47–48
Humean metaphysics, 39, 47, 54
humility, 33, 35, 41, 48–50

I

identity of properties, 2, 17, 20–22,
    28–29, 75–84, 114, 119,
    124–126, 129, 140, 142–143,
    145, 149, 158, 160, 168
indiscernability, 34, 36–37, 41, 45,
    49–51, 55

K

kinds
    biological, 93, 161, 164, 168
    natural, 12, 21, 56, 82, 93, 142–144,
        160–161, 163–164, 167–169,
        171
    physical, 163–164, 167

L

laws
    biological, 8, 99–100, 117–119, 121,
        124, 126–129, 135–139, 142,
        146, 160
    ceteris paribus, 7, 25, 73, 99, 126,
        134, 149, 163
    fundamental, 1, 9–10, 12, 147, 163
    physical, 1, 9–12, 18, 29–30, 40, 55,
        83, 92, 95, 97, 99, 107, 109,
        141, 143, 146–152, 154–158,
        160–163, 166
    special sciences, 2, 10, 18, 27–29,
        73–75, 83, 139, 141, 144, 146–
        152, 154–163, 166, 169–170
    strict, 7, 18, 163
    sub-types, 135–139, 158–161, 163

M

manifestation conditions, 58–60, 63,
    80, 99, 102–103, 114, 118–123,
    137
mass, 22, 35–36, 38, 40–44, 48, 59–60,
    70–72, 112, 163
measurement problem, 56–59
modes, 31, 45, 68–75, 78–83, 142–144,
    167
multiple realization, 2–3, 14–16,
    18–22, 24–28, 32–33, 35,
    50–51, 82–83, 99–100, 121–
    122, 127–130, 132, 134–139,
    143–144, 146–151, 157–158,
    160–161, 165, 167, 170
    of tokens, 19–21
    of types, 19–22

N

natural selection, see selection
necessity, 39–41, 47, 53, 59
neutralism, 102, 104–105, 108,
    132–133
niche, 90–91, 102–103
non-separability, 45, 64
normal conditions, 7–8, 13–15, 73,
    144–145, 149, 152–156, 159,
    161, 163

Index of Subjects 203

O

overdetermination, 17–18, 80

P

phenotype, phenotypic effect, 7–8,
14–15, 17, 23–24, 72, 74, 76,
92–94, 104–105, 118–130, 133,
137, 142, 145–147, 152–155,
163
physicalism, 27–28
primitive thisness, 19, 21, 45–46
probability, 7, 10, 31, 42, 44, 57,
59–60, 87, 91–95, 98, 102,
104, 106–111, 131–132, 137,
152–158, 163
processes, 40, 56–57, 60, 62–64, 67,
72, 86, 88, 95–97, 110–111,
119, 122–123, 133, 137–138
   causal, 62, 64
   irreversible, 60, 62–63
propensities, 59, 99
properties
   categorical, 22–24, 33–39, 46–51,
      54, 58, 77
   causal, 3, 13–14, 22, 24, 28–29,
      31, 36–41, 46–56, 58–61, 68,
      72–81, 91, 99–100, 102–103,
      106, 112–115, 118–130,
      141–160, 163–170
   determinable, 42, 70, 80–81
   determinate, 42, 71, 80–81
   emergent, 2, 9, 11, 13–14, 16, 18,
      27–28, 76, 80
   functional, 2–3, 13–29, 31–32,
      35, 75, 77, 79–82, 99–100,
      112–115, 120–122, 132–137,
      141, 167
   intrinsic, 22–23, 31–38, 41–51,
      53–55, 59–60, 64, 66–69,
      74–76, 80
   relational, see relations
   tokens, 18–23, 33, 39, 68–70, 73, 75,
      78–83, 113–114, 119–121, 124–
      134, 140, 142–147, 149–158,
      160, 163–164, 166–168
   types, 8, 13–15, 18–26, 34–39, 50,
      68, 81–83, 114, 118, 121, 127,
      136–139, 142, 146, 151–152,
      157–159, 164–171
powers, 22, 36–40, 46, 48–49, 51,
      53–54, 56, 58–60, 62–63,
      68, 72–73, 75, 77–78, 80–81,
      112, 128, 130, 143, 146–147,
      149–150, 165

Q

quantum theory, 8–9, 11, 42–45, 52,
55–68, 72
quiddity, quidditism, 33–35, 37, 41,
48–50, 55, 60

R

reduction, reductionism
   a posteriori, 170–171
   a priori, 170–171
   conservative, 2–3, 29, 31, 46, 55, 75,
      79, 81, 95, 117, 136, 141–142,
      148, 163–168, 170–171
   epistemological, 2, 29, 117,
      168–169
   methodological, 166, 170
   "new wave", 26–27, 165
   ontological, 29, 31, 77, 79–81, 83,
      117, 124, 128, 135, 138–141,
      145, 149, 163, 168–169
relations, 13, 15, 17–18, 22–24, 31–39,
      41–53, 63–64, 68–70, 73,
      75–77, 90, 96, 100, 116–120,
      123, 125–127, 129, 135–136,
      140, 144–146, 149, 151–158,
      163, 171
   metrical, 46, 63–64
   of quantum entanglement, *see*
      entanglement
relativity theory
   general, 8–9, 38, 41, 45–50, 52, 55,
      61, 63–65, 67, 71
   special, 8, 63, 71
replication, 8, 108–111, 161–162
reproduction, 87–89, 91–96, 99,
      102–103, 110–111, 114,
      131
resources, 87–92, 101–103, 110,
      131

S

selection
   natural, 14–15, 87–88, 91–102, 104–
      106, 108–109, 111, 116–118,
      120, 132, 138–139, 161, 163,
      165–167
   pressure, 92, 132
   selection for, 100
   selection of, 100
   unit of selection, 95, 102, 111,
      115
similarities, 70, 74, 78–79, 82, 87,
      92, 94, 96, 102, 106, 120,
      128–129, 142–143, 147–148,

204   *Index of Subjects*

160–161, 163–164, 166–167, 169, 171
imperfect, 142–143
perfect, 70, 142, 167
space-time, 5, 9, 22–24, 36, 45–50, 52, 58, 61, 63–65, 67, 71, 109
state reductions, 56–58, 60–61, 65–68, 72–73, 75–76
structural realism, 44–48, 52, 54–56, 69
  Cartesian, 47, 52
  Leibnizian, 47
  moderate, 44–45, 69
  radical, 44, 69
structures
  algebraic, 52
  biological, 107, 111
  categorical, 46–52, 54–56, 63, 68
  causal, 2–3, 29–31, 46, 49, 51–53, 55, 58, 60–65, 67–68, 74, 78–80, 85, 91, 107, 129, 142, 146, 164, 169–170
  geometric, 49, 52, 63
  living, 91, 107
  mathematical, 51–56, 65, 69
  physical, 31, 46, 50–53, 55–56, 61, 65, 67, 70, 73, 75–79, 81, 97, 125, 140, 145, 147, 149–150, 156, 160–162, 164, 168, 170–171

sub-types
  comparison between sub-type and realizer, 134–135, 138–139, 157–161, 165–166, 169–170
  comparison between type and sub-type, 148, 157–161
  construction of sub-types, 134–135, 139, 148, 156–157, 160, 170
  sub-type laws, 135–139, 158–161, 163
superpositions, 40, 42–43, 45, 49, 56–57, 60, 62, 66, 71
supervenience
  global, 11, 170–171
  Humean, 22, 46
  local, 17–18, 76, 96

T

theory realism, 53–54
tropes, 68, 75, 81–83, 142

U

uniformitarism, 86
universals, 21, 68–70, 78

W

worlds, possible worlds, 17, 19, 23–24, 33–35, 37–41, 50–51, 108